URBAN LEGENDS

CLARENDON STUDIES IN CRIMINOLOGY

Published under the auspices of the Institute of Criminology, University of Cambridge; the Mannheim Centre, London School of Economics; and the Centre for Criminology, University of Oxford.

General Editor: Robert Reiner
(London School of Economics)

Editors: Manuel Eisner, Alison Liebling, and Per-Olof Wikström
(University of Cambridge)

Jill Peay and Tim Newburn
(London School of Economics)

Ian Loader, Julian Roberts, and Lucia Zedner
(University of Oxford)

RECENT TITLES IN THIS SERIES

Urban Legends

Gang Identity in the Post-Industrial City

ALISTAIR FRASER

OXFORD
UNIVERSITY PRESS

Great Clarendon Street, Oxford, OX2 6DP,
United Kingdom

Oxford University Press is a department of the University of Oxford.
It furthers the University's objective of excellence in research, scholarship,
and education by publishing worldwide. Oxford is a registered trade mark of
Oxford University Press in the UK and in certain other countries

First Edition published in 2015
Impression: 1

Published in the United States of America by Oxford University Press
198 Madison Avenue, New York, NY 10016, United States of America

British Library Cataloguing in Publication Data
Data available

Library of Congress Control Number: 2015933281

ISBN 978-0-19-872861-0

Printed and bound by
CPI Group (UK) Ltd, Croydon, CR0 4YY

Fur Betty

He was standing on the bridge looking over the parapet into the dirty water, at the very spot where Boswell had stood and looked at the widest streets in the whole of Europe. Gles Chu! Glasgow! The dear green place! Now a vehicular sclerosis, a congestion of activity. He felt again a wave of nostalgia for another kind of existence...all the symbols of confidence, possibility, energy, which had lived before in this knotted tight, seized up reality which was around him had come to be.

Archie Hind, *The Dear Green Place* (1966)

General Editor's Introduction

Clarendon Studies in Criminology aims to provide a forum for outstanding empirical and theoretical work in all aspects of criminology and criminal justice, broadly understood. The Editors welcome submissions from established scholars, as well as excellent PhD work. The *Series* was inaugurated in 1994, with Roger Hood as its first General Editor, following discussions between Oxford University Press and three criminology centres. It is edited under the auspices of these three centres: the Cambridge Institute of Criminology, the Mannheim Centre for Criminology at the London School of Economics, and the Centre for Criminology at the University of Oxford. Each supplies members of the Editorial Board and, in turn, the Series Editor or Editors.

Alistair Fraser's book *Urban Legends: Gang Identity in the Post-Industrial City* takes on the challenging task of reinvigorating the criminological study of gangs. Despite its rich history, this area of scholarship has been somewhat waylaid in recent times, becoming overly preoccupied with messy issues of definition (what constitutes a gang?) and with somewhat unhelpful debates around alleged national differences or similarities. Fraser's starting point is to accept the variety and heterogeneity of gangs, over time, and within and between cultures, and to seek to navigate the choppy waters between those who think that we are witnessing the emergence of something radically different in gang membership, conduct and culture, and those who view the development of new concerns about gangs as little more than an indication of moral panic.

The ambitious aim of this volume is to understand the Glasgow gang phenomenon within that city's particular history, focusing not only on its socio-economic, geographical, and cultural moorings but, using ethnography and employing a Bourdieusian perspective, to understand the 'gang' through the eyes of its occupants. Glasgow is both a fascinating choice and, in many ways, an ideal one for such a study. As Andy Davies' work, among others, has shown, it is a city with a long history of gangs, but it is also one in which such worlds are very much the stuff of urban legend and where, in many respects, it can be hard to separate fact from fiction. Gangs are, in both senses, a part of the lifeblood of Glasgow's history and its present.

Glasgow is a city in which poverty has 'loomed large', but to which shipbuilding and other industries brought great wealth to some. As traditional industries have gradually, or not so gradually, disappeared so the city has been remade and reimagined. Whilst in many respects Glasgow may reasonably be described as a 'postmodern city', in reality many traditional neighbourhood, sectarian and social divisions and loyalties remain and, Fraser argues, the socio-spatial patterning of poverty and inequality are crucial in understanding gang identification. Moreover, whilst examining the ways in which territorial identity, violent masculinities, and neighbourhood nationalisms play a vital role in understanding the persistence of gangs in Glasgow, Fraser never loses sight of the fact that none of these are unchanging, and all are patterned in different ways in other postmodern cities. What is true for Glasgow will, at best, only be partly true for London and Los Angeles.

Fraser's role in this research was one of the embedded ethnographer – one who in Burawoy's terms sought to establish 'enduring human connection' – living and working in the local community in which his study was based over a very extended period. Very much in the tradition of William Foote Whyte, Howard Parker, and other of the classics of the field, Fraser's study of the 'Langview Boys' is a product of years of hard work, enabling him, in course, to get sufficiently close to a group of 'likely lads', young men whose offending was generally confined to vandalism, disorder and graffiti, with the majority also having engaged in some form of territorial violence. Several had stab wounds and though none had as yet been convicted of a serious offence, a number had older brothers in prison for violence.

With more than an echo of David Downes' *The Delinquent Solution* Fraser focuses centrally on the leisure pursuits of the Langview Boys and the role of leisure as a diversion from mundane everyday lives. Football remained central, cinema and gaming important, fighting was much talked about but less often engaged in, but represented an intermittent opportunity for boundary testing – both geographical borders and the limits of machismo. The street was of less importance to these boys than it would have been to their predecessors in the 1960s and 1970s and it had in part been replaced by shopping and by the transgressive excitement of what Fraser calls 'malling': using shopping malls, the new temples of capitalism, as 'centres for boredom-relief through consumption, and spaces bound by rules and constraints that can be subverted and played with'. Although there are differences between the leisure styles of the Langview Boys and those documented by Downes, Patrick, Parker, and Willis in earlier decades, intriguingly the continuities are much stronger than the contrasts.

In the tough, post-industrial environment in which the Boys were growing up, the crucial skills focus on learning to be a man – or more accurately learning particular forms of masculinity. In this connection, Fraser documents five 'ways of being': 'being a gemmie' (being, or appearing to be, fearless), 'taking (and giving) a slagging' (learning to deal verbally with other men), 'being best at stuff' (in particular all sport and most matters involving physical prowess), 'being in the know' (in essence being street smart), and 'being wan ae the boays' (through dress, talk, and conduct showing solidarity with the group). Challengingly for the Langview Boys and their peers, such attributes have much less utility in the world of work – if there is indeed any work to be had – in the post-Fordist world in which they live. Holding to such traditional masculine ideals in the new casualised, service-oriented labour market is especially challenging. Some successfully adapt, others retreat, most likely to marginalization and exclusion.

What Fraser is able to document is the continuation of an age-based, hierarchical street culture in Glasgow, and one which forms the basis for the persistence of gangs. Their membership, form and conduct reflect the continuing inequality, territorial mosaics, and embedded tough masculinity that continues to be a part of the city's make up. But as the city itself changes, so he argues its gangs do too. A critical approach to understanding such phenomena therefore, Fraser suggests, must jettison the universalizing and pathologizing approaches so prevalent in contemporary criminology, and embrace a social science that is sensitized to history, biography and culture. As Editors we commend this book as making a significant contribution to the field of criminology, and also to the study of the history and sociology of the city. It is a book to be most warmly welcomed to the *Clarendon Studies in Criminology Series*.

Tim Newburn and Jill Peay
London School of Economics
January 2015

Acknowledgements

In *Art Worlds* (1982), Howard Becker skewers the notion that artists are solitary types, ploughing a lonely furrow. Rather, Becker argues, art worlds are communities of artists and critics, working collectively. Though I make no claim to what follows being a work of art, academic works—artless as they so often are—nonetheless share a similar dynamic. In the years it has taken to move from blank slate to printed page, I have built up innumerable debts—personal, emotional, and financial—to a host of wonderful and remarkable individuals. This small acknowledgement does not do them justice; suffice to say they are between the lines of every page.

The Centre for Criminology at the University of Oxford, particularly Federico Varese, was instrumental in the original idea; the Violence Reduction Unit of Strathclyde Police, especially Karyn McLuskey, helped it develop. The Department of Sociology at the University of Glasgow provided a nourishing base for the study, where I had the fortune to work with a community of critical, engaged scholars and students—I owe Michele Burman and Susan Batchelor, who supervised the study, my eternal gratitude. My visit to the University of Illinois at Chicago allowed me an invaluable glimpse into the Chicago gang scene; the mentorship of John Hagedorn both during and after has been vital. In the Department of Sociology, University of Hong Kong, I have found a nurturing intellectual environment, and the psychological distance that enabled me to write this book; Karen Joe-Laidler and Scott Veitch have been much treasured readers and critics.

The Scottish Centre for Crime and Justice Research provided me with the opportunity to learn from a network of experienced scholars of youth gangs, urban environments, and violence—Mo Hume, Susan McVie, Johnny Pickering, and Jon Bannister, among them—and enabled my getting to know fantastic researchers from south of the border, particularly Tara Young and Rob Ralphs. I have gained greatly from working with historians of gangs and masculinities in Glasgow—Angela Bartie, Andy Davies, and Sean Damer—as well as those engaged in studies of other 'hidden communities' in Glasgow, most notably Colin Atkinson, Stephen Ashe, and Teresa Piacentini. The British Society of Criminology funded my attendance at several of their annual meetings; many of the friends I made there contributed to the development of this book. Special thanks to Jennifer Fleetwood and Jonathan Ilan, both of whom read and commented on earlier drafts. Lucy Alexander at Oxford University Press and Robert Reiner at the London School of Economics have been very supportive and patient with this first-time author.

My family and friends have supplied unstinting support throughout the process. My Mum and Dad (Hazel and Keith); Grandpa Fraser; Lisa, Graeme, and the boys; Sheila, John, and Laurianne; Iain and Christine; Kate, Jay, and Jess—thank you all. Many friends—too many to name—helped me in various ways: particular thanks go to Ryan and Linda, Dave and Vicky, Kathryn, Catherine and Jamal, Brendan and Caddy, who all generously let me stay with them during and after fieldwork. Special thanks to Andy Ross—who introduced me to LYP—to Jane Hamilton, proofreader extraordinaire, and Calum Hind, who generously allowed use of the opening quotation from 'Dear Green Place'.

Most importantly of all, I want to extend my warmest gratitude to all of the staff, young people and parents involved with Langview Youth Project, Langview Outreach Project, and Langview Academy—who generously allowed a stranger into their lives, and helped me with enthusiasm and resourcefulness. Particular thanks go to the project manager of LYP—whose strength, resolve, and determination have been a constant inspiration—and to the Langview Boys and the school-leavers who made this all possible. Lastly, unending gratitude to Beth. You have put up with me throughout with patience, love, and forbearance, and read and commented on drafts like only a loved one could. This one's for you.

Permissions

An earlier draft of Chapter 5 was published as 'Street habitus: Gangs, Territorialism and Social Change in Glasgow' by the *Journal of Youth Studies* 16(8), 970–85. Reproduced with permission from Taylor & Francis (<http://www.tandfonline.com>). Material from Chapters 1 and 8 were published as 'Making Up Gangs: Looping, Labelling and the New Politics of Intelligence-Led Policing' (co-authored with Colin Atkinson) in *Youth Justice* 14(2), 154–70. Reproduced by permission of SAGE Publications,

London, Los Angeles, New Delhi, and Singapore. Material from Chapters 3, 4, and 7 is drawn from a chapter in C. Phillips and C. Webster (eds), *New Directions in Race, Ethnicity and Crime*, titled 'We Belong to Glasgow: The Thirdspaces of Youth "Gangs" and Asylum Seeker, Refugee and Migrant Groups' (co-authored with Teresa Piacentini), pp. 55–79. Reproduced with permission from Routledge Publications. Extract from *The Dear Green Place* by Archie Hind is reproduced courtesy of Polygon, an imprint of Birlinn Ltd. <http://www.birlinn.co.uk>.

Contents

Introduction

The Glasgow Gang. For some, the phrase evokes grainy images from yesteryear; of post-war newsreels of pitched battles. For others, it conjures a more contemporary picture; CCTV footage of cornered young men huddled in tracksuits. These images—past and present, imagined and lived—represent an important starting point in making sense of the gang phenomenon. On one hand, the Glasgow gang has become deeply engrained in the popular imagination, reverberating around 'an infinite hall of mirrors where images created and consumed by criminals, criminal subcultures, media institutions and audiences bounce endlessly off the other' (Ferrell 1999, p. 397). In this sense the Glasgow gang has become something of a caricature: an urban legend where fact and fiction merge and blur. On the other, however, street-based territorial groups of young people, referred to as gangs, have been reported in Glasgow for over a century, with sporadic reporting indicating striking continuities over this period. This raises a number of searching questions relating to young people and social change that do not feature in the stereotypical image. Why, despite far-reaching alterations to the social, spatial, and economic landscape of Glasgow, have gangs persisted? And why, given the trajectories of other post-industrial cities, haven't they got any worse? In answering these questions, we must enter a jumble of fictional and factual representations, reflected and refracted, historical and contemporary; taking the city as a lens through which to analyse the history and present of the gang phenomenon.

Glasgow is a deeply storied and mythologized city. This mythology is a rich tapestry on which Gaelic folk-tales are woven alongside Highland legends, Orange marching bands are stitched in with Sunday Mass, socialist politics hemmed together with conservatism. These histories are passed down through the generations through word-of-mouth, art, and literature; a moving, shifting tableaux sustained by folk traditions and memory. Glasgow's coat of arms, indeed, represents a foundational myth—the legend of St Mungo, who founded the city based on four miracles: The bird that never flew/The tree that never grew/The bell that never rang/The fish that never swam. Like statues, legends form part of the character of a city; a representation of life that beats a deep rhythm beneath the movement of urban development. Just as the 'ancient function of statues was to immortalize the dead so that they would not harm the living' (Lefebvre 1974, p. 74), legends serve as a reminder of deeds past, an oral tradition in which culture is re-enacted. However, like the Duke of Wellington statue in the centre of Glasgow—notorious for its on–off adornment of a traffic cone—statues are not static but are points of interaction between past and present. They are reinterpreted and reimagined with the passing of time, moving yet stable.

Although there are no concrete representations to memorialize them, Glasgow is also littered with local legends; living histories breathed down through the generations, reinterpreted and retold for a new generation. Sometimes these take the form of cautionary tales or horror stories.[1] More often, they take the form of individuals: statuesque characters that symbolize a stability and continuity amid a changing urban environment. Names of political activists, comedians, musicians, and artists echo down through the generations, and reverberate around the world. Among these names, for better or worse, are those with a reputation for being 'hardmen'—tough, masculine figures that embody physical violence, inspiring both fear and respect. The novelist William McIlvanney puts it well:

This communal sense of identity found its apotheosis in a few local people. Thornbank knew itself most strongly through them. They were fixed as landmarks in the popular consciousness. If two expatriates from that little town had been talking and one of them mentioned the name of one of that handful of people, no further elaboration would have been necessary. They would have known themselves twinned. (McIlvanney 1985, p. 21)

---

[1] One recurrent legend—surfacing and resurfacing in different parts of Glasgow and beyond, from the 1980s to the present—is of a group of 'killer clowns', in a white transit van, abducting children in a manner similar to the character of the Child Catcher from the film *Chitty Chitty Bang Bang*. The legend varies but most often revolves around a group of escaped patients from a nearby asylum, offering children sweets to enter the van. Often too, there are sightings of the clowns in peripheral parts of the local area, where known space gives way to unknown. This story is infused with messages of stranger danger, staying close to home, and fear of territorial boundaries.

The title of McIlvanney's book—*The Big Man*—has particular resonance in the formulation of such legends. Being a 'big man' in the west of Scotland—and Glasgow in particular—often means adhering to a set of masculinities that were forged amid the unique alloy of industrialism, migration, and urbanization that form Glasgow's foundation. For industrial workers, a 'competitive spirit was part and parcel of *machismo* work culture, as was a high tolerance of danger and a propensity to take risks' (Johnston and McIvor 2004, p. 4); stoicism coupled with gameness, collectivism alongside individual distinction. In this context, local legends formed part of community mythology and lore, embodying these idealized forms of masculinity. These urban legends, critically, continue to represent a role model and pathway to recognition for young people growing up in the city; forming a meeting point of legend and reality that has contributed to the ongoing cycle of gang identification in the city's history. In the rupture brought on by the shift from industrialism to post-industrialism, gangs represent a root of identity—and a route to masculinity—that maintains this link with the past.

Glasgow has long held a reputation as a violent city: a 'Scottish Chicago' (Davies 2013), or 'murder capital of Europe' (McKay 2006) that is portrayed in the media as 'a filthy, slum-ridden, poverty-stricken, gang-infested city' (Damer 1990a, p. 5). Bound up with these depictions are constructions of street-based youth in Glasgow as 'Neds', or 'Non Educated Delinquents' (Law, Mooney, and Helms 2010; Law and Mooney 2012), echoing long-standing depictions of 'estate reputations' that are inscribed with class prejudice (Damer 1989; Hayward and Yar 2006; Hanley 2007). While these depictions of the city may be exaggerated, distorted, and warped by processes of 'territorial stigmatisation' (Gray and Mooney 2011), it is also clear that rates of violence in the city are comparatively high, and that territorially based violence is deeply rooted. Recent Scottish Government data report that Strathclyde region—encompassing Glasgow and its outlying districts—accounted for 51 of 88 murder cases in the years 2011–12, with 15 of these taking place in Glasgow itself.[2] A review of evidence on gangs, violence, and knife-carrying reports that

---

[2] Scottish Government (2013) *Homicide in Scotland, 2011–12*. Available at: <http://www.scotland.gov.uk/Publications/2012/11/6428/downloads#res-1> [Accessed 20 March 2013].

'Glasgow has the highest rate of murder of any city in Europe per head of population', a rate of 6.17 per 100,000 population for the period 2003–5, and that 'violent crime, in particular knife crime, have remained relatively constant for the last 40 years' (Squires et al. 2008, p. 86).

On another level, however, this street-based violence must be understood as a response to the structural violence that has deeply embedded inequality and disadvantage in Glasgow's socio-spatial fabric. Like the correlations between gang identification and social deprivation delineated in Edinburgh (Smith and Bradshaw 2005), historically gangs in Glasgow have emerged in areas of multiple disadvantage. As Davies notes of the 1920s and 1930s, '[g]ang formation was most heavily clustered in the poorer districts of the city's East End and South Side, but gang activity was also reported in working-class districts such as Maryhill and Anderston to the North and West of the city centre' (Davies 2007a, p. 408). Although the proportion has declined in the last decade, more than a third of the most deprived communities in Scotland are to be found in Glasgow.[3] In this context, Mooney and colleagues (2010, p. 24) report on the high correlations between areas of social deprivation and crime in Scotland—Houchin (2005), for example, found that 60 per cent of Glasgow offenders came from the city's poorest estates (Mooney et al 2010, p. 34). Although Glasgow has recently reconfigured from an industrial to service economy—from industrial powerhouse to 'call-centre capital of Europe'[4]—many of these communities have 'been left behind economically. In the context of this concentrated disadvantage, the importance of local space and reputation becomes more legible. The boundaries between communities become staging grounds for territorial conflicts, symbolically delimiting a space in which local status can be carved out.

While researchers scramble to articulate a universal definition of gangs—across time and space, cultures and continents—these insights should give some pause. Gangs in Glasgow have emerged and sustained as a result of the particular patterning of cultural, historical, and economic forces that have made up Scottish,

[3] Scottish Neighbourhood Statistics (2014) Available at: <http://www.sns.gov.uk/Simd/Simd.aspx> [Accessed 7 July 2014].

[4] Glasgow employs an estimated 20,000 staff in call centres. For further details, see <http://www.ckdgalbraith.co.uk/glasgow-calling> [Accessed 9 August 2014].

and in turn Glaswegian, history. Despite efforts to shift definitions of gangs from locally rooted understandings to 'global'
definitions—transferring one-size-fits-all social policy from the
United States—the distinctive character of individual cities cuts
directly against these tendencies. While conditions of global inequality have accelerated the preconditions for gang formation in
a wide range of contexts, these must be understood and located
within the particular cultural and historical path dependencies
of individual locales. In disaggregating the abstract and fearful
image of the 'global gang' in this way, the city can act as a prism
through which broader global, political, and economic forces are
refracted and rearticulated.

The Glasgow gang phenomenon, therefore, must be understood within the particular history of the city, incorporating
socio-spatial, cultural, and individual levels of analysis. In the context of locally specific cultures of machismo, persistent inequality, and fierce attachment to place, gang identification continues
to represent a path to individual reputation and status. Despite a
reorientation of Glasgow's economy away from the industrial context in which these battle lines were drawn, gang identities have
passed on through the generations via street-based age hierarchies.
As such, gang identity in Glasgow can be understood as an 'open
system of cultural codification' (Delanty 2003, p. 47) that is used
and drawn on in different ways by different individuals as they
grow up, but also by different generations. As a result, while the
city of Glasgow has undergone significant transformations over
the past century—in the form of deindustrialization, unemployment, rehousing, rebranding, and gentrification, not to mention
changes in employment, leisure, and demographics—there remain
considerable continuities in young people's experience from previous generations. While each of these aspects of Glasgow's development has made its mark, young people's habits and tastes continue
to resonate with those of previous generations.

The analysis that follows is based on an accumulation of almost
ten years of research, work and scholarship on the Glasgow gang
phenomenon. Beginning with a masters dissertation in 2005, my
interest matured through a period of work as an intelligence ana-
lyst for Strathclyde Police, where I saw first-hand the ways in which
gangs were analysed and policed. Thereafter, I engaged in a prolonged period of ethnographic fieldwork—a total of four years—in
Langview, a deindustrialized working-class community in the

Glasgow; gaining experience as a youth worker, street outreach worker, and high-school tutor in the process. Since completing this study, I have undertaken fieldwork on gangs in Chicago and Hong Kong, enabling a global and comparative perspective through which to analyse similarity and difference between the Glasgow case and gangs in other contexts. In presenting these accounts of similarity and difference, I aim to give voice to the views of young people who are frequently absent from political debate. Grounded in these qualitative accounts, I present a new theoretical perspective on gangs, which locates gang identities within the context of economic, social, and cultural changes to the post-industrial city. The book seeks to build on and ultimately move beyond constructionist and subcultural traditions by drawing on the conceptual vocabularies of French social theorist Pierre Bourdieu (1977, 1984, 2001, 2005); combining structural, cultural, and agentic scales of analyses to explore how gang identification 'survives' against a backdrop of social, economic, and political change.

The first half of the book makes a case for the cultivation of a global sociological imagination in reconnecting the study of gangs with urban sociology, social theory, and critical criminology. Against universalizing efforts to construct a homogenous 'global gang', gang identification will be presented as heterogeneous, contingent, and geographically specific—reflecting the unique patterning of history, biography, and culture in the cities from which they emerge. While comparative research is a critical component in understanding gangs in a global context, this must proceed from a recognition of *difference* rather than similarity. In using this approach, the unique case study of Glasgow will be presented. Unlike accounts that stress the novelty of gang identification in the United Kingdom, the waxing and waning of gangs over a period of 125 years will be described.

Chapter 1, *Shifting Definitions*, elaborates the divergent trajectories of gangs in the United States, England, and Scotland. The chapter identifies and analyses four clear shifts in gang research and response—street to database, subcultures to crime, local to global, ethnography to dataset—that cohere in the development of an imagination of a 'global gang' phenomenon that is ripe for media scaremongering and political entrepreneurialism. These shifts are representative of a broader set of changes in the academic field, wherein grounded ethnographic accounts are increasingly marginalized. The chapter draws attention, crucially, to a developing seam of critical research that acts as countercurrent to these increasingly homogenizing forces, making the case for a coherent theoretical and methodological agenda for advancing sociological knowledge of gangs in the UK and beyond. Chapter 2, *A Global Sociological Imagination*, sets out a vocabulary with which to pursue such a locally grounded, yet globally sensitized, exploration of the contemporary gang landscape. Highlighting three key areas missed by the 'global gang' discourse—history and social change, diversity and difference, structure and agency—the chapter argues for the critical mediating role of the city in shaping configurations of gangs. Introducing three key concepts—street habitus, the post-industrial city, and gang identification—the chapter presents a developed theoretical framework that seeks to account for both continuity and change in the gang phenomenon.

Chapter 3, *No Mean City*, elaborates this theoretical approach through detailed analysis of the particular historical trajectory of gangs in Glasgow. The chapter identifies five key meso-level variables that have contributed to the continuities of gang identities in Glasgow—persistent inequality, territorial identity, violent masculinities, neighbourhood nationalism, and economies of crime and justice—in an effort to delineate the particularities to Glasgow's gang phenomenon. Focusing on three historical periods in which gangs came to public attention, the chapter situates gang identities from these periods within the broader currents of social change occurring in the city at the time, whilst seeking out continuities between these epochal moments. Chapter 4, *The Best Laid Schemes*, weaves together this history with the development of the community that forms the focus for the study: Langview. Introducing the young people that populate the foreground to the narrative, as well the settings that form its background, the chapter unravels the complex ways in which global processes such as deindustrialization, gentrification, and regeneration have affected the community. The chapter also examines the path of my fieldwork in the community, and some of the research issues I faced as the research unfolded.

In the second half of the book—after a brief intermezzo in which I discuss the ways in which film-makers have made sense of the ruptures caused by Glasgow's shift from industrial to post-industrial economy—the perspective switches from theory to practice to elaborate these points as they are articulated and embodied at the level of lived experience. Seeking to renegotiate the trends that have evacuated meaning from gang research—street to database, local to global, subcultures to crime, ethnography to dataset—these chapters both ground and elaborate the theoretical framework presented in earlier sections. The everyday routines and rhythms of young people in Langview are presented within the long arc of history elaborated in earlier chapters—young people's gang identifications located between the fading light of industrialism and tractor beam of neoliberalism. These chapters present a complex and complicating picture to visions of the 'global gang', and pathologizing accounts of the 'gang menace'. While gang-related violence causes real and lasting harm to communities, limiting mobility and causing fear and injury to other young people, it cannot be understood outside of the structural violence that has been visited on communities across the country.

Chapter 5, *Street Habitus*, focuses on the role of place and space in the lives of children and young people growing up in Langview. As Glasgow has undergone significant cultural, economic, and spatial alterations in recent history, so too has young people's relationship to place and space altered and reconfigured. While certain youthful desires and identities have remained relatively consistent, the environment in which these play out has altered, with significant consequences. Processes of exclusion, gentrification, and commercialization of leisure have narrowed the opportunities for young people's use of public space and increased surveillance and policing on the few areas available. As a result, young people remain spatially constrained and seek out ways to own or appropriate these limited spaces. Chapter 6, '*Learning to Leisure*', extends this argument into the field of leisure, consumption, and technology. While the array of choices for youth leisure has expanded exponentially since the post-war period, the tastes and habits of children and young people in Langview are relatively consistent with previous generations (Jephcott 1967). Group activities that allow space for individual creativity, and individual activities revolving around mediated escapism, remain the most popular pastimes for young people in Langview. However, the narrowing of traditional leisure pursuits in the context of the growth of global capitalism—the closure of local cinemas, vast increases in admission prices to football matches, the trend towards out-of-town shopping complexes—has engendered a range of adaptive responses.

Chapter 7, *Damaged Hardmen*, focuses attention on everyday enactments of masculinities, group dynamics, and status politics; particularly on the ways in which these everyday interactions reproduce age, gender, and group hierarchies. These ways of creating and co-producing meaning—being a gemmie, taking a slagging, being best at stuff, being in the know, and being 'wan ae the boays'—cohere around a configuration of masculinities in which physical toughness, verbal aptitude, and group loyalty are highly prized; a form of masculinity that resonates throughout Glasgow and the west of Scotland, yet which is increasingly threatened by the dissolution of traditional routes to masculine status. These masculinities are regulated and policed through varying physical, verbal, and symbolic techniques—humour, insult, and violence—that continually challenge and contest the masculinities of group members. Chapter 8, *Generations of Gangs*, builds on the arguments in the previous chapters to probe the role of gang identity in the lives of children and young people growing up in Langview. In this chapter, I focus on the role of gang identities through various stages of transition, emphasizing the different roles the gang plays during different periods of social development. For many young people, gang identity represents a local rite of passage that is grown in and out of, replicated through street-based hierarchies based on age and status. This repetitive loop represents an ongoing adaptation to structural disadvantage in the context of local forms of 'hardman' masculinities, indicating the pattern through which territorial gang identification has reproduced in the city. Nonetheless, this pattern is neither fixed nor predetermined—for some young people the experience was preparatory for a smart, street-wise disposition which took them on to further education and economic success.

Chapter 9, *Come On, Die Young?* argues for an understanding of the gang phenomenon that is grounded in the experiences of children and young people yet is sensitive to the local and global structural contexts that pattern these experiences and identities. The city of Glasgow has undergone significant changes over the past century, reconfiguring the lived experience of young people growing up in the city. These developments have modified the nature of work, leisure, play, and space in Langview, alongside significant changes to the nature of youth identity and consumption. Young people grow up in an environment that is spatially constrained yet globally connected through new technologies and forms of communication. In this context, gang identities are perhaps best understood as a root of communal identity in a changing world—a means of establishing collective meaning in an increasingly constrained social landscape. The chapter concludes with a discussion of the implications and contributions of these arguments.

1

Shifting Definitions

Today's master symbol for excluded Others—the barbarian hordes threatening to crash the gates and destroy the foundations of civilization—is the gang member. The gang member is our urban savage, an all purpose devil figure onto which we project our deepest fears about social disorder and demographic change.

Conquergood (1996)[1]

In the aftermath of England's 'summer of violent disorder' in 2011, as television screens still fizzed with shaky images of blazing buildings and looted high streets, the British Prime Minister David Cameron was unequivocal in apportioning blame: 'At the heart of all the violence sits the issue of the street gangs. Territorial, hierarchical and incredibly violent, they are mostly composed of young boys, mainly from dysfunctional homes'.[2] A few days later, Cameron declared 'concerted, all-out war on gangs and gang culture... a major criminal disease that has infected streets and estates across our country'.[3] In stark terms, these statements marked a significant amplification of government rhetoric towards 'this thing we call a gang' (Morgan 2007), and a corresponding acceleration of gang-specific policy responses in the UK. More, they signalled a clear shift towards US-style definition and policing of the phenomenon, a country in which gangs have become one of the defining folk devils of the modern era.

---

[1] Quoted on <http://www.gangresearch.net> [Accessed 23 July 2013].
[2] BBC (2011) 'Riots: David Cameron's statement in full'. Available at: <http://www.bbc.co.uk/news/uk-politics-14492789 [Accessed 23 July 2013].
[3] UK Government (2011) 'PM's speech on the fightback after the riots'. Available at: https://www.gov.uk/government/speeches/pms-speech-on-the-fightback-after-the-riots [Accessed 23 July 2013].

This shift in political rhetoric has been accompanied, in part, by a change in academic approaches to gangs in the UK. Where once David Downes could pronounce with confidence on 'the absence of delinquent gangs in the East End [of London], except as a thoroughly atypical collectivity' (Downes 1966, p. 198), contemporary researchers are increasingly taking the existence of gangs as a given (Pitts 2008; Densley 2013). Debates sparked by this shift in emphasis (Goldson 2011) have, however, by and large taken place in the absence of new empirical material. In the absence of such a foundation, the field has lurched towards generalization about the 'UK gang phenomenon' that is often premised on the study of a single city, often London. This has in turn contributed to a conflicting and disunified knowledge base in relation to the UK gang phenomenon (Fraser 2012), and a corresponding lack of clarity on what gang identification might actually mean to young people in other parts of the UK. While the stigmata of 'the gang' must be approached with caution, it is clear that the term has real meaning for young people, and that new critical perspectives are required to make sense of the phenomenon.

In this chapter, I aim to clear a path for the development of new theoretical vocabularies with which to make sense of this reconfigured landscape, building a foundation for the nascent development of critical gang scholarship in the UK. This approach seeks to understand the meanings associated with gangs within the unique configurations of history, culture, and society in specific cities, grounding understandings at the micro-level of the community and the meso-level of city while tracing connections with the macro-level of global neoliberal economics. In building this foundation, I will first delineate some of the key indices of change in gang research—most notably the importation of criminal justice orientations towards gangs from the US, and the correspondingly negative implications for young people labelled as 'gang members'. In tracing the movement of this discourse, I explore the contrasts with British traditions of youth research, attempting to unpick the tangled knot of epistemological conflict, political positioning, and academic opportunism that have come to dominate the UK gang landscape. Tracing the intellectual lineage of gang research in the US, UK, and Europe, I identify four key shifts—street to database, subcultures to crime, local to global, and ethnography to dataset—that have cohered in an increasing convergence of approaches to gangs across a range of academic contexts.

These convergences, crucially, are rooted less in empirical realities, and more in efforts to 'internationalize' research through comparative agendas. As I will argue, while it is important to understand the *similarities* in gang formations in different global contexts—evidence as they are of the 'human consequences' of globalization (Bauman 2000b)—it is equally important to recognize and understand *difference*. Such 'global' research agendas mask wide divergences in the nature, form, and meaning of gang activity between linguistic, cultural, and geographical contexts. In the final section, I introduce the challenges posed by the case of Glasgow, where gang identification has remained remarkably resilient to change or evolution. The chapter makes a case against universalizing tendencies in gang research, emphasizing the heterogeneity and multiplicity of gangs both within and between nation states. The intention in reframing understandings of gangs in this way is as a bulwark against the importation of criminal justice policy that is explicitly targeted at a fearful global image of gangs, rather than in the lived experience of young people in specific urban contexts.

These shifts are particularly evident in US approaches to gang research as positivist and criminal justice approaches to gangs have come to dominate the field. Nonetheless, there are clear signs that this pattern is being followed in the UK and elsewhere. In drawing attention to the marked continuities in the Glasgow gang phenomenon over the course of the twentieth century, I hope to demonstrate the importance of challenging these shifts in narrative, and emphasize the geographical and cultural specificities of gang identity. This is not a call to return to a bygone era of research, but to urge for new theoretical and methodological advances that weave between street and data, that are informed by both sociological and criminological perspectives, that ground understandings at a local level while retaining a global reflexivity, and that blend insights from both qualitative and quantitative data.

Street to database

In *Keywords: A Vocabulary of Culture and Society* (1976), Raymond Williams traces the shifting meanings of the term 'culture' over time—from an emphasis on cultivation, to the development and process of the human mind, to an independent noun, and beyond. These changes occurred partly as a result of organic alterations to social life, but partly as a result of the changing forces of social order, power, and politics: linguistic development reflects not only changing social attitudes and mores but also the variable boundaries of official definition. A genealogy of the term 'culture' therefore exposes both the shifting nature of social life and the changing politics of society. As Williams states:

When we come to say 'we just don't speak the same language'...each group is speaking its native language, but its uses are significantly different, and especially when strong feelings or important ideas are in question. No single group is 'wrong' by any linguistic criterion, though a temporarily dominant group may try to enforce its own uses as 'correct'. (Williams 1976, pp. 11–12)

Clear parallels can be drawn with the genealogy of the term 'gang'. For much of its lifetime the term 'gang' was particular to specific cultural contexts—with separate etymological developments existing in Scotland, England, and the US—developing in step with changing social conditions, and subsequently with developing research agendas. It is only latterly that these specific meanings have become squashed under the weight of universalized definitions.

In the US, definitions of gangs have varied significantly according to social conditions. Initially used to describe frontier outlaws and prisoners, it was only in the wake of urbanization that usage became attached to street-based groups of young people (Sanchez-Jankowski 1991, p. 2). As Sanchez-Jankowski argues:

Looking at the history of the word *gang* in the United States, one finds that the term has perennially been used of certain social groups considered to be major social problems of the time. The social science academy's research on gangs has its own history, and the focus of this research has in turn been influenced largely by what society has considered the major social problems of the period. (Sanchez-Jankowski 1991, p. 1)

Early definitions of gangs, crucially, lacked the malignant criminal overtones of modern definitions—the gang was a relatively benign form of social organization, emerging in the interstices of the emerging cityscape; a by-product of population density, overcrowded streets, and poverty (Asbury 1927). Gangs were a vehicle through which to act out youthful fantasies and test developing social identities, in the search for creativity and excitement. In this sense, the gang was understood as serving a social function of maturation between childhood and adulthood, 'a manifestation of the period of readjustment' (Thrasher 1927/1963, p. 32) that served as a space for creating and mimicking adult identities, criminal or otherwise. Crucially, while early gang research sought to identify generic patterns of gang formation amid the social laboratory of Chicago, definitions and findings were firmly rooted in a specific time and place. Thrasher's (1963, p. 57) classic definition represents this balance of the general and the specific most clearly:

[The gang is] an interstitial group originally formed spontaneously, and then integrated through conflict. It is characterized by the following types of behaviour: meeting face to face, milling, movement through space as a unit, conflict, and planning. The result of this collective behaviour is the development of tradition, unreflective internal structure, esprit de corps, solidarity, morale, group awareness, and attachment to a local territory.

Subsequent research into youthful street groupings similarly looked to develop theoretical contributions from grounded definitions. In Shaw's classic biographical study, *The Jackroller* (1930/1966), Stanley's involvement in gang activity is fleeting and context-specific, part and parcel of his drift in and out of the slum areas of Chicago and further afield. Whyte's *Street Corner Society* (1943) emphasized a contextual and cultural explanation for gang activity—Whyte's detailed case study revealed the often banal routine that patterned the lives of Doc and The Nortons. Others that followed demonstrate a similar effort to comprehend the changing nature of social life through localized empirical study. Bloch and Niederhoffer (1958) discuss the role of developing sexual identity and group status in the push and pull towards gang identity; Miller (1958) describes the ways in which gang identities form part of the process of 'preparing the youngster for adult life within that culture' (Miller 1958, quoted in Klein 1971, p. 36); Matza, in *Delinquency and Drift* (1964), famously described the process of 'drift' between legal and illegal activities, which young people negotiate in making sense of the normative order. For Cloward and Ohlin (1960), youth groups and adult criminality had to be understood as an ecological whole—with development of a youthful street gang into a more organized criminal enterprise contingent on the illegitimate opportunities that exist in that locale. What these studies have in common is an effort to generate and refine sociological theory from specific case studies—definitions were rooted in particular contexts, with correspondent theoretical and epistemological underpinnings.

In the 1970s, however, a marked change occurred within the study of gangs, where the emphases shifted markedly to a universalist perspective whose starting point was not in specific sites but in efforts to delineate a universal social phenomenon (Brotherton 2008). The stimulus for this shift appears to be the first US conference on gangs, bringing together practitioners, researchers, and scholars (Klein 1967, p. v). Up until this point, Klein criticized 'findings from various studies and projects [which] tend to be limited to the geographical areas from which they emanate' (Klein 1967, p. v). Instead, consensus was sought in developing a universalized definition of gangs, which could be employed for comparative research and generalized social policy (Miller 1975).[4] The field shifted away from grounded qualitative work and towards attempts to categorize, compare, and design interventions. As a result, positivist methodologies were increasingly applied. While this was clearly intended as a means of tackling an emergent social problem, the unintended consequence was that of shifting attention away from the complex lived realities at street level. A chain reaction was set in motion that saw definitions of gangs moving from the public grammar of the street to the hidden logic of the database.

Subsequently, in the context of the broader ascendancy of positivism in mainstream criminological inquiry in the US (Young 2011; Joe-Laidler and Hunt 2012), funding streams have become directed towards quantitative methods and criminal justice policy and gang research geared increasingly towards assessing potential risk in police intelligence databases and informing judicial decision making (Spergel 2009; Jacobs 2009; White 2008). Today, gang research in the US has grown into a vast academic industry, as federal and state governments attempt to control the endemic violence affecting communities across the country. As Klein argues, summarizing the ascendancy of criminal justice orientations to criminological orthodoxy: 'Whatever may have been the history of the term *gang* and whatever may have been the desire—in many ways legitimate—to avoid stigmatizing youth groups with a

---

[4] The fact that Miller's consensus definition—involving a wide range of youth workers, criminal justice agents, and self-identifying gang members—had some 1400 features suggested (Ball and Curry 1995, p. 228) attests to the inherent difficulties of establishing a fixed definition.

pejorative term, it is time to characterize the street gang specifically for its involvement, attitudinal and/or behavioural, in delinquency and crime' (Klein 1995, p. 23).

The shift from particular to universal definitions of gangs is epitomized most clearly in the work of the Eurogang network, a group of European and US gang researchers who have developed a set of common definitional criteria for the purposes of cross-national research, comprising 'any durable, street-oriented youth group whose involvement in illegal activity is part of its group identity' (van Gemert 2005, p. 148). According to this broad definition, there are identifiable gangs in a range of European cities, exhibiting similar characteristics as their US counterparts. While this form of global surveying of gangs is instructive, implicit in these accounts is what we might call a 'cultural levelling' approach to gangs, in which gang meanings are removed from specific local contexts and re-imagined as a global universal. As when a range of local dialects are purged in favour of a singular 'official' language, the search for a universal definition purges the divergent linguistic and cultural histories of local contexts. While it is one thing to sketch the contours of a definition for the purposes of comparison—with colour and texture added through careful localized study—it is another to impose a definition wholesale.

This shift in approach to defining gangs—from particularism to universalism, bottom up to top down—can also be read as an indice of the changing means through which power and control have been exerted towards 'risky' populations. In the context of broader shifts towards risk management and actuarial justice (Feeley and Simon 1992; O'Malley 2001), it is clear that 'the gang' is becoming an increasingly potent lens through which social policy is directed. Like Hacking's description of the construction of 'human kinds' (2004), 'gang membership' has increasingly become a technique of classification in police databases, a form of data that exists independently of the real world. As Hacking describes, these can create a 'looping effect' that is constituted by 'interactions between classifications of people and the people classified' (2004, p. 279). While gang intelligence systems in the US have generated a lively debate of attendant problems (Spergel 2009)—resulting in 'undeserved law-enforcement attention... statutory sentencing enhancements... segregation in jail and prison, as well as causing a host of other consequences' (Kennedy 2009, p. 711)—in the UK similar systems have 'slipped unquestioned into mainstream policy and practice', with important consequences for gang labelling processes (Ralphs et al. 2009, p. 485).[5] Ralphs and colleagues (2009) point to the ways in which the definitional ambiguities surrounding gangs can have real and lasting consequences for children and young people growing up in communities designated 'gang areas'. In these areas, unjustifiable labelling of young people as 'gang associates' has resulted in school exclusions and heavy-handed police tactics:

> Being labelled as a gang member or associate created a greater vulnerability to police attention and surveillance. Armed police raids on family homes in search for firearms were common and brought stigma, stress and feelings of violation to the families involved. Young people living in these areas and labelled as 'gang associates' were often subjected to police checks and exclusion from community events including carnivals and family fun days. (Ralphs et al. 2009, p. 491)

The rendering of young people as 'gang members' through police intelligence is inherently problematic not only due to the difficulties in defining membership but also due to the role of civilian intelligence analysts, for whom the 'gang' may represent an abstract entity, composed of records from a database (Fraser and Atkinson 2014). In the process, local histories and individual identities are increasingly erased in the construction of the 'global gang'.

The shift from street-based understandings of gangs to definition by database represents the changing techniques of classifying and controlling 'risky' populations in the US. Despite a different etymological history, responses to gangs in the UK have become increasingly contiguous with mainstream US approaches. This shift stands in contrast with the critical approaches to youthful deviance that have dominated British research for several generations of scholarship.

---

[5] The recent introduction of Gangbos is further evidence of universalism in policy making (see Guardian 2009). Crucially, there is no empirical evidence for the efficacy of gang-specific intervention. A recent comprehensive review of UK gang interventions—a report of some 155 pages—found that 'overall, the comprehensive interventions had a positive, but not statistically significant, effect on reducing crime outcomes compared with usual service provision' (Hodgkinson et al. 2009, p. 5).

Subcultures to crime

Early meanings of the term 'gang' in English reflect a journey, movement,[6] or a 'set of things or people'. Later, these threads cohered to suggest a collective movement such as a band of travellers or company of workmen; in short, a collective noun for a group of men. Despite evidence indicating a longer genealogy (Pearson 2006), the first dedicated academic studies of 'delinquent' gang behaviour in the UK were not published until the 1950s and 1960s, in the form of an article in the *British Journal of Delinquency*[7] by Scott (1956), and Downes' book, *The Delinquent Solution* (1966). Both involved applications of the burgeoning US research and theory to youth groups in London, and both found comparable examples difficult to trace. As Scott describes, 'It is indeed difficult to find good examples of gangs, nor do the few that are found conform with the picture of healthy devilment, adventurousness, pride of leadership or loyal lieutenancy, that is often painted' (Scott 1956, p. 11). Basing his conclusions on 10 years of experience with young offenders and youth groups, Scott finds that the majority of group offenders were more frequently 'fleeting, casual delinquent associations' or 'adolescent street groups' than 'gangs proper' (Scott 1956, p. 20). Downes' *The Delinquent Solution* (1966), based on 'informal observations' in the streets of the Stepney and Poplar boroughs of London, similarly found 'US-style' gangs to be absent, and contemporaneous theories to be inapplicable: 'observation and information combined point to the absence of delinquent gangs in the East End, except as a thoroughly atypical collectivity' (Downes 1966, p. 198). Parker's classic study of youthful deviance in Roundhouse in the 1970s found similarly that '[t]he Boys are not a gang, they do not possess such rigid defining criteria; they are a network, a loose-knit social group' (Parker 1974, p. 64). Wilmott's *Adolescent Boys of East London* (1966) presented a similar picture of class and community-based groupings, grounding analysis at street level and disavowing gang labels.

---

[6] The Oxford English Dictionary lists the early uses of the term as an 'action or mode of going or moving' or 'action or an act of travelling', dating from around the tenth century: <http://www.oed.com/view/Entry/76566?rskey=DxrTSZ&result=1&isAdvanced=false#eid> [Accessed 15 January 2015].

[7] Now the *British Journal of Criminology*.

In recent years, however, the issue of youth 'gangs' in the UK has become an area of intense scrutiny, generating a range of policy, policing, and media responses. Sparked by a series of high-profile teenage deaths, and inflamed in the aftermath of the English Riots of 2011, 'dealing with gangs' has become a central plank of political discourse on law and order. A report from the Centre for Social Justice is emblematic of this change in rhetoric:

Over the past decade British society has seen an increase in gang culture and its associated violence. In addition, the composition and nature of gang culture has shifted: gang members are getting younger, geographical territory is transcending drug territory and violence is increasingly chaotic. (Centre for Social Justice 2009, p. 19)

David Cameron's declaration of a 'concerted, all-out war on gangs and gang culture'[8] marked a significant shift in rhetoric towards youth crime in the UK and has now been followed by a corresponding acceleration of gang-specific policy responses (HM Government 2011), many of which have a distinctly US flavour.[9] Summarizing the impact of such developments in England, Smithson and colleagues (2013, p. 114) recognize the importance of policy transfer from the US, noting that many English cities have developed dedicated police gang units, such as Trident in London, Matrix in Liverpool, Xcalibre in Manchester, and Stealth in Nottingham.[10] These developments signal a clear shift towards US-style understanding of gangs, with policing by database a central strategic move (Fraser and Atkinson 2014). In many ways this pattern of policy transfer from the US to the UK is the wrong way around, as the rates of 'gang' violence in the US are substantially higher than that in the UK (Hallsworth and Brotherton 2011). Given the trajectory described above, there are clear signs that

---

[8] HM Government (2011) 'PM's speech on the fightback after the riots'. Available at: <https://www.gov.uk/government/speeches/pms-speech-on-the-fightback-after-the-riots> [Accessed 23 July 2013].

[9] For a cogent critique of this policy document, see Cottrell-Boyce (2013).

[10] Katz and Webb (2006, p. 206) note that as violence associated with gangs increased in the 1970s, there has been a steady consolidation of gang policing within specialized taskforces. The defining characteristic of the units studied by Katz and Webb was the 'primary responsibility for collecting, processing, and disseminating gang intelligence for the police department was a defining characteristic'.

gangs are becoming the folk devil *par excellence* for twenty-first-century Britain (Fraser and Piacentini 2013).[11]

Rather than drawing on the language of 'gangs', the study of youth groups in the UK has largely, to date, been analysed through the subcultural studies of the Birmingham Centre for Contemporary Cultural Studies (BCCCS) and the National Deviance Conference.[12] The Birmingham School, founded by prominent members of the New Left in the 1960s, brought Chicago School methods of participant observation[13] to the study of youth culture in 1970s Britain, emphasizing the collective routes through which cultural identities are formed. Drawing together sophisticated Marxist theory and grounded methods, studies focused on the symbolic meanings and identities involved in the spectacular youth cultures of the 1970s—punks (Hebdige 1979), skinheads (Clarke 1975), and Teddy Boys (Jefferson 1975)—in seeking to make sense of the growing tensions caused by unemployment within wider working-class culture (Mungham and Pearson 1976). As Phil Cohen summarizes: 'the latent function of subculture is this—to express and resolve albeit "magically", the contradictions of the parent culture' (P. Cohen 1972, p. 23). The shift towards

---

[11] In England, as the perceived threat posed by gangs has become inflated, so a range of other popular fears have been collapsed into the gang phenomenon—notably those related to gender and 'violent women' (Batchelor 2009; Young 2011), ethnicity, and marginalization (Aldridge et al. 2007), gun and knife crime, immigration, asylum, and violent extremism (Alexander 2008).

[12] Although originating in a different time and place, the National Deviance Conference (NDC) brought similar methodological and theoretical agendas to bear on the study of crime and deviance, breaking away from what was perceived to be the positivist dogma of the period.

[13] The Chicago School sought to distinguish patterns of interaction, association, and order amid the rapid population and urbanization of the city. One of the most prominent methods of discovering these patterns was through direct observation of the phenomenon being studied. As Park, a former journalist, famously exhorted his students: 'Go and sit in the lounges of the luxury hotels and on the doorsteps of the flophouses; sit on the Gold Coast settees and on the slum shakedowns; sit in the Orchestra Hall and in the Star & Garter Burlesk. In short, gentlemen, go get the seat of your pants dirty in *real* research' (Robert E. Park, speaking *c*.1920, quoted in Lofland 1971). This instruction was taken up by a generation of graduate students (Faris 1967), leading to the publication of scores of observational studies of Chicago during this period—famous examples including *The Hobo* (Anderson 1923), *The Taxi-Dance Hall* (Cressey 1932), *The Ghetto* (Wirth 1928), *The Gold Coast and the Slum* (Zorbaugh 1929), and, of course, *The Gang* (Thrasher 1927/1963).

gang rhetoric therefore represents a marked contrast to critical traditions of youth research in the UK, exposing clear epistemological and methodological tensions between academic researchers.

Drawing on the subsequent critical vocabularies of moral panic, labelling, and cultural rebellion pioneered by Cohen (1972), Parker (1974), Hall and colleagues (1978), Robins and Cohen (1978), and Corrigan (1979), British studies of youthful deviance have, until very recently, pointedly avoided recourse to 'gang talk' (Hallsworth and Young 2008). One of the few studies of gangs in the early part of the millennium argued, for example, that:

'The Gang' exists more as an idea than a reality—a mode of interpretation rather than an object, more fiction than fact. It becomes self-fulfilling prophecy, self-fulfilling and axiomatic, impossible to disprove and imbued with the residual power of common-sense 'Truth'. (Alexander 2000, p. xiii)

Alexander's powerful ethnography demonstrates the distance between representation and reality in most 'gang talk' and highlights the necessity of constructionist approaches to the gang phenomenon. More recently, however, something of an accepted wisdom has developed in relation to gangs in the UK—not only are there no 'US' gangs, but any implication otherwise represents either a cynical form of moral entrepreneurialism or an uncritical acceptance of criminal justice authoritarianism. In general, however, the behaviour of youth groups studied by the BCCCS and successors were relatively peaceable and non-violent in comparison to the level of violence attributed to youth gangs. The sudden wave of violence in contemporary London and elsewhere, alongside the frenzy of media interest in the apparent influx of 'US-style' gangs, therefore presented some academic researchers with a conundrum. Prefacing their report on gang behaviour in the UK, Squires and colleagues (2008, pp. 5–6), point out:

Throughout the period during which this report was being compiled, virtually every other news bulletin, every day, featured stories about another person, often young, being stabbed or shot on Britain's apparently dangerous streets…Drafting this report [on gangs and knife crime] in such a climate has been like trying to negotiate a river crossing in full flood.

Notably, the empirical basis for knowledge of gangs in the UK remains weak. Put simply, quantitative surveys invariably find relatively high levels of fixed gang membership—though varying by the cohort involved, and questions asked—while qualitative and ethnographic accounts demonstrate the fluidity and situational specificity of gang identities (Batchelor 2009). For example, Bennett and Holloway's study, involving adults arrested across 14 sites in England and Wales, found that 15 per cent of those arrested defined themselves as having 'current or past experience as a gang member' (Bennett and Holloway 2004, p. 311); the Offending, Crime and Justice Survey found that 6 per cent of 10- to 19-year-olds were members of a 'delinquent youth group' (Sharp et al. 2006, p. v); and the 'Edinburgh Study of Youth Transitions and Crime' reports that some 20 per cent of 13-year-olds report gang membership (Smith and Bradshaw 2005, p. 3). Contrastingly, qualitative and ethnographic research consistently finds that gang membership is fluid and in most cases indistinguishable from other peer associations. As Aldridge and colleagues state, 'gangs are very much like informal friendship networks whose boundaries vary according to whom you ask in the network. Indeed the notion of "membership" was somehow alien to the vocabulary of young people we interviewed' (Aldridge et al. 2007, p. 17). A Youth Justice Board report (Young et al. 2007) found that distinguishing between gang members and young people who offended in groups was inherently problematic, due to 'young people's own claims to gang status in order to boost their credibility; labels ascribed by others to any form of group offending by young people; [and] the groups young people are involved in tending to overlap and continually change' (Young et al. 2007, p. 15).

This level of debate and controversy, coupled with the number and breadth of competing actors and agencies, has left researchers struggling to gain purchase in public debate. As Alexander notes, ' "the gang" has developed a public life independent of any empirical foundation or conceptual exploration—full of its own sound and fury, but signifying very little' (Alexander 2008, p. 3). For many schooled in the critical traditions of labelling and subcultural theory, academic 'gang talk' is encoded with racialized, gendered, and class-based stereotypes. In the fast-flowing currents of government policy and public opinion, however, these critical voices have become embroiled in something of a log-jam. The rapid rise of apparently 'gang-related' youth violence has not been easily located within the Birmingham School tradition, creating something of a theoretical vacuum. In criticizing gang research that leans too heavily on these traditions, Laurie Taylor put this dilemma succinctly:

Although I'm sure it's a very valuable exercise to explode the conventional nonsense about a Golden Age...and although I'm also sure that it's valuable to show how the alleged causes of street violence constantly recur...it does often strike me that this knowledge can seem irrelevant, almost an academic distraction, when we're emotionally confronted by the sad fact of yet another wasted life. And perhaps that's the enduring dilemma in this area. How to reconcile our commendable empathy with victims of violence with an intellectual appreciation of how, given an historical context, that violence is sadly nothing new. (Laurie Taylor, *Thinking Allowed*, 31 December 2008)

As Taylor suggests, scholars have struggled to locate this violence within critical British intellectual traditions and have been keen to avoid recourse to US gang research, yet there has been little new empirical research on which to build understanding. As a result, UK gang scholarship has become an increasingly tangled web of methodologies, political agendas, and definitions, underpinned by a relatively static set of epistemological conflicts.

On one hand, based on a series of community studies in London, Pitts (2008, 2011) argues forcefully that the UK gang phenomenon represents a fundamentally new and unique set of dangers and instabilities, cohering around a set of social, cultural, and economic circumstances similar to that of the US. Pitts mounts a forceful, left-realist critique of constructionist perspectives on gangs, arguing that youth gangs in the UK represent a novel, cogent, and distinctive threat, addressing 'the thorny academic debate about whether or not "youth gangs" exist and, if they do, whether or not we should be worried about them. It concludes that they do and we should' (Pitts 2011, p. 161). On the other, Hallsworth (2011, 2013), also drawing on a series of qualitative studies of young people in London, argues that violent street worlds are not reducible to the 'garrulous discourse' of 'gang talk' (Hallsworth and Young 2008, p. 177)—and that the subcultural and critical academic traditions of the UK are more apt to describe these experiences. For Hallsworth, 'the problem of "the gang" is not "the gang" itself, but the media-driven "moral panic" and "gang control industry" that surrounds it' (Hallsworth 2011, p. 184). Listing compelling evidence of moral entrepreneurialism within the gang phenomenon, Hallsworth locates the societal reaction to gangs within the oeuvre of classical critical criminological perspectives.

These polarized positions have come to dominate gang research in the UK, with researchers impelled towards deciding 'Whose Side Are We On?' (Becker 1963). In what follows, I seek to navigate these contested waters by emphasizing divergences in the history and present of gangs in different cities in the UK. By looking at the contingent lineage and path dependencies of gangs in Glasgow, I hope to demonstrate the importance of locating understanding within the contexts of different urban environments while remaining sensitive to the dangers inherent within the growing 'gang industry' (Hallsworth 2013). This step is particularly critical in the current context, as Squires and colleagues (2008, p. 105) note: when 'popular concern and political reactions drive the debate along, the danger often is that policy making begins to outrun the available evidence base'. While the critical traditions of British youth sociology remain an indispensable tool in puncturing popular stereotypes and drawing attention to particular historical contexts, it has become equally clear that new conceptual lenses are also required. Without this foundation, the vacuum will be increasingly filled by entrepreneurial research that is directed more towards funding and 'impact' on this heavily politicized issue than in understanding the phenomenon in a grounded way. Indeed, there is a danger that gang researchers in the UK may, 'like U.S. journalists in the Iraq war...become embedded in the law enforcement bureaucracies that are waging war on gangs, drugs, terror, practicing a kind of domestic orientalism' (Hagedorn 2008, p. 135).

In developing these new conceptual vocabularies it is notable that there is a new generation of gang scholarship emerging in the UK. Aldridge and colleagues, for example, basing their findings on an intensive two-year ethnography in an unnamed English city, argue that debates over the existence—or non-existence—of gangs in the UK in fact obscure the lived realities of children and young people growing up in communities where violence and gang labels exist (Aldridge et al. 2007). Instead, they seek to ground their research in the experiences of participants, for whom 'gangs are very much like informal friendship networks whose boundaries vary according to whom you ask in the network. Indeed the notion of "membership" was somehow alien to the vocabulary of young people we interviewed' (Aldridge et al. 2007, p. 17). Tara Young (2009, 2010) and Batchelor (2010) have done much to challenge the 'malestream' in UK gang criminology, setting out an exploratory agenda for research that draws on the complex meanings and motivations for women's violence. Others (Ralphs et al. 2009; Smithson and Ralphs 2013; Densley 2013) have started exploring the divergent forms of gang identification and implications for social policy in a range of ways. Crucially, too, this new generation of scholarship draws on empirical data that is geographically diverse—as Medina and colleagues (2013, p. 200) point out, there are 'diverse scenarios across cities' where change over time must be understood within particular urban contexts.

In cultivating this critical foundation, it is important to exercise caution regarding generalization or importation of US gang definitions. In the fearful rhetoric of the 'global gang', local experiences and identifications remain pivotal.

Local to global

As the youth gang phenomenon has become a sensitive issue in communities from Los Angeles to Rio, Cape Town to London, the locally rooted understandings that constituted the wellspring of contemporary gang research have become supplanted by research that seeks out *comparison* of gangs across diverse global sites. As myths and stereotypes relating to gangs circulate via the global media of film and TV, so a hyper-mediated global consciousness of gangs as a fundamental social evil has developed momentum. From the reproduction of US gang 'style' in Europe (Decker et al. 2009) to televised 'tours' of gangs in different cities around the world,[14] from film representations to videogames that turn gang life into commodified thrills, 'the gang' has become a global brand. In this context, academic researchers have become increasingly alert to the global nature of gang activity, and have sought to survey the global topography of gangs (Klein et al. 2001). In the process, however, both the broader forces that structure life in gang communities and the lived experiences that compose them have become blurred and glossed.

Despite clear political and economic convergences between the US and Europe, particularly the UK, in recent years (Young 1999; Garland 2001; Pitts 2008; Jones and Newburn 2007), there

[14] For example, the Sky One television series, *Ross Kemp on Gangs* (2008).

remain equally clear points of cultural and historical divergence (Wacquant 2008a). As Venkatesh and Kassimir (2007, p. 7) note:

the similarities among and the connections across the Atlantic do not erase or make meaningless the distinctiveness of each locality in terms of their cultural, political, and historical landscapes—a point that recent research on global processes has made quite evident, and that complicates any simplistic notion of homogenisation.

Nonetheless, the predominant response among gang researchers to 'globalization' has been to *reach backwards* to previous debates regarding definitions, rather than to *reach outwards* towards literature that considers the unique predicament of researching gangs in the global context. Comparative study has to date focused on the similarities of the gang phenomenon in diverse sites, rather than focusing on understanding and explaining differences. As the Eurogang group concedes:

[W]e have a very limited understanding of how local and national contexts shape the particular ways in which the gang phenomenon is socially constructed and developed across different national and local contexts outside the US... it could be argued that in its current configuration the Eurogang set of tools is well designed to illustrate similarities and differences in gang dynamics and behavior across national locations. However, a lot of work needs to be done to *explain those differences*. (Emphasis added; Weerman et al. 2009, pp. 22, 24)

The nature and meaning of 'gangs' vary tremendously across time and space. In Glasgow, gangs are street-based groups of teenagers, affiliated with specific territories, that engage in territorial violence. In cities like Chicago, however, gangs play a pivotal role in organized violence (Dowdney 2007) and international drug trafficking (Castells 2000). As such, cross-national definition may obscure as much as it reveals.

There are, moreover, deeply uncomfortable convergences of geopolitical and intellectual power in the construction of 'global' definitions of gangs, as there are in contemporary criminological knowledge more broadly (Aas 2011). As critical anthropologists have demonstrated (Comaroff and Comaroff 2012), despite claims to 'global' research, the majority of knowledge production remains concentrated in the global North, in particular the US. Similarly, research and practice emanating from the US—often with a crime-control orientation—have exerted a gravitational pull on gang research, policing, and policy making in cities across the global North and South. All too often we view the issue of gangs through a blinkered lens: blinkered by the fact that most research, and most researchers, are based in the global North and that US stereotypes and definitions cast a long shadow. The genealogy of gangs in Hong Kong, for example, is culturally rooted in the unique colonial and post-colonial politics of the region, alongside the particular history of political dissidence and underground resistance in China. As such it is not only incorrect but also arrogant—constituting a kind of knowledge-based colonialism—to impose definitions and constructions developed in the North to explore the unique aspects of cities within the global South (Fraser 2013b).

Although there is little doubt that global processes have led to convergences in the spaces of 'advanced marginality' in which gangs most frequently emerge (Wacquant 2008a), these are always refracted through the prism of local historical and cultural conditions. As Dowdney (2007, p. 28) notes, gangs in the global context most often emerge in:

urban enclaves of poverty that are underdeveloped and distanced from the state via differentiated policy and poor provision of public services, and densely populated. Furthermore, these areas tend to be in cities or countries that have populations comprised of a notably high percentage of adolescents and youths, where adolescent labour in the formal and informal markets is common despite disproportionately high levels of unemployment and low levels of education amongst this group.

Processes of globalization have accelerated the development of this form of urban enclave in a wide range of countries (Davis 2006). Yet, as Wacquant's work demonstrates, there are critical divergences in the particularities of these global trends that require investigation of lived experience, cultural difference, and institutional change (Wacquant 2008a). Gangs are deeply rooted in the social, economic, and political histories of the urban environments from which they emerge (Coughlin and Venkatesh 2003; Sanchez-Jankowski 2003), in some cases becoming powerful political actors in their own right (Brotherton and Barrios 2004; Hagedorn 2008).

As definitions have shifted from street to database, local to global, so the study of gangs has become increasingly allied to criminal justice orientations beyond the US. Although individual nation states have diverse and varied histories of street-based collectives, and unique histories of crime control systems, the logic of the 'global gang' has become increasingly dominant—aided by the mobility of gang 'experts' and policy transfer. In the process, local meanings and understanding are increasingly undermined. In order to compare these divergent social and cultural environments, definitional accuracy is substituted for breadth—such that a wide range of street-based youths are subsumed, and groups that do not fit the US archetype are excluded. Global comparisons are important, but must be constructed in such a way as to recognize and understand difference. In order to construct these meso-level variables in a way that is grounded in reality there is a need to reinvigorate the ethnographic study of gangs in a way that responds flexibly this new global context.

Ethnography to dataset

From the eight-year, city-wide qualitative study of gangs carried out by Thrasher (1927/1963), the field of gang research developed critical mass in the post-war period, with a wide range of close-up, on-the-ground studies of gangs in different neighbourhoods and contexts. These contributions, crucially, were rich in theoretical sophistication, and were operating at the leading edge of new sociological understandings of society; in different ways, all were searching for broad theoretical knowledge that was applicable in different times and places whilst remaining grounded in the lived experiences of young people. Indeed, it can be said that gang research, as it is known today, was formed through ethnographic, qualitative, and participatory research (Hobbs 2001). As Decker and Pyrooz note, '[p]erhaps no substantive area in criminology is as closely tied to a methodology as gangs are to ethnography' (Decker and Pyrooz 2013, p. 274). The illicit nature of gang activity precludes in-depth 'outsider' understanding—ethnography, 'as a *sensibility* about the external world and a *sensitivity* to its nuanced ambiguities' (Ferrell 2009, p. 16), has been particularly well suited to documenting the lived experience of street life. It is paradoxical, therefore, that the recent increase in attention to gangs coincides with a marked decline in interpretivist ethnographic accounts from street level. Grounded accounts have latterly become sidelined as quantitative methodologies have become the new orthodoxy in both US and comparative gang research.

Adler and Adler (1998a) map the history of ethnographic studies of deviance in the US, broadly, onto the history of artistic
movements. They see key formative eras as the 'Impressionism'
of the Chicago School of the 1920s and 1930s, followed by the
'Renaissance' of the Second Chicago School in the 1940s and
1950s, then the 'Abstract Expressionism' of ethnographies of
counter-culture in the 1960s. The 1970s to 1990s signalled a
return to the 'Dark Ages', where criminal justice orientations, statistical universalism, and Institutional Review Boards drowned
out the wave of creative ethnographies from the earlier eras.
Nonetheless, the Adlers see the turn of the twenty-first century
as evidence of a new 'Enlightenment', a gasp for breath amid the
stifling airlessness that had come to dominate criminological
research. This new period is marked by the ascension of 'ethnographies at the edge'—studies of graffiti writers, motorcyclists, sky-
divers, firefighters—that represented an injection of energy into an
increasingly despondent field (Ferrell and Hamm 1998).

This trajectory translates well as a lineage of methodological approaches to gangs. Gang research found its feet in the
'Impressionist' mix of journalistic methods, cutting-edge social
theory, and rapid urbanization that composed the Chicago School
of Sociology. Thrasher (1927/1963) had the time and space to
spend eight years composing a city-wide picture of gangs—the
depth and range of the observations generated by this approach
have truly stood the test of time. Although published later, and
researched in Boston, Whyte's *Street Corner Society* (1943) owed
much to the Chicago School, steeped as it was in participant
observation. Yet Whyte's intervention was also a break from the
Chicago School's thesis of 'social disorganization'—Whyte's careful study demonstrated a firm social order and street hierarchy in
the midst of an apparently unorganized space. The critical period
for gang research, however, was the 'Renaissance' of the 1950s
and 1960s, and the surge of theoretically informed empirical studies published during this period.[15] Unlike the focus of the Second
Chicago School—on the 'total' institutions of asylums, prisons,
factories—these studies were tracing sociological threads from
Merton, Sutherland, and Blumer and shaping them into a budding

---

[15] Cohen 1955; Bloch and Niederhoffer 1958; Cloward and Ohlin 1960;
Yablonsky 1962; Matza 1964; Short and Strodtbeck 1965.

sociology of deviance (Fine 1995). They took place, too, amid the New Deal optimism of post-war America, and efforts to remedy social problems through social inclusion and welfare, rather than the 'Abstract Expressionism' of countercultural studies.

The 'Dark Ages', in the US at least, are characterized by the increased dominance of positivist methodologies, resulting in a lack of normalized critique and debate within studies of gangs (Katz and Jackson-Jacobs 2004)—mirroring the broader ascendancy of 'Abstracted Empiricism' (Young 2012) in the social sciences more generally. As Hallsworth and Young, from a British perspective, write: 'the empirically driven gang research tradition not only fails to grasp group life as a space of cultural production, it actively misrepresents the reality of group life in the reductive empiricist analysis the phenomena brings to bear to describe it' (Hallsworth and Young 2008, p. 187). As gang definitions have moved from street to database so researchers have increasingly shifted from grounded ethnographic approaches to statistical datasets. This is problematic because of the demonstrable difficulties in ascertaining membership—as Jock Young argues, while certain phenomena are capable of definition, 'there are many others that are blurred...because it is their nature to be blurred' (Young 2004, pp. 25–6)—but also in the distance between researcher and research context. As Hacking describes of criminological classifications more generally:

[t]he use of these categories often has real effects upon people. Not necessarily direct effects, related to the mere knowledge that the authorities or experts classify you in a certain way. The effect can be indirect, when the classifications are incorporated into the rules of institutions, for example prisons. Few criminals know the elaborate theories and structures of criminological classification. (Hacking 2004, p. 297)

While participatory research has a stronger tradition in the UK,[16] and ethnographic methods have underpinned a number of recent studies (Aldridge et al. 2008; Gunter 2008; Densley 2013), there

---

[16] Downes' *The Delinquent Solution* (1966) was based on 'informal observations' in the streets of the Stepney and Poplar boroughs of London. Similarly, classic studies of gang identification in Glasgow during this period drew on participatory and ethnographic approaches (Armstrong and Wilson 1973a; Patrick 1973). The Birmingham School's methodological approach leaned heavily on to ethnography; 'not [as] a single method, but a repertoire of methods, even including survey techniques and statistics' (Roberts 1976, p. 245).

are also clear signs that data-driven research—with its attendant difficulties—is coming to define the field (Fraser and Atkinson 2014). As Ericson and Haggerty argue:

[t]he more the abstract system of specialized knowledge becomes embedded in communication formats and technologies, the more it takes on a life of its own. As it deskills, it also produces alienating and fragmenting effects on the occupational culture and the self. (Ericson and Haggerty 1997, p. 38)

There are, perhaps, signs of a nascent 'Enlightenment' in ethnographic approaches to gangs, in light of the broader movement to understanding global 'forces, connections, and imaginations' by seeking out new ethnographic fieldsites in which the lived experiences of globalization can be captured (Burawoy 2000), and critical reflexivity in the social sciences (Bourdieu and Wacquant 1992).[17] As Brotherton (2007, p. 378) has argued, in the context of a 'highly mobile, stratified and globalizing society' in which marginalized groups must maintain identity and community within a 'global sphere of production and exchange', some gangs have evolved into transnational organizations exhibiting isomorphic traits. In this context, Brotherton finds 'significant comparability at the transnational level between the research findings' on the Latin Kings gang/collective in Barcelona, Genoa, Milan, Santo Domingo, Quito, and New York City (2007, p. 378). This new wave of critical ethnography attends to issues of power, reflexivity, and globalization that mounts an explicit critique of the structures of power through which knowledge is created, and the intellectual legacies of 'telling stories' about peripheral populations.[18] As Behar

---

[17] Nonetheless, grounded ethnographic and qualitative accounts of gangs in the US have never quite vanished—Moore's *Homeboys* (1978), Campbells' *The Girls and the Gang* (1984), and Hagedorn's *People and Folks* (1998b), among others, were published during this broader lull in critical ethnographies. More recently, Sanchez-Jankowski's *Islands in the Street* (1990), J. Miller's *One of the Guys?* (2001), and Brotherton and Barrios' *The Almighty Latin King and Queen Nation* (2004) have all continued this critical tradition.

[18] Critical ethnography consists of a merging of a range of critical perspectives from feminist, anthropological, and post-structuralist perspectives, seeking to challenge the epistemological and ontological foundations of ethnographic research, while unearthing and confronting relationships of power and domination (Clifford and Marcus 1986; Clifford 1988).

(2003, pp. 15–16) argues, ethnography is a loaded term, coded with specific claims to, and methods of, knowing the social world:

Ethnography began as a method, which was discovered, perfected, and institutionalized in western centers of power, for telling stories about the marginalized populations of the world. It has its origins in the flagrant colonial inequalities from which modernity was born and in the arrogant assumptions that its privileged intellectual class made about who has the right to tell stories about whom.

In order to situate the study of gangs back within specific local contexts, these insights are critical. In building a foundation for knowledge of the gang phenomenon in the UK, this stable of 'critical gang studies' should form an important strut.[19] While ethnographic methods are invaluable as a means of excavating lived experience, situated meaning, and cultural adaptation, the 'ethnographic imagination' (Willis 2000) must be located within history, biography, and culture. Gang identification is a contextual practice, and must be understood not as a generalized phenomenon but as a local articulation of structural processes. In the next section, this argument is elaborated through analysis of continuity in the face of change—of the persistence of a certain formation of gang identity in Glasgow, apart from the vicissitudes of academic research so far described.

Continuity amid change

Fittingly, the development of the meaning of the term 'gang' reflects a slightly different etymological history in Scots than that of US or English history. Although cognate with the development of the word in English, 'gang' was used as a verb 'to go'—in Robert Burns famous couplet, 'the best laid schemes o' mice and men/gang aft agley'. In this context, it is worth remembering that groups of men, associated with particular territories, dress and names, drinking alcohol, and carrying knives, have a long history in Scotland. From the thirteenth century, Scotland was subdivided by a clan structure

---

[19] See, for example, Alexander's *The Asian Gang* (2000), Mendoza-Denton's *Homegirls* (2008), Garot's *Who You Claim?* (2010), Hagedorn's *A World of Gangs* (2008), Brotherton and Barrios' *Banished to the Homeland* (2011), Ward's *Gangsters without Borders* (2012), and Brenneman's *Homies and Hermanos* (2012).

that was premised on a blend of territorial, familial, and kinship ties, with mythologized foundations and shared allegiances.[20] These clans, crucially, were associated with movement through territorial space—Scotland was sliced up into clearly demarcated territories. As gangs have become a central focus for the rhetoric of law and order in the wider national context, however, so the history and present of gangs in Scotland has become elided into a UK-wide gang phenomenon, overlooking historical distinctions and continuities. As these particular local histories are collapsed into a universal narrative, so further weight is added to the discursive shifts from street to database, subcultures to crime, local to global, and ethnography to dataset.

These shifts are also reflected in the mainstream media. For example, a *Dispatches* series about gangs in the UK—focusing on London, Liverpool, Manchester, Birmingham, and Glasgow—combined examination of the issues of gangs in England with those in Scotland.[21] The *Breakthrough Glasgow* report, published by the Centre for Social Justice, explicitly links the Glasgow and London gang issues:

There are estimated to be more than 170 gangs in the Glasgow city region—this compares to 169 identified by the Metropolitan Police Service in London, a city over six times the size. By Glasgow's ratio of gangs to population, there would be over 1,000 gangs in London. (Centre for Social Justice 2008, pp. 12–13)[22]

This figure, notably, was based on a reference to an uncited source in a newspaper article from the year before, but in a process typical of the social construction of social problems (Loseke 2003),

---

[20] To this day, the modern Scottish kilt attire includes a *sgian dubh*, a small dagger secreted in the right sock.

[21] Channel Four (2009) *Dispatches: The War against Street Weapons*; Broadcast 3 August 2009.

[22] Another report on gangs in the UK is more circumspect with this statistic, noting that 'Strathclyde Police "have no definitive description for gangs" and their database on gangs operates on a rather loose definition of gang membership: it is based on known facts, criminal convictions, but also softer intelligence and simply associations. Therefore, a number of the people on the database are likely to not be strictly involved in gangs themselves but may be associated with a gang member, that is, related, partner, etc.' (Squires et al. 2008, p. 82).

became quoted again and again until it became a taken-for-granted aspect of debate.[23] As Best notes:

[p]eople trying to draw attention to some social problem tend to be convinced that they've identified a big, serious problem. When they come up with a big numeric estimate for the problem's size, they figure it must be about right. (Best 2005, p. 210)

This figure, crucially, played into a long-standing stereotype of Glasgow as a 'violent city'—depicted most famously in the novel *No Mean City* (McArthur and Kingsley-Long 1936/1956),[24] and in the films *Small Faces* (1990) and *NEDS: Non-Educated Delinquents* (2008). Nonetheless, despite the apparent correlation between gang activity and the English Riots of 2011, there were no incidents of violent disorder in Glasgow. Indeed, the Violence Reduction Unit, based in Glasgow, has been identified as a model of good practice in dealing with gangs.[25]

Glasgow has long been synonymous with gangs.[26] Groups of young people engaging in territorial violence have been reported since the 1880s, in the midst of population increases during Glasgow's high point of industrialism as 'Second City' of the British Empire. Since then, there have been persistent and recurring reports of similar territorial groupings,[27] in certain cases, with the same gang names

[23] For a critical discussion of the media construction of 'girl gangs' in Scotland, see Batchelor (2001).

[24] *No Mean City* is a controversial novel depicting Glasgow slum life in the 1920s. The novel was based on the notes of Alexander McArthur, an unemployed baker (Damer 1990b), but written by Kingsley Long, a London journalist assigned the task of translating the notes into a publishable novel (Damer 1990b, pp. 27–8).

[25] CIRV, based on the Community Initiative to Reduce Violence project in Cincinnati, USA. The project seeks to target gang members in Glasgow, with individuals signing a 'no-violence' contract in return for access to the CIRV team—composed of a range of police, health, social work, and education workers offering professional advice and support. In addition, the project has access to a large number of apprenticeships, as well as counselling services and alcohol and drug support. More information available at: <http://www.actiononviolence. co.uk/node/160> [Accessed 29 August 2010].

[26] For discussion of gangs in Dundee, see Fitzpatrick (1972); for Edinburgh, see Bradshaw (2005). For a broad account of gangs in different Scottish cities, see Bannister et al. (2010).

[27] On portrayals in the 1930s, see Davies (1998, 2007a, 2007b); on the 1960s, see Bartie (2010). For an overview of media portrayals throughout the twentieth

recurring consistently for nearly a century.[28] While the longevity and character of gangs in Glasgow has been the subject of popular and academic discussion for at least 40 years, there have been surprisingly few serious efforts to analyse the conditions through which this persistence has emerged. The one notable exception is James Patrick's *A Glasgow Gang Observed* (1973), researched almost concurrently with Downes' *The Delinquent Solution* (1966) which for some 25 years remained the sole academic account of youth gangs in the UK. Patrick's study—now infamous in methodology textbooks for the authors' use of covert participant observation—is based on 12 outings with 'The Young Team', a group of teenage boys in a working-class neighbourhood in the west of Glasgow. For Patrick, contrary to the 'fashionable approach' of labelling and deviance amplification (Patrick 1973, p. 200), the Young Team exhibited pathological tendencies and evidence of psychological disturbance, attracting and acting as vehicle for 'the most disturbed, the most violent boys, those with lowest impulse control' (Patrick 1973, p. 178). Patrick argued further that 'available evidence…points to the conclusion that there is no English equivalent of the Glasgow gang' (Patrick 1973, pp. 164–5).

Yet Patrick (1973, p. 170) is also careful to locate this interpretation within a broader structural context, in particular the lack of economic opportunities in the neighbourhood:

The city's high rates of slum housing and unemployment, of delinquency and violent crime, of alcoholism and disease, are not discrete areas of deprivation but inter-connecting and cumulative forms of inequality. And it is from this 'interlocking network of inequalities' that the subculture of gangs in Glasgow has grown. This subculture shows in the starkest possible way how poverty, inferior education, the lack of even minimum opportunities, and a steadily deteriorating economic situation all combine to produce feelings of frustration, rage and powerlessness.

While the language of psychopathology may be one reason Patrick's analysis has been marginalized in recent analyses of gangs in the UK, this approximation of structural and socio-psychological

century, see Damer (1990a) and Spring (1990). For a history of cultural representations of Glasgow as a 'violent city', see Fraser (2010).

[28] For example, the Baltic Fleet, from Baltic Street, Dalmarnock, in Glasgow's East End, were first reported in 1916 (Patrick 1973, p. 123) and remain listed on police databases to this day (Donnelly 2010).

explanations of violence is in fact quite prescient. Though couched in different language, these ideas resonate with recent theoretical approaches that combine structural, cultural, and agentic accounts, for example in the work of O'Malley and Mugford (1994), Young (2003), Lyng (2005), and Sandberg (2008). In the context of an excavation of the genealogy of gangs in Glasgow—and in view of the subsequent critique of Patrick's study (Damer 1990)—it is worthwhile reappraising these arguments in light of contemporary knowledge.

As Patrick's analysis makes clear, the persistence of gangs in Glasgow must be understood within the broader context of persistent poverty, unemployment, and associated social problems in the city. Consistent with comparative studies of gangs in a global context (Dowdney 2007; Hagedorn 2008), throughout their history, gangs have been reported in working-class communities in Glasgow marked by a lack of amenities, frequently accompanied by high levels of overcrowding and high populations of young people (Davies 2007a, p. 408; Armstrong and Wilson 1973a; Bartie 2010). A recent study of gangs and 'troublesome youth groups' in Scotland found some continuity in gang names across generations in Glasgow, and clear correlations between gang identification and areas of multiple disadvantage (Bannister et al. 2010, p. 16):

Some gangs in Glasgow were said to stand out as having a semi-continuous history of serious conflict. In most instances, though, it was just the gang name that had lasted. A gang name might be revived by a different group of young people after a period of disuse, with no retrospective social connection. These represented a perennial problem for communities and law enforcement agencies; however there was no clear sense that their prevalence and impact were changing, although recent years had seen much greater attempts to get a grip of the problem.

This continuity presents a challenge to both academic and political claims that gangs are a qualitatively new and distinct phenomenon in the UK—or indeed that responses to gangs in the UK are necessarily dramatized and polarized—but also to the dialectical relation between globalized social change and everyday lived experience. Amid the build-up of fearful rhetoric surrounding gang identification in the UK, there is a need to recognize the role of history, diversity, and social change in the development of gangs in different cities.

Conclusion

This chapter has outlined four marked shifts in the study of gangs in the US, UK, and Europe that have important implications for the nascent development of critical gang research in the UK. In the US, as the centre of gravity in gang research has shifted from the street to the database, grounded perspectives rooted in local understandings, community contexts, and historical circumstances have become increasingly marginalized. Localized understanding has become sidelined as positivist research has become the new orthodoxy. This shift has come in tandem with an increasingly repressive approach to gangs in US social policy, with gang membership viewed as a risk or aggravating factor within the criminal justice system. In the process, the cultural meanings and structural causes of gang identification have been rendered opaque. Nonetheless, there remains a strong critical tradition in US gang research, acting as a countercurrent to pathologizing discourse.

Despite this critical counterweight, the logic of mainstream US gang research has globalized. Through the work of the Eurogang group of researchers, sustained efforts have been made towards unifying definitions of the gang phenomenon to improve comparability between jurisdictions in comprehending this increasingly global phenomenon. While this form of comparison is important, a universal approach to definition masks critical divergences in the nature, form, and meanings of gangs in divergent geographical contexts and encourages the importation of social policy from apparently similar contexts. In the UK, this has involved the transplantation of several repressive and ill-defined policies targeting gangs (HM Government 2010, 2011; Cottrell-Boyce 2013). This shift in UK-based approaches to gangs, set off by a spike in youth violence and disorder, created a range of difficulties for researchers—not least the problem of locating 'the gang' within critical traditions of British youth research. In light of a lack of empirical evidence and new critical vocabularies, debate has become increasingly polarized and static. There is therefore a need to build a foundation for new scholarship in this fraught area. The history and present of Glasgow's gang phenomenon presents a challenge to claims of universalism or novelty of gangs in the UK. New sociological accounts of gangs must therefore attend to issues of continuity and change, similarity and difference, structure and agency in ways that are attentive to the global and local contexts of the contemporary gang landscape.

2

A Global Sociological Imagination

The facts of contemporary history are also facts about the
success and failure of individual men and women. When a
society is industrialised, the peasant becomes a worker; the
feudal lord a businessman...Neither the life of an individual nor the history of a society can be understood without
understanding both.

Mills (1959, p. 3)

The shifts in definitional and methodological approaches to gangs
described have created a disconnection between the study of
gangs and the broader currents of social theory. While the early
clutch of post-war American gang research was rich in sociological theory—local analyses of gangs were transposed into general theories of youth development, social class, and community
formation—sociological approaches have more recently taken a
back seat to ascendant criminal justice orientations. In reconnecting gang research with sociology, Mills' celebrated delineation
of the contours of modern sociology—of the shuttling back and
forth between 'private troubles' and 'public issues' in an effort
to comprehend the unique configuration of history, biography,
and culture that compose social phenomena—represents a critical starting point. However, Mills' cultivation of a 'sociological
imagination' must now be located within a global context; now
society has globalized, the worker has become a call centre opera-
tive, the businessman a knowledge broker. In making sense of the
impact of these changes at an individual level, therefore, we must
aim to add a global layer to Mills' classical formulation of the
sociological imagination; in short, to cultivate a global sociological imagination that attends to the locally constituted yet globally shaped patterning of history, culture, and biography. This
approach seeks out 'lines of connection or parameters which make

for a global relevance allowing "place-bound", necessarily always local, ethnographic writing to carry across the world' (Willis and Trondman, 2000, p. 7); infusing localized perspectives with a comparative sensibility that is attentive to the heterogeneity of the global era.

In this chapter, I aim to develop this approach through engagement with the work of the French 'maverick of ideas', Pierre Bourdieu (Jenkins 2002). Like Mills, Bourdieu saw the task of sociology as being 'to uncover the most profoundly buried structures of the various social worlds which constitute the social universe as well as the "mechanisms" which tend to ensure their reproduction or their transformation' (Bourdieu and Wacquant 1992, p. 7). The intention in analysing gangs through this lens is to re-engage with structure, agency, and culture in understanding the gang phenomenon, recognizing that there may be similarities between gangs in diverse geographical contexts while exploring levers of differentiation. The chapter is structured in two main sections. In the first, I specify a number of key absences in existing approaches to gangs: the role of history and social change on gang evolution; the impact of globalization on gangs in divergent social environments; and the relationship between gangs, structure, and agency. In the second, Bourdieu's conceptual schema of habitus, field, and capital are suggested as a set of 'thinking tools' with which to build a new conceptual vocabulary. Bourdieu's method of practice is then applied to the study of gangs through three connected concepts: street habitus, gang identification, and the post-industrial city. This approach seeks to reconstruct the sociological imagination in a global urban context, examining the history, biography, and culture of different cities in accounting for contemporary configurations of gangs, while remaining attentive to similarities in specific patterns of exclusion in geographically distant communities.

Theorizing absence

Where once issues of history, culture, and class were at the heart of theories of gangs, latterly issues of crime, policing, and risk management have come to dominate. As a result, gangs are too often reduced to an alien other—a fixed, static, and universalized entity, homogenized into statistical equations or criminal definitions—which is presented as a universal social form. In the shifts described in the previous chapter, nuance and subtlety have become 'lost in much of contemporary scholarship in which the gang may be depicted as a monolithic entity, with a single-mindedness of purpose and outlook' (Venkatesh 2003, p. 8). As such, much gang research today is of an autopoeitic nature, self-referential and self-sustaining, and often operating at a distance from the lives of the children and young people who comprise them. In laying a set of foundations with which to build a critical approach to gangs, it is therefore important to establish the absences in current approaches.

History and social change

A primary difficulty in contemporary gang research is the lack of an adequate account of history and social change on gang activities. As historians and gang scholars have documented (Adamson 2000; Sanchez-Jankowski 2003; Davies 2013; Coughlin and Venkatesh 2003), in certain contexts gangs have adapted and evolved over time, transforming into street-based political organizations (Brotherton and Barrios 2004), political parties (Hagedorn 2008), or transnational criminal organizations. In other contexts, however, gangs have remained relatively unchanged over time, a finding at variance with accounts of increasing homogeneity. In efforts toward a universal definition, these heterogeneous histories are lost, decontextualizing the study of gangs from the sociological imagination. As Sanchez-Jankowski notes

> missing from the sociological literature on gangs is an appreciation of how progressive social changes have produced concurrent transformations in the functional shape and behaviors of gangs. Gangs operate in society, and societies remain in a constant process of social change; both alter dialectically in relation to each other... Thus, to fully understand gangs in a particular era, one must consider broad social changes that have affected them at specific times. (Sanchez-Jankowski 2003, p. 202)

In seeking to remedy this deficiency, Sanchez-Jankowski locates different gang formations within the context of successive changes to the political and economic infrastructure in the US—immigration, blue-collar expansion, drug deregulation, mass incarceration, and market monopolization. Honing in on a particular city, Hagedorn locates the history of gangs in Chicago within the context of the racial segregation, political nepotism, police brutality, mass incarceration, and drug capitalism that has dominated the history of Chicago (Hagedorn 2009). Drawing on the concept of 'polygenesis', which seeks to weave together the 'multiple threads of structure and agency that combine over time to form a gang's particular shape' (Hagedorn 2009), Hagedorn firmly grounds his analysis at the level of the city and the particular institutional, social, cultural, and economic patterns of power and powerlessness shaping the experiences of young people in gangs.

Since the publication of Geoffrey Pearson's *Hooligan: A History of Respectable Fears* (1983), British criminologists have long been sensitized to the recurring nature of popular fears over youthful deviance. As Pearson has documented, 'youth crime and disorder are better understood as persistent, if somewhat intermittent, features of the social landscape' (2011, p. 20). However, this glowing insight has become slightly warped with time; often this is taken as proof that contemporary concerns over youth crime are groundless, and that the public are simply replaying an age-old set of popular fears. This default approach has, perhaps, obstructed meaningful analysis of the role of social change on youth. Pearson's point was not that youth cultures do not themselves change over time, but rather that societal reaction alone remains a poor barometer of youth behaviour. Like E.P. Thompson, we must look to ordinary voices rather than official accounts in retelling history, and pay attention to the structuring influence of social and economic forces in reshaping society.

An example of this approach can be found in Hobbs' characterization of the evolution of gang collectivities in London—specifically, an East London borough known as Dogtown—through the lens of socio-structural change and post-industrialism (2013). For Hobbs, organic, territorial collaborations of working-class youths belong to a bygone era of greater predictability and stability within socio-spatial class formations—in which family ties and organized criminal networks were densely woven into the fabric of life, and gang identifications existed as a fragment of this broader culture. In short, for Hobbs, previous generations of Dogtown gangs belonged to a previous generation of theory—differential opportunity, strain, resistance through ritual—that was rooted in more predictable industrialist social patterning. Post-industrial Dogtown, however, is at once more fragmented, diverse, and dissolute, dominated by diasporic identities and fractious alliances in which 'bored youths, entrepreneurs, and would-be gangsters alike have become embedded in the fissures between households, neighbourhoods, and generations' (Hobbs 2013, p. 132). For some in this environment, the industrial-era masculinities into which they have been socialized are well suited to the drug trade and illicit economy; many others, however, fall into the cracks of dissolution and decline. In the post-industrial city, where work opportunities are uncertain and unstable, there are conflicting, paradoxical relations, evincing both continuity and change (Hayward 2004; Taylor et al. 1996).

These studies point the way towards a reinvigorated engagement with history and social change in the study of gangs. An appreciation of how individual identities and collective behaviours are shaped by the broader forces at play in society—gentrification, migration, inequality—encourages a social understanding of gangs and discourages pathologizing stereotypes.

Diversity and difference

Since the model of gang formation formulated by Thrasher (1927/1963) nearly a century ago—of juvenile 'play-groups' integrated through conflict—the social and cultural environment inhabited by gangs has altered irrevocably. Gangs today take on a wide array of forms worldwide and vary by city, neighbourhood, country, age, ethnicity, religion, and gender, and they can change radically over time (Hagedorn 2008). In this context, the interlocking processes that have developed under the heading of 'globalization'—namely 'the progressive enmeshment of human communities with each other over time and... the complex social, economic and environmental processes that stretch across their borders' (Held 2000, p. 394)—have had important ramifications for the study of gangs. In an era where global flows of capital, culture, and technology cut across all areas of social life, and where structural and cultural forces are increasingly global in reach, researchers must be sensitized to the globally interconnected nature of social problems (Brotherton 2007).

The current era has been conceptualized as the 'Age of Migration' (Castles and Miller 2009), in which predictable large-scale population shifts from colonizing to colonized nations, or from Old World to New World, have been replaced by a complex cycle of flow, ebbs, and eddies, in which movement from global South to global North represents the principal current. As Bauman notes, refugees are 'perhaps the most rapidly swelling of all the categories of world population' (Bauman 2002, p. 343) today.[1] In this context, developed nations have increasingly sought to enforce ever stricter border policies—criminalizing immigration for those seen as unproductive to economic development,[2] with deportation or imprisonment the ultimate consequence. As Aas notes, 'globalisation, far from being a progress of global mobility and de-territorialisation, also represents immobility, re-territorialisation, and localization' (2010, p. 427). For those locked on the margins of society, social and spatial mobility may be a distant possibility. Thus, for Bauman, mobility—and its converse, immobility—has become a principal pivot of social stratification in the global era:

Alongside the emerging planetary dimensions of business, finance, trade and information, a 'localizing', space-fixing process is set in motion...freedom to move...fast becomes the main stratifying force of our late-modern or postmodern times. (Bauman 2000a, p. 2)

In this context, attempts to rationalize this diversity into a single, unifying definition become deeply problematic. The second central absence in extant studies of gangs, therefore, is the lack of an account of diversity and differentiation between gangs in divergent geographical contexts. In this regard, it becomes increasingly critical to comprehend the complex convergences and divergences in gang activities in distal geographical contexts.

Global processes of neoliberalism, segregation, and marginalization have cohered in the development of spaces of 'advanced marginality' in urban locales across the globe; areas 'perceived by both outsiders and insiders as social purgatories, leprous badlands at the heart of the post-industrial metropolis where only the refuse of society would accept to dwell' (Wacquant 2007, p. 67). The interconnections between these areas is exhibited in the development of informal 'grey' economies, street justice, and territorial protectionism, conditions in which the informal social order of gangs can play a functional role (Sanchez-Jankoswki 1991). Processes of

---

[1] For further discussion, see Ferrell (2012a).

[2] Stumpf (2006) has coined the term 'crimmigration' to summarize these processes. Aas (2012) has also written perceptively of the localized identity politics and community conflicts engendered by these new migrations—encapsulated neatly in the phrase 'global flows meets criminology of the other'.

globalization, urbanization, and marginalization are closely connected, and gangs—and other groups of non-state actors—have emerged in a wide range of cultural contexts, from the favelas of Rio de Janeiro to the banlieues of Paris, from the ghettoes of Chicago to the schemes of Glasgow, from the townships of Cape Town to the urban villages of Beijing. In the absence of a legitimate state presence in such spaces of 'advanced marginality'—wherein regularized work has been replaced by increasingly precarious, flexible work, often in the service economy—street-based forms of justice and entrepreneurialism have come to form an intrinsic aspect of the local ecology. As will be elaborated below, these new 'geographies of exclusion' (Sibley 1995) form a key analytic for understanding gangs in the global context and a central means of explicating the similarities and differences between gangs in the global context.

Beyond these processes of immobilization, however, globalization has also created new geographies of mobility that have impacted materially on contemporary configurations of gangs. As people, labour, technology, capital, and culture have become increasingly fluid, so processes of 'deterritorialization' and 'reterritorialization' (Deleuze and Guattari 1984) have impacted on gangs in marginalized communities in diverse geographical locations. As Hagedorn and Rauch (2007) have demonstrated in relation to rehousing and gentrification, powerful global forces have reshaped the inner city, displacing communities and disrupting entrenched territorial boundaries. Areas of marginality must therefore be understood as areas in which global trends of forced migration and competition for scarce resources are played out at a local level (Fraser and Piacentini 2013), as new migrants seek out fragile communities in what are often tense and violent social environments.

Long-standing territorial boundaries are therefore overlaid with a chequerboard of conflicts reflecting divergent ethnic, national, and community ties. While globalization has created conditions that favour certain convergences in lifestyles, dispositions, and habits in geographically distant locations, it is equally necessary to attend to the distinctive hybridities of culture—what Robertson (1995) terms 'glocalization'—that occur at a local level; in short, the divergences in social forms in apparently similar environments. In shuttling back and forth between these subjective and objective layers of analysis, there is a need to develop a more nuanced understanding of the historical levers that have facilitated these divergent trajectories, to understand the path dependencies of contemporary configurations of gangs in different cities. In moving towards this framework, a more developed understanding of the dialectic between gangs, structure, and agency is a critical step.

Structure and agency

In the context of the increasingly contested relationship between local, national, and global influences for social action, there is a need for a more rounded understanding of the relationship between gangs and political economy. As Giddens (2000) quips, citing Daniel Bell, the nation-state is too small to deal with many global issues yet too big to deal with many local issues. The third absence within the oeuvre of existing gang studies, therefore, is the relationship between structure and agency—too often, gangs are understood and explained at the level of the individual, with structural and cultural factors relegated. Administrative gang research, by and large, looks at gang membership as a deficiency—and thus a question of individual choice—neglecting broader questions of structure and socio-economic position. While studies that fall within more critical sociological traditions have been more attentive to issues of social structure, there is unquestionably room for greater sensitivity to the dialectic relationship between structure and agency in this context.

In a globalizing climate, clear connections can be made between the economic and cultural patterning of distant geographical contexts. The neoliberalizing logic of economic globalization has resulted in clearly defined hierarchies both between and within nation-states: between 'winners' and 'losers', those leading the pack and those left behind. Gini-coefficients attest to rising inequalities in all advanced capitalist societies, and increasing populations of individuals rejected by the logic of global modernity—a population Standing refers to as the 'precariat' (2011)—that are in a state of spatial and economic 'drift' from traditional societal roots (Ferrell 2012a). At the same time, cultural and technological global trends have exposed increasing numbers of people to comparable patterns of consumerism, consumption, and taste—for example, the desirability of certain consumer products in both established and emerging economies—resulting in convergences in cultural aspiration right round the world. Currie delineates a clear correlation between this form of neoliberalizing, globalizing inequality, and the rate of violent crime, demonstrating that post-industrial market societies tend to produce more violence (1997). He proposes a mid-range theory that articulates key mechanisms that link this global scale with the meso level of societal difference. While recognizing the local path dependencies of gangs in different contexts, it is equally important to develop understandings of such meso-level convergences.

However, global connections are premised upon 'contingent lineages' (Tsing 2005, p. 145) and are therefore both unpredictable and inchoate. To put it another way, social phenomenon that emerge from the same primordial soup of global change may take very different forms and evolve in different ways. Wacquant (2008a), for example, draws attention to the comparable impact of neoliberal logic on processes of urban marginality in Chicago and Paris—territorial stigmatization, punitive welfarism, and socio-spatial segregation—yet draws close attention to their differences, filtered through the cultural and institutional contexts of the American and French models of statehood. In this context, *scale* emerges as a central issue in comprehending the nature of contemporary social phenomena. The operation of scale—not just between local, national, and global, or micro, meso, and macro levels, but within the new geographies of global immobility—represents a primary means of grasping the emergent nature of social reality in a way that is both grounded in lived experience, yet sensitized to the contingent and contested nature of 'multiple modernities' (Appadurai 1996; Beck 1999). To date in the critical gang literature, there has not been sufficient attention paid to the complex realities thrown up by these new social conditions. While authors such as Hagedorn (1998) and Vigil (2002) firmly locate gang identification within a framework of political economy—for Hagedorn, in a context of poverty, alienation, and racism, for Vigil in the context of 'multiple marginality'[3]—more work is required in *reconciling* structural constraints and individual decision making.

Just as global forces have created new geographies of immobility in the city, so too have certain groups drawn on a transnational

---

[3] As Vigil argues: 'Basically, the street gang is an outcome of marginalization, that is, the relegations of certain persons or groups to the fringes of society, where social and economic conditions result in powerlessness' (Vigil 2002, p. 7).

discourse of gang identification as a means of seeking solidarity in the context of shared adversity—a process akin to Aas' description of alienated teenagers coming together to create a sense of community beyond and apart from the nation-state, under the banner 'AlieNation is My Nation' (Aas 2007, p. 93). In the context of these new forms of insecurity, precariousness, and uncertainty, for Nilan and Feixa, young people 'form localized networks of "sociality" to survive and be powerful in uncertain economic and social times when mechanical solidarity has broken down' (2006, p. 149). In developing this approach, and reconciling the tensions noted, the social theory of Pierre Bourdieu—which shares crucial philosophical and conceptual foundations with the Birmingham School traditions (Bourdieu and Wacquant 1992, p. 80)—is particularly instructive.

Reconceptualizing gangs

Stated broadly, Bourdieu's concept of habitus refers to the set of durable character dispositions—habits—that all individuals possess. These dispositions are both intellectual and physical—habits of thought and habits of behaviour—and frequently operate at an unconscious or *pre*conscious level, giving the feeling of being instinctive (Bourdieu and Wacquant 1992; Bourdieu 2005). These traits allow individuals to negotiate, or 'improvise', the situations that present themselves in daily life—what Bourdieu refers to as 'practice' (Bourdieu 1977). While each human interaction is different and the range of responses infinite, these interactions are structured by our habitual range of responses, learned during early childhood and repeated ad infinitum. Bourdieu likens this to a 'feel for the game'—an instinctive response to learned rules, like playing a sport one is proficient at (Bourdieu and Wacquant 1992, p. 128). Behaviours that are experienced as spontaneous and unplanned, therefore, are in fact patterned by the hinterland of individual history, biography, and physicality.

This experiential and improvized set of unique practices represents the internalization of external social structures. For Bourdieu, the world is patterned by relationships of domination and subordination, power and powerlessness—existing both on an objective level 'out there' and a subjective level 'in here'. Hierarchical structures of gender, age, and class form part of the learned dimension of habitus. As illustrated in *Language and*

Symbolic Power (Bourdieu 1991) and *Masculine Domination* (Bourdieu 2001), these structures are also implicit in our use of language. For Bourdieu, these structural patterns are reproduced insidiously, through an endless cycle of minute actions, practices, and vocabularies. This results in an unquestioning attitude to inequality, as actors become complicit in relationships of power and subordination. Bourdieu calls this process *symbolic violence*:

The realistic, even resigned or fatalistic, dispositions which lead members of the dominated class to put up with objective conditions that would be judged intolerable or revolting by agents otherwise disposed . . . [that] help to reproduce the conditions of oppression. (Bourdieu 2000, p. 217)

Unlike physical violence, which is tangible and immediate, the operation of symbolic violence is an intangible and slow-burning process—akin to Foucault's conceptualization of disciplinary power, in which the micro-dynamics of power invisibly constrain and channel lived experience (Foucault 1977). For Bourdieu, symbolic violence is detectable in a wide range of minute phenomenological moments and is ingrained in the language, thought, and action of habitus. This is a theory of internalized social structure, of inequality made concrete and reinforced through socialization—experienced as natural, a 'second skin'. As Bourdieu notes, symbolic violence operates with some degree of complicity, as the unequal structures and strictures of society are inculcated at a deep level: 'dominated lifestyles are almost always perceived, even by those who live them, from the destructive and reductive point of view of the dominant aesthetic' (Bourdieu 1998, p. 9). This conceptualization, crucially, allows for an account of the interplay between social change and individual dispositions, the embodied process through which cultures can become replicated in a way that is out of step with broader social and economic shifts.

In explicating this concept of habitus, Bourdieu makes reference to two other distinct but complementary concepts: field and capital. In simple terms, field refers to spheres of activity that we enter into in our daily life—examples from Bourdieu's writing include the academic, scientific, economic, and educational fields, as well as the field of cultural production (Bourdieu and Wacquant 1992). Continuing the metaphor of habitus as 'feel for the game', field refers to the various fields of play on which individuals act out daily life. In this sense, the metaphor of field functions in a similar way as a sports field—a space in which the game of practice is played out. On another level, however, the concept of field also relates to the structures of power operating within each of these spheres—each field has its own unique logic, hierarchy, and system of social relations that shape the experience of actors within it (Jenkins 2002, p. 85), just as each sport has its own set of explicit and implicit rules, which every player must embody when playing on that field. In Bourdieu's conceptualization of field, however, these rules relate to power and status, the logic to which every player must submit. In this sense, field also functions as a metaphor for the force of these relations of power—a gravitational field similar to that exerted by planets. For Wacquant, therefore, field is defined as 'a *relational* configuration endowed with a specific gravity' (Bourdieu and Wacquant 1992, pp. 16–17).

For Bourdieu, every field is relational and contingent and is thus the site of competition and conflict. Jenkins, paraphrasing Bourdieu, defines field as 'a social arena within which struggles or manoeuvres take place over specific resources or stakes and access to them' (Jenkins 2002, p. 84). Each actor within a field occupies a position of 'domination, subordination or equivalence' (Jenkins 2002, p. 85) in relation to other actors within the field. Power, status, and authority within any given field are conferred through a system of agreed currency, or capital. Bourdieu distinguishes a number of forms of capital—principally economic capital (money), social capital (contacts), cultural capital (distinction), and symbolic capital (respect or recognition)—which cohere to form an actor's position within any given field. To achieve power and authority in the economic field, for example, more than money is necessary; having the right 'distinctions' for status, knowing the right people, and harbouring their respect are also important. Importantly, forms of capital exist in a market for capital—economic capital can be traded for cultural capital in the form of qualifications, or symbolic capital in the form of philanthropy.

Bourdieu's conceptualization of habitus, field, and capital provides a powerful framework for comprehending lived experiences of power and powerlessness in the contemporary era. In the field of criminology, these concepts have been employed as a means of blending structural and agentic accounts, illuminating the violent street-worlds of drug dealers in Oslo (Sandberg and Pederson 2011; Sandberg 2008), the 'subcultural capital' of club-drug users in England (Thornton 1995), victimization and agency in the lives of young women who commit violent offences (Batchelor 2007), and persistent violence in the north-east of England (Hobbs et al. 2003; Winlow and Hall 2009a). For the field of gang research, these concepts have the potential to advance a sophisticated account of history, social change, and structure that is nonetheless attuned to issues of agency, diversity and difference. These potentials are articulated below, under the conceptualizations of *street habitus, the post-industrial city*, and *gang identification*.

Street habitus

Street habitus can be conceptualised as the relatively permanent and sometimes unconscious dispositions of individuals committed to street culture. It is the embodied practical sense that is seen in hypersensitivity to offences and frequent displays of violent potential. (Sandberg and Pederson 2011, p. 34)

For Sandberg and Pederson, street habitus represents the habituation and socialization of actors within a violent street-world (Sandberg and Pederson 2011; Fraser 2013a), in which street-smarts—an innate understanding of how to survive on the street – and bodily strength are crucial forms of street capital. Winlow and Hall (2009a), discussing violent men in England, draw on the *pre*-conscious dimension of habitus (Akram 2014), explicating the 'retaliate first' habitus of seemingly senseless violence through a subtle depiction of deep-seated experiences of victimization, humiliation, and symbolic violence. What these authors have in common is an effort to draw on habitus in a contextualized and historically specific context, connecting structural marginalization with agentic violence. Building on these concepts, I use the term street habitus as a means to explore the deep-seated, preconscious connections between young people and territorial space as a response to limited spatial autonomy in the post-industrial city. Just as Bourdieu, drawing on Merleau-Ponty, delineated the ways in which objects external to the body can be incorporated into the habitus—a typewriter, for example (Crossley 2001)—so *street habitus* refers to an unconscious attachment to the streets of a well-known locale, experienced as instinctive and improvised, but an adaptive response to urban marginality. This approach seeks to develop an understanding of the mutually constitutive role of culture and space in the formulation of habitus.

In short, street habitus refers to the fusion of space and self, developed through repetition of behaviours in physical space. Leach describes this process (of territorialization) in the following terms: '[t]hrough habitual processes of movement, by covering and recovering the same paths and routes, we come to familiarise ourselves with a territory, and thereby find meaning in that territory' (Leach 2005, p. 299). Geography thus becomes part of the unconscious of habitus, forming a backdrop on which to enact identity. Local places and spaces, bound up with individual and collective memory, become fused with self-identity and the family, friendships, and relationships which occur there. In this framework, performance of 'gang' identity creates a form of 'practice' in which space *as self* is protected. While dispositions and character traits are personal and individual, however, there are nonetheless significant overlaps between individuals sharing the same social space. Bourdieu most famously elaborated this idea in *Distinction* (1977), demonstrating that tastes, political beliefs, and predilections are fiercely patterned by the matrix of class position at an objective level, whilst simultaneously differentiated and unpredictable at the subjective level. As Wacquant summarizes:

These unconscious schemata are acquired through lasting exposure to particular social conditions and conditionings, via the internalization of external constraints and possibilities. This means that they are shared by people subjected to similar experiences even as each person has a unique individual variant of the common matrix (this is why individuals of like nationality, class, gender, etc., spontaneously feel 'at home' with one another). (Wacquant 2008b, p. 267)

This account of habitus offers a framework for understanding the emergence of comparable social formations in a wide range of contexts, countries, and cultures. If it is true that national boundaries are no longer the governing force in individual identities, and that global forces are creating marked similarities in geographically distant communities, it follows that there may exist *homologies of habitus* between these diverse locations.

Research carried out on what has been termed 'inner-city street culture' indicates some support for this conclusion. Bourgois, basing his ideas on extended participant observation in *El Barrio* in Brooklyn, New York, distinguishes the set of dispositional qualities that obtain in this community:

a complex and conflictual web of beliefs, symbols, modes of interaction, values, and ideologies that have emerged in opposition to exclusion from mainstream society. Street culture offers an alternative forum for personal dignity. In the particular case of the United States, the concentration of socially marginalized populations into politically and economically isolated inner-city enclaves has fomented an especially explosive cultural creativity that is in defiance of racism and economic marginalization. (Bourgois 1995, p. 8)

Anderson, in his celebrated work *Code of the Street* (1999), identifies a similar set of 'street' dispositions in low-income communities in Philadelphia. For Anderson, the 'code' is a 'partly specified but partly emergent' (Anderson 1999, p. 99) matrix of informal rules, character traits, social cues, and self-presentations that enable individuals to navigate street-life in communities in which 'violence is just below the surface' (p. 23). This violence, moreover, is an adaptive response to the structural violence of socio-economic alienation, stigma, and marginality—for Anderson, the 'inclination to violence springs from the circumstances of life among the ghetto poor' (1999, p. 33). These bodily dispositions entail a 'careful way of moving, of acting, of getting up and down the streets' in which 'the toughest, the biggest, and the baddest individual prevails' (Anderson 1999, pp. 23–5), and the notion of respect is a governing force. The wariness, lack of trust, and fragile social relations render participants in street life extremely 'sensitive to advances and slights' (Anderson 1999, p. 34).

Sanchez-Jankowski, elaborating a theory of gang persistence in the US, draws a similar picture. Basing his findings of ten years of ethnographic fieldwork in low-income communities, Sanchez-Jankowski draws attention to a recurring character trait among his participants, which he terms 'defiant individualism'. Defiant individualism—constituted by, among others, competitiveness, mistrust, self-reliance, and survivalism (1991, p. 24–6)— is an example of internalized psychological traits, a 'social character' that has evolved in relation with the experience of lived marginalization. Like *habitus*, social character is both individualized and collective:

The concept of social character does not refer to the complete or highly individualized, in fact, unique character structure as it exists in an individual, but to the 'character matrix', a syndrome of character traits which has developed as an adaptation to the economic, social, and cultural conditions common to that group'. (Sanchez-Jankowski 1991, p. 23)

Researchers in a range of other locations have uncovered similar articulations of street-based sensibilities. Sandberg's research in Oslo (Sandberg 2008), for example, employs the terminology of *street habitus* to denote an embodied, streetwise disposition among street-based drug dealers—in which bodily capital, language, and street-smarts are employed to navigate violent social terrain—that represents the internalization of the experience of marginality and the strategic employment of forms of available capital. Ilan, writing about a group of street-based youth in Dublin (Ilan 2013), decouples such dispositions from locale, in arguing for a street capital that *enables* mobility in the underlife of the 'liquid' city: as 'young disadvantaged men...relocate around Dublin between archipelagos of less-desirable addresses they must re-orientate themselves, make new friends and find new opportunities for leisure, income, support and dignity' (Ilan 2013, p. 4). A 'street habitus', in this formulation, represents the habituation and socialization of actors within this violent street-world (Sandberg and Pederson 2011), but also an adaptive subcultural response to the increasingly volatile and precarious social environment of the modern city.[4] In a society composed of a rejecting, exclusionary logic, gang identification can become a resource through which to gain status and respect.

These 'homologies of habitus' between diverse geographical locales represent adaptive responses to convergent economic trends. As Young summarizes:

> Young men facing such a denial of recognition turn, everywhere in the world, in what must be almost a universal criminological law, to the creation of cultures of machismo, to the mobilisation of one of their only resources, physical strength, to the formation of gangs and to the defence of their own *'turf'*. Being denied the respect of others they create a subculture that revolves around masculine powers and *'respect'*. (Young 1999, p. 12)

Street habitus is therefore formulated in dialectical relation with existing material relations—that is, as a deliberative, encultured, and agentic adaptation to a specific configuration of structural positions. In the context of globalization—with its attendant intensification of inequality, socio-spatial segregation, and consumerism—these structural conditions have demonstrated

---

[4] For further depictions of street cultures in diverse global contexts, see Mullins (2006), Gunter (2008), and Brenneman (2013).

marked *convergence* across diverse geographical contexts. In this sense, therefore, it might be said that globalization has amplified and intensified the preconditions for gang formation.

Nonetheless, like culture (Conquergood 1991, cited in Ferrell et al. 2008, p. 4), *street culture* functions best as verb rather than noun—as something premised on movement and change rather than stasis and solidity—so too is it equally important to recognize the *divergence* of street-based cultural forms in different locations. To date, this has not been effectively accounted for in studies of street culture. In attending to this deficiency, focusing on meso-level variables that exist at the level of the city—the cultural, economic, and social patterning of global forces that refract through the unique lens of individual cities—is an important analytic tool. For the purposes of this book, the concept of the *post-industrial city* is particularly apt.

The post-industrial city

While Bourdieu's theory of practice most frequently takes French society as an exemplar from which to extrapolate *universal validity* from investigation of this particularized case (Bourdieu 1998), Wacquant (2008a) roots understanding at the level of the city. In his comparative analysis of 'advanced marginality' in Chicago and Paris, Wacquant analyses the urban environment as a space in which processes of neoliberalism become articulated. For Wacquant, comparisons between diverse geographical contexts are necessary, but only 'become intelligible once one takes caution to embed them in the historical matrix of class, state and space characteristic of each society at a given epoch' (Wacquant 2008a, p. 2). In constructing an analytical frame through which to understand gangs in a comparative context, therefore, the city—as a microcosmic exemplar of these matrices of class, state, and space—becomes a lens through which broader social and cultural forces are filtered and refracted.

Early gang research was firmly located in the broader intellectual currents of the Chicago School, which took the city as its site, focus, and 'social laboratory'. Part of the enduring reputation of the Chicago School was in discerning regular structures amid seemingly chaotic or disorganized urban terrain (Downes and Rock 2003, pp. 64–9). The emergence of gang behaviour took place against a backdrop of urbanization, industrialization, and mass migration in so-called zones of transition, existing in the interstices between affluent areas. However, as Snodgrass, in a critique of Chicago School methods, argues:

[t]he interpretation was paralysed at the communal level, a level which implied that either the residents were responsible for the deteriorated area, or that communities collapsed on their own account. Instead of turning inward to find the causes of delinquency exclusively in local traditions...their interpretations might have turned outward to show political, economic and historical forces at work. (Snodgrass 1976, p. 10)

Since the work of Thrasher and the Chicago School, cities have become much more complex and multi-layered; the shift from industrial to post-industrial forms of organization has been neither straightforward nor smooth. Forms of spatial organization, patterns of migration, and economic growth are increasingly uncoupled from local contexts and relocated into the global marketplace of transnational corporations and post-Fordist manufacture. Urbanization has become a defining feature of late modernity; more than 50 per cent of the world's population now living in cities (Davis 1998), and rural-to-urban migration has become the dominant form in many developing economies. The twenty-first century has inaugurated the hyper-speed growth of so-called megacities—consisting of 20 million or more inhabitants—many of which are situated in developing economies in the global South. As Hagedorn notes, 'gangs today organize in response not just to industrialization and urbanization but primarily to social exclusion and the changing spaces of globalizing cities worldwide' (Hagedorn 2007, p. 6). In turning understanding of gangs back toward the city, therefore, it is necessary to understand the multiplicity of forms that exist in the 'age of urbanism' that constitutes the contemporary era. In this context, there have been a number of concepts suggested to encapsulate this new complexity.

Primary among these is Sassen's formulation of the 'global city' (1991). For Sassen, in a context of the declining relevance of the nation-state in which flows of capital, labour, and communication are increasingly organized in a networked and borderless way, cities have become critical 'hubs' or 'nodes' in the management of the global economy—with cities such as New York, London, and Tokyo exerting more influence than many nation-states. This captures the *contingency* and *co-dependence* of the global economy, and the sense of jockeying for position among cities in a hyper-competitive economy. While processes such as informalization of economies, obsolescence of traditional working-class industries, and shifts to precarious working (Harvey 2000) may be occurring globally, they are experienced locally. As Sassen notes, '[t]he term *global city* captures a partial condition: much of what happens in these cities may have little to do with globalization' (Sassen 2007, p. 98). As such, there is a need to comprehend the lived experience of what Appadurai terms *multiple modernities*, being the specific, localized configurations of global processes—the outcome of the 'increasingly non-isomorphic paths' (Appadurai 1996, p. 37) forged on the frontier of the new global exclusions.

As certain cities become globally connected 'hubs' for financial and economic sectors, so new 'global elites' operate in 'non-spaces' which are reproduced identically across the globe: airport lounges, coffee chains, hotels. These processes are represented by a 'footloose economy' of new world citizens moving flexibly between cities—globally connected and locally disconnected (Aas 2007, p. 58). The flipside of these developments are those left behind by the developing global economy. Cities operate as concrete examples of the consequences and causes of globalization. Castells' concept of a 'dual city' seeks to capture the persistence of relative inequality and social stratification in this new geography of marginality, arguing that contemporary cities remain marked by fault lines of class, ethnicity, and power. As Young has documented, these processes do not always result in spatial immobility for those individuals most marginalized in the global city (Young 1999). Life on the margins of the global city is often composed of a structurally patterned mobility of commutes between multiple jobs, shopping for low-cost food, and attendance at welfare offices (Danson and Mooney 1998). This complicates the binary image of the 'dual city' of rich and poor in the era of 'liquid modernity'; mobility in this case is constraining rather than liberating (Young 1999). For Ilan (2013), indeed, it is this exclusionary logic of mobility that necessitates the cultivation of defiant 'street capital' for precariously housed young men.

Moreover, not all cities are 'global'. In an international hierarchy of cities, there is space for only a few lead actors; many more compete for supporting roles. Sassen (2007) has written of the role of regional cities in feeding the broader global city networks—as a means, for example, of understanding the role of Hong Kong as a hub between the rising second-tier cities of South China and the global economy—as well as the decline of former centres of economic growth and productivity in the post-industrial era.

Alongside the new global and regional hierarchies of cities is a vast territory that has become increasingly peripheral, increasingly excluded from the major processes that fuel economic growth in the new global economy. Many formerly important manufacturing centers and port cities have lost functions and are in decline, not only in the less-developed countries but also in the most advanced economies. The formation of these new geographies of marginality is yet another meaning of economic globalization. (Sassen 2007, p. 101)

Since Glasgow's slow decline from its position as a global powerhouse of manufacturing, it has become increasingly peripheral to the functioning of the global economy, fulfilling service functions such as tourism and acting as the location for call centres. In this context, as Glasgow has become marginalized by the global economy, young people have experienced the jobs market as increasingly precarious. The notion of post-industrialism captures well the problems that these reconfigurations have wrought in Glasgow—and many other British cities—and the impact this has had on identity in formerly working-class communities. Former models of working-class masculinities have been fundamentally ruptured, rendering 'hard graft' increasingly marginal. This shift, occasioned at a global level, has therefore had considerable social impact at a local level. The concept of the 'post-industrial city' is intended to engage with broader-based changes in the nature of urban life, while remaining grounded in lived experience—operating as a meso-level lens that refracts between the local and global.

As Bourdieu points out, 'in all the cases where dispositions encounter conditions (including fields) different from those in which they were constructed and assembled, there is a *dialectical confrontation* between habitus, as structured structure, and objective structures' (Bourdieu 2005, p. 46). Crucially, the habitus does not automatically accede to the new conditions of the field; as the saying goes, 'old habits die hard'. Rather, as the behaviours and traits of the habitus are contained within the body and frequently exist at an unconscious level, they may reproduce and perpetuate largely independent of the material conditions that gave rise to them. As Nash (1999, p. 184) argues: 'since it is embodied, the habitus develops a history and generates its practices, for some period of time, even after the original material conditions which gave rise to it have disappeared'. Bourdieu referred to this as 'paradoxical relations', in which the dispositions inscribed in the *habitus* are experienced as being out of synch with the new *field* logics—these are experienced as unsettling (McNay 2001).

Many cities, like Glasgow, have suffered crushing declines in forms of industrial manufacturing that once breathed life into their urban heartlands. Cities in the north of England—Liverpool, Manchester, Sunderland, and Bradford—have experienced declines in manufacture and attempts at rebranding, gentrification, and regeneration. In picking through the impact of these neoliberal alterations to British cities, the loss of this form of industrial identity—and its corresponding forms of masculinities—cannot be overstated. The power of Glasgow's industrial heritage, coupled with the rupture caused by deindustrialization, has resulted in a legacy of industrial masculinities that no longer tally with the economic realities of life in the new service economy. In post-industrial contexts, wherein deeply rooted community ties and working-class identities have been confronted with new logic and circuits of capital, a 'tormented habitus' can occur at the level of the individual, wrestling between old and new. In the north-east of England, Nayak argues, young men have responded to this struggle 'by intertwining new and old cultures…the determined preservation of older drinking customs in new times; the redeployment of "grafting" through a cultural apprenticeship of crime; the enactment of a muscular, body-capital to gain credibility on the street; and a fierce commitment to traditional notions of "respect"'' (Nayak 2006, p. 828). Elsewhere, as Sassen argues, these new configurations of long-standing social and spatial geographies of marginality 'might be contributing to the formation of a new type of gang, the postindustrial gang' (Sassen 2007, p. 112).

These continuities and changes over the lifetime of a city—of broad-based economic change engendering both predictable and unpredictable results at a local level—also speaks to the importance of individual life trajectories in making sense of the global gang phenomenon. In the following section, gangs are conceptualized as a form of identity, or *identification*, that alters and reconfigures over the life-course.

Gang identification

Too often, definitions of gangs are fixed, conceptualizing gang membership as a constant and unwavering force in individuals' decision making. For some critical gang scholars, however, gangs are not static entities—with universal characteristics and forms—but a fluid identity, to be used and drawn on in different ways, by different individuals, at different times. This approach, which locates gangs in the broader context of identity and social development, has important implications for the study of gangs. Rather than conceptualizing gangs as alien others, to be researched to target criminal justice interventions more effectively, the enactment of gang identities becomes a way of understanding the interleaving structures of age, gender, and ethnicity in young people's lives. Garot (2010), for example, locates these gang identities within the broader context of social development in young people's lives; contrasting this everyday image with the repressive machinery of the 'gang industry':

Adolescence is especially recognized as a time when one needs to experiment with identity, as the choices one makes in terms of career and family may have long-lasting ramifications...Yet such insights tend to be overlooked when we speak of inner-city youth, and especially when we talk about gang-members: fear clouds our thinking. When we feel threatened by those commonly referred to as 'monsters' or 'superpredators', it seems irresponsible or even dangerous to appreciate the artful nuances of their ways of performing identity'. (Garot 2010, p. 1)

Jenkins (2008) suggests two dialectical forces in the construction of identity: identification and categorization (see also Brubaker and Cooper 2000). Identification, in this context, refers to self-identification—a temporary attachment, or 'suturing' (Hall 1996) to an imagined community (B. Anderson 2006) with an attendant set of values and behaviours. Categorization, on the other hand, refers to external categorization—the 'placing' of an individual within a constructed category—in a similar conceptualization to that of labelling theory (Becker 1963). While positivist gang definitions frequently focus on the various ways in which young people might be *categorized* as gang members, gang identity refers to the 'fluid, contextual, and shifting' (Garot 2010, p. 3) ways in which individuals identify with, and enact, the persona of a gang member. For Jenkins, moreover, identity is by its very nature fluid and contingent: 'a process—*identification*—not a "thing"' (Jenkins 2008, p. 5). Much like habitus, identification is both improvized *and* structured by experience and socio-structural positionality (Jenkins 2008, p. 42), representing both shared belonging and differentiation. Conceptualizing gang activity as a form of identity—or *identification*—therefore brings 'the gang' into the realm of structured agency, and resolves some of the tensions latent in social theory surrounding the gang; specifically the issues of continuity, change, diversity, and difference.

For Bourdieu 'the body is a mnemonic device upon and in which the very basics of culture, the practical taxonomies of the habitus, are imprinted and encoded' (Jenkins 2002, pp. 75–6). Gang identification is one means through which this habitus can be embodied, but one that changes and alters during different stages of social development.[5] Crucially, for children and young teenagers, this may represent a form of experimentation rather than a commitment to a criminal lifestyle—Brenneman's work in Central America, for example, reveals that 'joining the gang is not a one-time, momentary decision but an interactive process in which youth "try on" the gang-member identity' (Brenneman 2012, p. 15). Similarly, Anderson describes how the 'code of the street' is learned and internalized: 'by the age of ten, children...are mingling on the neighborhood streets and figuring out their identities. Here they try out roles and scripts in a process that challenges their talent and prior socialization' (Anderson 1999, p. 68).[6] The processes through which young people grow into adult roles and identities are riven with conflict, doubt, impulse, and apprehension; the habitus is therefore

[5] In Scotland, for example, the Edinburgh Study reports that, at the age of 13, a higher percentage of females claim gang membership (21.5 per cent girls versus 18.8 per cent of boys); by the age of 17, however, the figure reverses (8 per cent males; 3.5 per cent females) (Smith and Bradshaw 2005, pp. 9–11).

[6] For much of the period since the 'invention of childhood' in the fifteenth century (Aries 1967), childhood was viewed as a stasis before adulthood, where children were controlled before entry into the adult world; the freedom of children was not emphasized (Jenks 1996). Research from the 'new social studies of childhood' has focused on problematizing the traditional view of children and young people as 'human becomings rather than human beings' (Holloway and Valentine 2000, p. 5). Current thinking instead views young people as active agents, within certain restraints set out by adult society (James et al. 1998).

variously developing, melding, and congealing throughout the process of growing up.

Conceptualizing gang identity in this way suggests a complex range of factors that compose young people's relationship with gangs. At a global level, the acceleration of inequality and social-spatial marginalization has created urban enclaves where gangs have emerged as an alternative social order. These groups vary tremendously, however, and one must look to the divergent social, cultural, and economic histories of different cities in making sense of this difference; these forces operate as a mediating factor in shaping the particular *habitus* of individuals sharing social space. Within this specific habitus, however, identities reshape and reform over time—both in the lifetime of the individual, and the lifetime of the city. As such, just as gangs can evolve into different forms of social organization, so too can the meanings attached to gangs alter for the individual. For Bourdieu, where the habitus no longer accords with field conditions, individuals may experience discord or ambiguity—what Bourdieu referred to as *habitus clivé*—resulting in alterations to individual dispositions. In the context of gangs, this can mean active *dis*-identification:

The pull of different ideologies may also be located within the same person so that the system of predisposition—'habitus' in Bourdieu's terminology—may reflect varying and possibly discordant cultural structures...not only will the gang as a social group display variance in terms of the motives and interests of its members, but any one individual affiliated with the group may have different reasons for investing time and energy. And, these may change over time, especially over the life course as youth mature and move in and through other social institutions. (Venkatesh 2003, p. 9)

Conceptualizing gang identity in this way crucially emphasizes the role of agency and individual choice in making sense of gangs. For some young people, the gang may be a temporary rite of passage that is cast off as an individual enters the economic field as an adult, or indeed as the city enters a different phase of economic development. Nonetheless, the *pre*conscious dimension of habitus also indicates a deeply buried pattern of social reproduction in gang identification, suggesting a clear structural link between continuities of inequality and disadvantage and the persistence of gangs.

Conclusion

As the field of gang research has shifted from sociological to criminological orientations—from issues of history, culture, and biography to crime, rational choice, and risk—research of gangs has become separated from lived experience and relocated into a free-floating academic field of knowledge. More, this field has become increasingly insulated from broader debates in cognate fields—anthropology, social theory, youth studies—resulting in a self-perpetuating, self-sustaining research agenda that is increasingly autopoeitic. In the process, theoretical accounts of gangs have become disengaged from the critical relationships—history and social change, diversity and difference, structure and agency—that influence the nature and form of gangs in the contemporary era. In this context, this chapter has argued for the need to reconnect studies of gangs with social theory, infusing Mills' 'sociological imagination' with a global and comparative reflexivity.

In developing a new vocabulary with which to analyse the gang phenomenon, Bourdieu's concepts of field, habitus, and capital have great potential in filling in the absences identified in extant theory, reconciling the tensions identified, and re-engaging sociological approaches to gangs. While Bourdieu's 'thinking tools' allow for an appreciation of the historically contingent nature of social action—the 'glacial force' (Appadurai 1996, p. 6) of habitus contrasted with the rapidity of changing economic conditions—they also create space for understanding the divergence and difference between gangs in different cultural contexts. Bourdieu's approach indicates that individuals in similar social spaces may share comparable dispositions—a clustering of characteristics, or homologies of habitus, that exists at a cross-national level. Since the habitus is the confluence of past, present, and future, however, it also ambiguous, somewhat randomized: 'the logic of practice is logical up to the point where to be logical would cease being practical' (Bourdieu and Wacquant 1992, pp. 22–3). As such, while gangs may be comparable across diverse geographical contexts, they are always locally constituted.

Building on this framework, the chapter introduced three complementary concepts with which to make sense of gangs: street habitus, the post-industrial city, and gang identification. These concepts apply Bourdieu's concepts to gangs in a global context, emphasizing structured variability in gangs between different cities; in a UK context, indicating the relationship between post-industrialism and gang identities; and in an individual context, demonstrating the agentic and structurally positioned nature of gang identification. These concepts are intended to build a foundation for new critical gang scholarship in the UK. In the following chapter, they are elaborated through analysis of the history and present of gangs in the post-industrial city that is the site, focus, and inspiration for this study: Glasgow.

3

No Mean City

The deepest problems of modern life flow from the attempt of the individual to maintain the independence and individuality of his existence against the sovereign powers of society, against the weight of historical heritage and the external culture and technique of life.

Simmel (1903/2002, p. 11)

For Simmel, writing at the dawn of the twentieth century, the development of the modern industrial city represented a qualitative shift in the nature of social interaction. As compared with the ideal typical 'village' environment, founded on kinship and community, the sheer breadth of experience and rapidity of pace of urban life necessitated the construction of a layer of indifference to one's surroundings—a 'protective organ' from the hyper-stimuli of everyday life that Simmel called the *blasé*. Just as the blasé catalysed individuality of fashion, taste, and habit, so too did it stimulate the growth of new forms of community. As cities grew, ethnic enclaves and urban villages emerged alongside new forms of association that were not tethered to neighbourhood of residence—social clubs, sport fandom, public recreation. While the development of cities created a desire for individual distinctiveness, it also threw up a range of new opportunities for commonality through shared living environments.

Drawing inspiration from Simmel, Thrasher argued that gangs first emerged in Chicago as a result of similar processes of individuation and collectivism. Gangs emerged in neighbourhoods with high population densities where large numbers of children and young people populated public spaces, with little in the way of amenities or resources (Thrasher 1963, p. 23). Forming into natural playgroups, children were forced to defend their space or play privileges from other groups: in 'its struggle for existence a gang has to fight hostile groups to maintain its play privileges, its property rights, and the physical safety of its members' (Thrasher 1963, p. 117). In this way, for Thrasher, groups become gangs via a process of being 'integrated through conflict', developing a group consciousness, a 'high-sounding name', and a territory (Thrasher 1963, p. 193), simultaneously creating a protective environment, and a space for individual distinction. In this sense, the gang represented 'the struggles of American ethnic and racial groups to gain or maintain a toehold in urban social systems' (Moore 1998, p. 65). Crucially, these efforts were carried out between the cracks of the developing city landscape—in the interstices between affluent areas, the nooks and crannies of the city (Thrasher 1963, p. 57)—where space became an important resource for constructing a sense of self.

While Thrasher's model of gang formation—of street-based youth, integrated through conflict—is perhaps the closest thing to a universal criminological theory that has been developed, cities have changed immeasurably in the century or so since his experiments in Chicago. While groups of young people continue to gang together in communities across the world, they now do so in increasingly varied and evolving ways; from economic organizations institutionalized in urban communities (Sanchez-Jankowski 1991) to political social actors (Brotherton and Barrios 2004). To make sense of this, we must look beyond the apparently 'natural' development of gangs in the urban environment to the broader forces that shape urban segregation and settlement (Burawoy 2000), and their interrelation with local history and culture. As Snodgrass writes of the Chicago School more broadly: '[i]nstead of turning inward to find the causes of delinquency exclusively in local traditions, families, play groups and gangs, their interpretations might have turned outward to show political, economic and historical forces at work' (Snodgrass 1976, p. 10). While seeking commonalities in gangs around the world, we must be sensitized to the contingency of the persistent presence of gangs, their evolution and sometime institutionalization on locally specific levers of difference.

Tracing these continuities in the face of change, this chapter will probe the distinctive character of the city of Glasgow, interrogating the context in which gangs have persisted. In the first section, blending 'soft' interpretations with 'hard' statistics, I sketch the distinctive characteristics of Glasgow that intersect with the history of gangs: persistent inequality, territorial identity, violent masculinities, neighbourhood nationalism, and economies of crime and justice. In the second, I relate these characteristics to the historical development of territorial gangs in Glasgow, examining the waxing and waning of gang identification in relation to the changing fates and fortunes of the city of Glasgow. In this way, I seek to excavate a genealogy of gangs in the city—delving deep into the unique and historically contingent configurations of class, space, and identity in Glasgow, while seeking out similarities with other post-industrial cities.

Soft city, hard city

The city as we imagine it, the soft city of illusion, myth, aspiration, nightmare, is as real, maybe more real, than the hard city one can locate on maps and statistics. (Raban 1974, p. 10)

It was Glasgow on a Friday night, the city of stares. (McIlvanney 1983, p. 1)

Raban's *Soft City* (1974) distinguishes the 'soft city' of interpretation, experience, and meaning from the 'hard city' of facts, numbers, maps, and graphs. The city can be viewed from above, through urban planning and design, and from below, through the subjective experience of everyday life and experience. For Raban, there is creative potential in public spaces that exists apart from the decisions of town planners—a spontaneity of experience and adaptability of identity that taps directly into Simmel's concept of the blasé. However, as Suttles' work *The Man-Made City* (1990) demonstrates, urban experiences must be understood in relation to these structuring forces. Decisions by urban designers and housing departments have a material impact on individuals' experience of cities, and it is necessary to understand the dialectical relation between 'hard' and 'soft' in this context. This in-betweenness speaks to Soja's notion of 'thirdspace', defined as 'a simultaneously real and imagined, actual and virtual locus of structured individual and collective experiences and agency' (Soja 1998, p. 11). Probing the connections between urban history and social life in this way emplaces identity and culture, and is characterized by resistance to the 'either/or' world of urban planners (Soja 1998, p. 10). For the field of gang research, this approach recognizes the critical role of space, urban history, and subjective experience in making sense of the differences between gangs in different urban environments.

The second quotation, the opening line from McIlvanney's classic Glasgow novel, *The Papers of Tony Veitch*, refers to a different interpretation of the 'hard city'. This is the cultural representation of Glasgow as a tough, violent city of mean streets: 'Britain's most murderous city, where only the ruthless survive'.[1] This image of the city has proven remarkably resilient, despite considerable diversification in representations of the city. One need not look far to find contemporary examples. Most recently, in the context of the Glasgow East by-election, Mooney's discourse analysis of media reports found, '[o]verwhelmingly, the portrayal of this area and the people who live in it during the election campaign was highly negative, drawing upon stereotypical representations of poverty in disadvantaged urban localities' (Mooney 2012, pp. 437–8; see also Gray and Mooney 2011). In the case of Glasgow, therefore, it is not only important to analyse 'soft' and 'hard' versions of the city but also the tensions that exist between different constructions and interpretations. In probing the unique blend of fact and fiction—legend and reality—that compose the Glasgow gang phenomenon, the 'thirdspace' that exists between experience and imagination is therefore of critical importance.

This section will outline the forces that have shaped the particular character of gangs in Glasgow today: persistent inequality, territorial identity, violent masculinities, neighbourhood nationalism, and economies of crime and justice. These characteristics are introduced as meso-level variables that exist at the level of the city, that represent the refraction of broader global forces, but that have had a structuring role on local experiences within communities. While not unique to Glasgow, they nonetheless establish a layer of analysis that allows for comparison with cities that have experienced similar economic and social ruptures in the post-industrial era. They are intended to operate as a lens through which to understand the micro-level of gang identification over time, discussed in the subsequent section.

---

[1] Channel Five (2005) *MacIntyre Uncovered*; broadcast 19 April 2005.

Persistent inequality

Throughout Glasgow's history, poverty has loomed large. Even during the boom years of 1875–1914 when the city became the shipbuilding capital of the world (Checkland 1981, p. 1; Maver 2000, p. 113),[2] the living conditions in the poorest districts were notorious. As Engels famously noted, after visiting the city:

I have seen human degradation in some of its worst phases, both in England and abroad, but I can advisedly say, that I did not believe, until I visited the wynds of Glasgow, that so large an amount of filth, crime, misery, and disease existed in one spot in any civilized country…These places are generally, as regards dirt, damp, and decay, such as no person of common humanity would stable his horse in. (Engels 1871, quoted in Damer 1990a, pp. 73–4)

At the same time, the city's captains of industry—following a pattern established by the so-called 'Tobacco Lords' in the eighteenth century—built empires, exploiting both the city's workforce and the favourable shipping routes available to the 'Second City' of the expanding colonial Empire. To the east and west of Glasgow was a strong mining tradition, and in Glasgow itself heavy engineering was well established (Checkland 1981, p. 5). Coupled with these natural advantages, the dredging of the River Clyde created a crucial transport hub for the fruits of the industry's labours. As Oakley quips, '[t]he Clyde made Glasgow, and Glasgow made the Clyde' (Oakley 1946, p. 211). The class distinctions between the working population of Glasgow and the emergent industrialist class—many of whom were part of a lineage of feudal lords and land-owners in Glasgow—found concrete form in the spatial patterning of the city. The east of the city was a less desirable area to live in because the wind blew much of the smoke from the manufacturing plants in this direction. Working-class districts were therefore largely constructed around the manufacturing plants that patterned the area. At the same time, the spoils of industry were spent in the west and south of the city, constructing the spectacular Victorian architecture for which Glasgow is now famous.

In the 1920s and 1930s, Glasgow lost much of its industry and with it the dubious honour of being 'Second City of Empire'. In

[2] In 1914, Glasgow produced three-quarters of the ships for the British Empire, as well as half the locomotives (Mitchell 2005).

the space of three years (1920–3), the shipbuilding tonnage of the Clyde fell from 672,000 to 175,000 (Maver 2000, p. 204), and the city experienced significant decreases in population.[3] The processes of urban separation between the rich and the poor—the 'virtuous cycles of growth and vicious cycles of decline' (Maver 2000, p. 218)—quickened, as the wealthier classes moved increasingly to the west, and the worse off were left with the overcrowded, unsanitary mass slum accommodation, which became associated with Glasgow in this period. Although Glasgow has seen successive waves of regeneration and redevelopment—from the Clyde Valley Plan of 1949 to the 'City of Culture' campaign of 1990—these improvements have not been felt equally. To this day, some 40 per cent of Glaswegians live below the poverty line (Dorling and Pritchard 2010), and life expectancies in the most depressed wards is less than 70 years (Glasgow Centre for Population Health 2008). The Scottish Index of Multiple Deprivation—the national measure of a range of factors of deprivation—rates Glasgow as having over one-third of the 10 per cent most deprived areas in Scotland, although this has decreased from nearly half in 2004.[4] As Maver summarizes, the acute losses of industry have been well-nigh impossible to correct.

Despite sustained efforts to introduce new industries and bolster shipbuilding via substantial state subsidies, the scale of Glasgow's structural defects proved impossible to overcome. From the 1970s the emphasis shifted decisively away from the old manufacturing base. The city was channelled towards an overwhelmingly service-based economy, where culture and tourism were promoted assiduously as key components of the post-industrial age. (Maver 2000, p. 203)

The move to a service economy—reimagining the city as a post-industrial haven of shopping, global tourism, and service industries—has done little to ameliorate the embedded inequalities in many of Glasgow's communities. While this process of rebranding has created new jobs and economic investment—Glasgow is 'regularly distinguished as a successful model of place-marketing

[3] Later, Glasgow lost residents at a rate of almost 10,000 a year for three decades: in 1951, the population stood at 1.1 million; in 1991, that had decreased to 681,228 (Maver 2000, p. 218).

[4] Scottish Index of Multiple Deprivation (2012) *SIMD 2012 results*. Available at: <http://simd.scotland.gov.uk/publication-2012/simd-2012-results/overall-simd-results/key-findings/> [Accessed 9 August 2014].

and urban entrepreneurialism' (MacLeod 2002, p. 603)—there are many who argue that this has come at great cost. The neoliberalizing policies that have stimulated development have simultaneously polarized wealth in the city, accelerating and amplifying processes of socio-spatial marginality and territorial stigmatization.[5] For many, this new, sand-blasted image of the city suppresses the experiences of poverty and worklessness which still characterize the experiences of many[6]—an example of neoliberal policy making that 'has further excluded and peripheralized sections of the population long considered disadvantaged' (Danson and Mooney 1998, p. 218).

In Bourdieu's terms, the shared experience of persistent inequality might be said to form part of a shared habitus that, while individuated by biography, economic position, and social capital, constitute a situation in which 'the objective conditions in which the habitus operates are similar to the objective conditions of which it is a product' (Hillier and Rooksby 2005, p. 30). As Robson summarizes in his discussion of a 'south-east London habitus', it is possible to identify certain shared characteristics at the level of the city:

It is indeed possible, I would suggest probable, that particular structures of feeling and patterns of culture have been generated by London, its history and its people. These have assumed specific forms, dimensions and characteristics out of the historical process of the growth of London and its at times spectacularly novel and particular social dynamics. As an historically unique kind of city it has produced unique and arguably specific forms of working-class metropolitan culture. (Robson 1997, p. 3)

Similarly, it could be argued that there are certain shared characteristics among the people of Glasgow that have emerged as a result of shared experience—for many in the city, of shared adversity—and communal cultural history. In this sense, habitus

---

[5] Following Boyle, 'Neoliberalism here is not taken as a static entity but an emergent and contingent political process... [while taking] seriously the need to examine the complex ways in which the doctrine has taken root in specific locales, has metamorphosed with different local path dependencies' (Boyle et al. 2008, pp. 313–14).

[6] The 'Worker's City' collective, including Alasdair Gray, James Kelman, Jeff Torrington, and many others, railed against the 'City of Culture' rhetoric. For discussion, see McLay (ed.) (1988, 1990) and Kemp (1990); for a later appraisal, see Garcia (2005).

might be conceived of at city level, delineating common characteristics among individuals sharing social space.

For Checkland, the proximity of social classes in tenement dwellings created a 'sense of common identity among Glaswegians [which] was strengthened by shared experience: there was a real sense in which Glasgow was one' (Checkland 1981, p. 22). Although the city has undergone two world wars, a significant decline in population, loss of heavy industry, several waves of decline and regeneration—and most recently the reinvention and rebranding as a post-industrial shopping mecca and service economy—there has been a remarkable constancy in the character of the city. In the face of change, 'habitus changes constantly, continuously, but within the limits inherent in its original structure, that is within certain bounds of continuity' (Hillier and Rooksby 2005, p. 31). As Damer concludes of Blackhill, a long-standing housing scheme in the east of Glasgow:

if their culture appears to have more in common with the Glasgow of the 1930s than the 1990s, it is because it represents the determined struggles of the very poor people of Blackhill to cope with the grim economic realities of post-Thatcherite Britain—in much the same way that their grandparents coped with the exigencies of the Depression. (Damer 1992, p. 60)

This continuity, it will be argued, forms the underlay for the persistence of gang identification in Glasgow. Glasgow is by no means unique in experiencing persistent and embedded inequality; however, the related issue of territorial identification forms part of the unique historical continuities of the city.

Territorial identity

A recent study of territoriality in six British cities (Kintrea et al. 2008)—Bradford, Peterborough, Sunderland, Bristol, London, and Glasgow—found curbs on economic and spatial mobility have created a 'hyper place attachment' to local territories in all sites, but found that territorial 'identities were historically embedded, with names and myths' only in Glasgow and Peterborough (Pickering et al. 2012). Similarly, a wide range of qualitative research on territoriality in Scotland[7] has uncovered deep-rooted attachments to

---

[7] MORI Scotland 2003; Seaman et al. 2005; Turner et al. 2006; Bannister and Fraser 2008; Frondigoun et al. 2008; Kintrea et al. 2008; Suzuki 2007; Deuchar 2009; Bannister et al. 2010.

place, with corresponding fear of travelling beyond the local area. Consequently, young people report a restriction on mobility both within their local areas and beyond, impacting on both friendship networks and leisure opportunities (Bannister and Fraser 2008, pp. 102–3; Frondigoun et al. 2008, pp. 43–50; Deuchar 2009). This deeply rooted attachment to place—or territorial identity—is an important factor in comprehending the persistence of the Glasgow gang phenomenon; the development of both can be traced back through time.

In broad terms, as with many other industrializing cities, the cleavages of economic inequality have been expressed in spatial terms—with working-class communities clustered in the east of the city while the more prosperous middle classes became established in the west of the city. Nonetheless, unlike the classical 'concentric zone' model of urban inequality, in which a depressed inner-city ripples its way to extreme affluence in the suburbs (Shaw and McKay 1942), social boundaries in Glasgow have always been relatively porous. For one thing, Glasgow's older housing is patterned by the coexistence, cheek by jowl, of traditionally working-class communities alongside the extremely affluent. For another, Glasgow's working-class roots run deep, and the community interdependence in tenement life forms part of the shared experience of the city's history. As McIlvanney observes, 'Glasgow has always been in my experience a city where boundaries are not very vigorously observed, full of socially mixed blood' (1987, p. 15). Will Fyffe's classic Glasgow folksong of the 1920s, *I belong to Glasgow*, expresses this sentiment most evocatively: 'I'm only a common old working chap/As anyone here can see/But when I get a couple of drinks on a Saturday/Glasgow belongs to me'.

As Glasgow flourished in industry in the nineteenth century,[8] waves of migrants from Ireland, Europe, and the Scottish Highlands were attracted to the city for work. In this context, the density of housing became increasingly extreme:

There were by 1914 no less than 700,000 people living in three square miles, thus creating the most heavily populated central area in Europe... One of the consequences of this concentration was to... [create]

---

[8] The Glasgow Story (undated). Available at: <http://www.theglasgowstory. com/storyd.php> [Accessed 9 August 2014].

strong sub-loyalties, to the many former villages of which Glasgow was composed. (Checkland 1981, p. 18)

As Checkland argues, one of the consequences of housing density in Glasgow's past was the development of fierce loyalties to these communities. Deeply wrought relationships between families and friends enabled survival in these harsh social environments: 'a *common* way of adapting had to be found, or individuals and families would have gone under—as many did' (Damer 1990a, p. 86).

For Taylor and colleagues (1996), drawing on a study of local 'structures of feeling' amongst adults in the post-industrial cities of Manchester and Sheffield, territorial identification emerges as a response to persistent inequality. This 'substance of locality', they describe, is characterized by 'routinised relations, reproduced over time, because of the dependency of actors condemned to geographical immobility' (Taylor et al. 1996, p. 14). This interlacing of inclusion and exclusion in community identification—evoking Elias and Scotston's description of 'Established vs Outsider' (1965/1994) relations—neatly captures the complex dialectics of territorial identity in Glasgow, in which competitiveness, distrust, and conflict can shape local communities: a Glaswegian gloss on the phrase 'tuppence ha'penny looking down on tuppence'.[9] While *social* boundaries may not be well-observed, however, *spatial* boundaries are less fluid. As Newman notes:

[w]hile public discourse tends to focus on the national scale of territorial conflict, such as the demarcation of state borders or the relationships between neighbouring states, the vast majority of people are affected at the local and micro scales of territorial behaviour…Such borders may be perceived; they do not necessarily have clear demarcators. They may be based around highways or other transportation arteries within the city…they are resilient in that they facilitate the processes of inclusion and exclusion through which territories and spaces retain their spatial homogeneity'. (Newman 2005, p. 6)

The city of Glasgow inspires fierce loyalties—a territorial identity representing a blend of class loyalty, shared history, and cultural memory which are all shaped by the broader structure of economic and political shifts in the city's history. On one hand, this shared

---

[9] Both 'tuppence' and 'tuppence ha'penny' are very small denominations of money. The phrase is used to indicate social divisions between the very poorest communities in the city.

territorial identity finds its roots in the community interdependence fostered by structural disadvantage. As Wacquant argues of territorial identity in Chicago and Paris: 'identification with one's place of residence can assume exacerbated forms that reflect the closure of one's lived universe' (Wacquant 2008a, p. 271). On the other hand, however, social divisions based on class, ethnicity, and religion are intertwined with this broad-based territorial identification; Glasgow is criss-crossed by urban fault lines that inspire equally fierce loyalties, be they sectarian, territorial, or institutional. Community inclusion, therefore, is an inherently double-edged sword—inclusion laced with exclusion, pride laced with shame. As Sibley argues, '[t]he construction of community and the bounding of social groups are a part of the same problem as the separation of self and other' (Sibley 1995, p. 45). Overlaid with the history of industrial-era machismo and violence in Glasgow, this territorial identity has formed a crucial element in the persistence of gang identification in Glasgow.

Violent masculinities

Glasgow has long had the reputation as a 'hard city' (Damer 1990a), with an image of hardened street-based masculinities evident in a range of cultural representations. Most notable among these is McArthur and Kingsley-Long's *No Mean City: A Story of the Glasgow Slums*, set in the Gorbals during the Depression (1956). The novel set a precedent for cultural representations of Glasgow that remains a powerful part of the mythology of the city to this day (Spring 1990, p. 112). As Sylvia Bryce-Wunder argues, '*No Mean City* is the paradigmatic Glasgow novel whose themes of violence and poverty have characterized many Glasgow fictions ever since, nourishing a tenacious image of hard men, mean streets and gangs' (Bryce-Wunder 2003, p. 122).[10] The narrative

---

[10] The novel's graphic descriptions of violence, drunkenness, and poverty, though dismissed by some with a snort of 'incredulous amusement' (House, quoted in Damer 1990b, p. 33), was nonetheless the cause of a great deal of controversy at the time of publication. For McArthur, however—an unemployed baker who documented life in 1930s Gorbals—conditions were of such extreme poverty that it demanded to be brought to the attention of the wider world. In a rejoinder to some of the reviews of the novel, he explains in a letter to the *Daily Record and Mail* that 'for working-class people to go on living and ignoring their weaker brethren, not caring how low they may have fallen is to me a social crime of the most dangerous kind' (Burrowes 1998, p. 20).

revolves around the rise and fall of violent 'hardman' Razor King, also known as Johnnie Stark, and his wife Lizzie, with parallel plot lines relating to two other young couples seeking to raise their heads above that of the masses, one through hard work and diligence, the other via celebrity at the local dance halls.

For the writer William McIlvanney, while the *No Mean City* stereotype of hardmen and street violence may have been exaggerated, it nonetheless taps a deep vein within Glasgow's working-class history: 'the legend may have been fed on the steroids of publicity but it originally earned its muscles on the streets' (McIlvanney 1987, p. 18). This 'hardman' persona evokes the 'fighting men' identified by Davies' historical work in the 1920s—urban legends whose names stand like statues in Glasgow streets: 'Each of Glasgow's tenement districts had its "fighting men"—those who were renowned locally and sometimes further afield both for their prowess as street fighters and for their ready resort to violence' (Davies 2013, p. 251). This image of the hardman runs like an electric current through Glasgow's cultural history, interlaced with varying forms of territorial identification. Writing of his childhood in the Gorbals area of Glasgow in the 1950s, Jimmy Boyle recalls:[11]

There would be occasions when Big Ned [a local 'fighting man'] used to mess his opponents up very badly, and in some cases they were seriously hurt, but the following morning he would walk down the street and people who had seen the fight the previous night would chat away to him as though nothing had happened. In a sense this was socially acceptable and no one ever made a big deal over it. (Boyle 1977, p. 15)

The hardman legend was forged in the very real context of hard labour and heavy industry, an embodied response to harsh *working* conditions similar to the territorial identification that emerged from harsh *living* conditions. As Jimmy Reid[12] famously declared in the 1970s, 'We don't only build ships on the Clyde. We build

[11] Boyle's autobiography relates his childhood involvement in violent street gangs in Glasgow, his later involvement in organized crime, and the brutal conditions of his imprisonment. Through the pioneering rehabilitative work of the Barlinnie Special Unit, Boyle has since been released and embarked on a career as a writer and sculptor. For a broader discussion of prisoner autobiographies, see Nellis (2010).

[12] Jimmy Reid was a renowned trade unionist and political leader who famously acted as spokesperson during the Upper Clyde Shipbuilders 'work-in' in 1971. He later became Rector of the University of Glasgow.

men'. Like Bourdieu's formulation of a gendered habitus, capitalist exploitation of bodies intertwined with the development of masculinities. As Hall argues of similarly formed masculinities in the north-east of England, 'violent hyper-masculinity' emerged in the context of 'an enforced practical relationship with specific material conditions' (Hall 2002, p. 45). For Damer, similarly, there is 'cachet in Glasgow in having the reputation of a "hardman"', which operates as a form of 'symbolic compensation' for the violence of poverty (Damer 1992, p. 52).

Although the imagery projected from the city of Glasgow has changed markedly over the past two decades, most memorably through the 'Glasgow: City of Culture' and 'Glasgow's Miles Better' campaigns (Damer 1990a, pp. 7–8)—and latterly the rhetoric surrounding the 2014 Commonwealth Games (Paton et al. 2012)—it is notable that *No Mean City* remains a touchstone in much media commentary on the city. As Davies notes of the London-based press in particular, riffs on the phrase 'No Mean City' remain central to headlines relating to Glasgow (Davies 2008). The phrase is used in everything from fashion catalogues advertising the 'new Glasgow' to the title theme to the quintessential Glasgow crime drama, *Taggart*. While these constructions are filtered through the distorting lens of media stereotypes, however, violent masculinities continue to form a backdrop for territorial gang fights. As will be seen in the next section, these violent masculinities have also formed a basis for the formation of a tough police force and a fiercely competitive landscape of organized crime.

Economies of crime and justice

From Cloward and Ohlin's *Delinquency and Opportunity* (1960) onwards, researchers have been sensitized to the broader social ecology of crime in gang evolution. While information on organized crime is difficult to collate and assess (Hobbs 2000), there are a number of autobiographies written by prominent ex-gangsters in Glasgow (Boyle 1977; Campbell and McKay 2001; Ferris and McKay 2001), from which the broader relationship between youth gangs and organized crime can be glimpsed.[13] The criminal careers of Boyle (1977),

---

[13] In fact, some of the most powerful and illuminating accounts of gang experiences are to be found within biography, though as Thompson notes, 'memories

Steele (2002), and Weaver (2008), for example, describe a movement from youthful gang activity into adult crime that is largely entrepreneurial, exploiting the continuities between the forms of violent masculinities prized within street gangs and adult criminal markets. Unlike the systematic links between street-based groups and drug distribution and organized crime in cities like Chicago (Venkatesh 2008) and Hong Kong (Lo 2012), in Glasgow youth gangs are more likely to operate in a relatively unorganized, non-economically motivated way, independent of more organized adult criminal groups.

In Glasgow, organized crime has traditionally been the preserve of a number of established 'crime families' with firm ties to traditional working-class communities. Starting in the late 1960s, groups of former safe-breakers and housebreakers began to carve out territorial zones in which money lending, illicit 'shebeen'[14] drinking, and gambling could be controlled. Walter Norval, a former gangster who served a 10-year term for armed robbery, has been quoted as follows:[15]

When I went into prison in the early 60s, there were wee gangs of hooligans that wanted to fight but when I came out in 1967, the place had changed, they were starting to thieve. In the old days they wanted to fight with each other but by then it was about making money. I controlled the hard cases from those areas. We were after money. There were smarter people taking over at that time. When I came out of the jail I realised we had been stupid before, that we really should be going after the cash, while still guarding our districts.

Boyle (1977) similarly mentions the late 1960s as marking a shift towards more organized crime in the city; from youthful ad hoc criminal collectives to more organized, purposive criminal groups. While the history of organized crime remains a topic for further investigation, this suggests that the development of tightly knit 'crime families' in Glasgow may have prevented a more open criminal marketplace in which gangs might have evolved. Since this time, serious and organized crime has increased significantly and is

will have faded but also there are axes to grind, scores to be settled, no longer with knives but in print' (Thompson 1995, p. xiv).

[14] After-hours drinking dens.

[15] Daily Record (2011) 'Glasgow Gangland: How 1970s saw street battles turn to organised crime'. Available at: <http://www.dailyrecord.co.uk/news/uk-world-news/glasgow-gangland-how-1970s-saw-1092584> [Accessed 6 August 2014].

now estimated to cost the Scottish economy up to £2 billion annually (Scottish Police Authority 2014). Law-enforcement authorities estimate that much of this activity clusters around Glasgow, with dense networks stretching from the illicit economy into the grey and licit economy in the form of taxi firms, car washes, and private security. In this context, one of the few studies to discuss the issue in Glasgow found links between youthful gang activity and 'the world of organised criminal networks were considered to be weak or non-existent' (Kintrea et al. 2011, p. 65).

Hobbs (1997) has written insightfully about the fragmentation of traditional organized crime families/territories in London and the impact this has had on street-based youths—with organic, territorial collaborations of working-class youth giving way to more diasporic, diverse, and dissolute alliances. However, in one industrial area he calls Upton, traditional loyalties retain a stronghold:

Despite the destruction of its industrial base, Upton's cultural inheritance is one of a static population grounded in traditional notions of family and neighbourhood, both of which remain coherent and relatively intact. The principal crime groups reflect this traditional profile by being family based and territorially orientated and are persistent features of the local landscape across generations. (Hobbs 1997, p. 410)

While some media commentators suggest an evolution in the landscape of organized crime in Glasgow—from 'local hard man to an educated foreign criminal whose contacts spanned the globe'[16]—organized crime does not appear to have offered regular opportunities for young people to move into the illicit economy.

The other critical variable in assessing the opportunities for economically motivated gang activity in Glasgow is the role of the police. The police force in Glasgow—initially Glasgow Police, latterly Strathclyde Police, now subsumed into Policing Scotland—was the first municipal police force in the United Kingdom, established in 1800, some 29 years before London's Metropolitan Police was constituted (Dinsmor and Goldsmith 2010, p. 55). The force became professional during the industrial

---

[16] Scotsman (2008) 'The changing face of gangland crime'. Available at: <http://www.scotsman.com/news/the-changing-face-of-gangland-crime-1-1158587> [Accessed 6 August 2014]. See also Herald (2012) 'Scotland's FBI warns 25 foreign mafia gangs are now at large'. Available at: <http://www.heraldscotland.com/news/home-news/scotlands-fbi-warns-25-foreign-mafia-gangs-are-now-at-large.16460653> [Accessed 6 August 2014].

era in Glasgow, and experienced institutional fluctuations that mirrored wider urban concerns over the course of the twentieth century—most notably the economic difficulties in the midst of the Depression (Dinsmor and Goldsmith 2010, p. 61)—and gathered strength in the post-war period as well-trained army volunteers were recruited. Despite considerable changes over time, Glasgow has maintained a robust police force, and continues to have one of the highest ratio of police officers to citizens among world cities. For Damer, this is a key factor in understanding the equilibrium of crime and justice in the city:

the biggest and most successful gang in Glasgow was always the city's police force. Organised professional crime on any scale was impossible in the city under such a tough and efficient force. So one aspect of local crime was sporadic and highly ritualised gang fights. (Damer 1990a, p. 149)

As such, the configuration of crime and justice in Glasgow has served as a limiting factor in the evolution of gangs into more organized, economically oriented groups. While organized crime has established deep roots in the city, the absence of a developed open-air drugs market—as in cities in the United States—has prevented the development of connections between organized drug distribution and street-based youth. The strength and weight of Glasgow's police force has also played a key role in the prevention of this development. Unlike cities where youth gangs have become organized and institutionalized, too, social divisions based on ethnicity have not been pronounced.[17] To date, commonalities rooted in territory—or 'neighbourhood nationalism' (Back 1996)—have been a more common characteristic in Glasgow.

Neighbourhood nationalism

Back (1996) develops the concept of neighbourhood nationalism as a means of capturing the new identities, ethnicities, and affiliations that have emerged in the 'multiculture' of contemporary London. Although racial discrimination and prejudice remains an everyday occurrence, Back identifies a process through which differences based on ethnicity are subordinated to a collective loyalty

---

[17] Hagedorn (2008), for example, argues that racialized politics, socio-spatial segregation of ethnic groups, and police discrimination have formed a critical variable in the development of gangs in Chicago.

to a geographical area. In short, neighbourhood nationalism 'attempts to banish the racial referent and replace it with a simple commitment to local territory' (Back 1996, p. 55), in a pattern similar to the 'Established–Outsider' relations described by Elias and Scotston (1994). The concept of neighbourhood nationalism incorporates a form of territorial inclusiveness that supersedes, but does not erase, distinctions on the basis of ethnicity (see also Watt and Stenson 1998).[18]

Similarly, while Glasgow's territorial identity is firmly tied to deeper social divisions in the city—seen most clearly in the 'Old Firm' rivalry between Celtic and Rangers football clubs (Murray 1996), representing long-standing sectarian tensions between Irish Republicanism (Celtic) and Protestant Unionism (Rangers)—this is not a solely exclusive or divisive impulse.[19] On the contrary, it is a protective instinct, representing affiliations to a local community that invoke deeply embedded familial and friendship ties. Paradoxically, the same fierce community loyalties that inspire territorial or football violence form a strong backbone of local volunteerism, mentorship, and inclusion that has prevented street-based violence developing to the levels of other post-industrial cities. There are a great many tireless local organizations working for poor pay in inferior facilities, relying on a core of community spirit that can be found across the city.[20]

In Glasgow, new migrants—often refugees and asylum-seekers—are frequently housed in areas of persistent poverty (Fraser and Piacentini 2013). In certain circumstances, this co-location has led to heightened tensions, discrimination, and conflict (Wacquant 2008a)—for example, a recent survey of young people in dispersal areas highlighted an increased sensitivity to difference and potential conflict (Ross et al. 2008). The blend of persistent inequality, community interdependence, and violent masculinities in

---

[18] Robins and Cohen (1978) in fact hint at this form of inclusion and exclusion in their discussion of racialised conflict between groups from different areas (1978, pp. 115–18).

[19] Davies (1998, p. 254) notes that in the 1930s relationships between gang rivalries and sectarian tensions were by no means clear cut: 'conflicts in the East End of the city ended to be strongly sectarian in character, while those in the South Side tended to be rooted more in territorial rivalries'.

[20] The following section details a number of important historical examples of this work. In the contemporary context, FARE in Easterhouse stands out as a clear contemporary example of this characteristic.

Glasgow has proven, surprisingly, less combustible than in comparable cities in the United Kingdom (Runnymede 2009; Deuchar 2011). This is demonstrated most clearly in the 'riot that never was'. In 2011, as widespread instances of youthful disorder spread across post-industrial cities in England in what have been labelled the 'consumer riots', (Treadwell et al. 2013), young people in Glasgow—a few exceptions aside[21]—did not respond. This suggests, if nothing else, that we must consider the unique cultural, spatial, and social patterns in different cities.

Although Scotland has experienced several waves of immigration—predominantly different groups of Irish, Jewish, Italian, Chinese, East European, and Indian sub-continent immigrants (Croall and Frondigoun 2010, pp. 112–13)—the country remains an overwhelmingly ethnically homogenous nation, with approximately 4 per cent of the population categorized as belonging to black and minority ethnic (BME) communities; though this increases to 12 per cent in Glasgow (Haria 2014). To date, statistics indicate a relatively proportionate representation of minority ethnic groups in the Scottish criminal justice system, and that ethnicity play a less significant role in victimization in Scotland than in other jurisdictions (Croall and Frondigoun 2010). For some, this attenuation of the race–crime relationship reflects a particular form of civic liberal nationalism in Scottish identity (McCrone 2001), which Miles (1993, p. 78) has argued focuses on perceived economic and political disadvantages of the Union without reference to race.[22] For Maver, despite a 'strand of conservatism' in Glasgow's character, this is supplanted by a 'cosmopolitan and progressive' attitude to migrants. Recent increases in the number of racist incidents in Scotland, however, suggest that this picture may be changing (Haria 2014).[23]

[21] BBC News (2011a) 'Scottish Youths Arrested over Facebook "Riot" Messages', 9 August. Available at: <http://www.bbc.co.uk/news/uk-scotland-glasgow-west-14461393> BBC News (2011b) 'Glasgow Boy, 16, Charged with Incitement', 10 August. Available at: <http://www.bbc.co.uk/news/uk-scotland-glasgow-west-14481665>.

[22] However, there is evidence that racial hate crimes are under-reported (GARA 2009; de Lima 2005), linked on the one hand to a lack of confidence in police to recognize the 'racist' elements in offences, and on the other hand to a less pervasive antagonism between police and ethnic minority groups in Scotland (Croall and Frondigoun 2010).

[23] The racially motivated murder of Kriss Donald, in 2004, is until now one of the few high-profile instances of racial youth violence in Glasgow. As Haria

Despite a comparative absence of racial conflict (Croall and Frondigoun 2010), there remain deep-seated social divisions and histories of discrimination in Scotland—in relation to Roma Gypsy communities, Irish Catholics, and white, working-class youths, labelled 'neds' (Poole and Adamson 2008; Croall and Frondigoun 2010)—that might mask the lived experiences of prejudice and 'othering' that exist on a day-to-day level.

The bringing together of soft and hard interpretations of the city of Glasgow—historical, statistical, cultural—is intended to allow a glimpse of those shared traits that constitute Glasgow's unique character; the core of the city's character that is not amenable to short-term refashioning. Persistent inequality, territorial identity, violent masculinities, and neighbourhood nationalism—in varying configurations, and interacting with a range of other forces—have formed a critical aspect in the formation of a shared *habitus*. Critically, this is not intended to denote a fixed or predetermined model of agency—habitus is a generative grammar for action, and is therefore socially learned and encoded. Neither is it to suggest that there have not been marked improvements in living conditions in Glasgow, or that grassroots activism and political interventions have not played an important part in changing communities for the better. It is, rather, intended as a means of exploring the deeper causes for the striking persistence of gang identification in Glasgow over time in order to locate this continuity in the context of persistent poverty, unemployment and associated social problems in the city. In the following section, I trace these links through excavation of a *genealogy* of gangs in Glasgow, connecting these city-level analyses with the historical development of gangs in the city. This section will argue that gangs in Glasgow have altered, reconfigured, and evolved in dialectic relation to broader social and economic forces at play in the city—emerging in cyclical patterns that follow the vicissitudes of the local economy.

A genealogy of gangs in Glasgow

Groups of young people engaging in territorial violence have been reported since the 1880s, during the peak of Glasgow's industrial

(2014) argues, however, recent increases in the BME community in Glasgow have been accompanied by increases in racially motivated crime.

productivity, with continuity in reportage throughout the twentieth century (Patrick 1973, p. 150)—in certain cases, with the same gang names recurring consistently throughout this period. First reported during the period of mature industrialism, at times gangs have evolved into more organized criminal units in periods of severe economic hardship, at others they have fallen away as large numbers of young men went to war. Gang formations during different generations—from industrialism to the Depression to post-industrialism—have reflected the changing economic and social circumstances of the city, waxing and waning according to broad-based shifts over time. In today's post-industrial economy, gang identification embodies continuing structural exclusions and cultures of machismo, in the absence of an established organized criminal hierarchy providing work in an illicit economy. Unlike Hagedorn's (2007) depiction of gang institutionalization in the United States—with role differentiation, adaptability, community involvement, and a subcultural outlook—gang identification in Glasgow has been looser and more subject to change. As McCallum recalls in his history of gangs in Glasgow: 'All gangs had a very fluid membership and with the coming of each generation the gangs took on a new character which was generally based on the influence of their leader affs [leaders]... Generally this osmosis would take place every decade' (MacCallum 1994, p. 98). As such, gang identification carries forward through generations (Davies 1998; Bartie 2010) and is appropriated in ways which reflect and refract broader processes of social change.

Although gangs have a long lineage in Glasgow, it has only been during particular historical periods that the issue has become an object of popular outrage and political attention. While conditions of life for young people in former working-class communities have continued to be structurally similar to those experienced by previous generations, gang formations have also operated cyclically, with certain periods—notably the 1930s and 1960s—attracting more interest and publicity. As Murray (1996, p. 120) warns, this impression is warped by the fact that the voices of young people are often silenced by history:

A major problem in tracing the history of gang warfare... is that most of the evidence comes from old folks' whose memories have been distorted with time, and newspapers with a middle-class bias reporting what is essentially a working-class phenomenon. Nevertheless, there do seem to have been periods when gang warfare assumed significant proportions, most notably in the 1930s and the late 1960s.

Focusing on early accounts of gangs in the 1880s alongside these two periods, in this section I build on the core aspects of Glasgow's character as a city to excavate a genealogy of gang identification in Glasgow.[24] I will examine the early origins of the gang phenomenon, locating this within the broader history of Glasgow. Gang identities emerged most prominently in areas of Glasgow with high densities of housing, large youth populations, and a severe lack of work and amenities. These conditions have existed in communities throughout Glasgow's history, and the institutionalization of gang identities in these communities should be read in the context of these ongoing social conditions. In short, gang identification represents a cultural continuity in the face of economic change, that nonetheless waxes and wanes in dialectical relation with socio-structural forces.

1880s: Gangs and early industrialism

While there are sketchy reports of territorial groups prior to this period, the majority of gang histories in Glasgow focus on the 1880s as a key starting point. These early accounts of gangs in Glasgow focused on their emergence in communities with high densities of population—principally composed of poor migrants from Ireland and elsewhere in Scotland—where large numbers of children and young people populated public spaces, with little in the way of amenities or resources, in the classic Thrasher mould (Thrasher 1963, p. 23). Early reports of territorial gangs are therefore co-terminous with the development of industrial 'hardness'. Oral historians Johnston and McIvor (2004, p. 1) have written of the layering of historical and economic factors that cohered in the development of working-class masculinities in the industrial era.

Evidently, as in other industrial regions, Clydeside working class masculinities were initially incubated in the tough street culture of the neighbourhood. Many boys' games centred around the acting out of heroic

---

[24] I am indebted to John Hagedorn for the suggestion of the term 'genealogy' for this exercise (Hagedorn 2009). The term is intended to invoke Foucault's use of the term, which implicates the operation of power through complex social machinery over time.

roles—emulating the glamourised danger faced by cinema and comic book heroes, including Tarzan and John Wayne.

The formation of industrial masculinities—risk aversion, rugged competitiveness, and dark humour—in this way finds a youthful equivalent in the street-based cultures of gang identification. Further, this period was also notable for the increases in population that Glasgow experienced in the context of industrial success, and the waves of migration from Ireland and the Scottish Highlands, as well as the social and religious divisions that this new configuration generated.

Davies, in his recent periscopic overview of gangs in Glasgow between the 1880s and 1930s (2013), draws close attention to the linkages between migration, religion, and early reports of territorial violence. Davies' analysis of newspapers and court records of the period demonstrate a close correlation between neighbourhood, religious affiliation, and resulting conflict—particularly in the rivalries provoked by Orange marches and St Patrick's Day parades in the city (see also Archibald 2013). As Davies notes, however, this was not simply a matter of nationality, but a more complex chequerboard of class, religion and institutional identity in a rapidly developing urban environment (2013, p. 12).

In the wake of mass Irish immigration, religious divisions had become inextricably bound up with, and inflamed by, the Ulster conflict. A substantial minority of the Irish migrants to Glasgow were Protestants, and they brought with them the Orange Order with its aggressive assertion of Protestant ascendancy.

Records of these violent skirmishes that have survived appear to have been related to sectarian divisions between the variously affiliated social clubs of the city. 'Recollections of the gangs of the 1880s were entwined with memories of parades by sectarian "party" bands' (Davies 2013, p. 11). It was in this period, too, that both Rangers and Celtic Football Clubs were established (Rangers in 1873, Celtic in 1888)—both teams grew out of social clubs run by local Protestant and Catholic groups, from working-class communities in the south and east of the city (Murray 1996). This coming together reflected a solidification of social divisions rooted in religion, but also reflected aspects of neighbourhood nationalism, community interdependence, and violent masculinities. Davies (2013, pp. 33–4), however, traces an abatement in gang rivalries in the post–First World War era to the politics of 'Red Clydeside', quoting news sources from the period that suggested that 'hooliganism had ceased to exist in Glasgow' as strikes and demonstrations took their place.

1920s–30s: Gangs and the Depression

In the 1920s and 1930s, in the midst of the Depression, Glasgow saw a resurgence of fears over the 'gang menace'. Gangs were linked to 'an epidemic of thefts and small burglaries, a "sex war" between young wives and their husbands, and a spate of aggressive begging' (Davies 2007a, p. 415), thus serving as a 'focal point for a host of economic, social and cultural anxieties' (Davies 2007a, p. 409) relating to the rising rates of unemployment in the city. Coupled with this, stories of Al Capone and Chicago gangsters were increasingly published alongside stories of Glasgow gangs, eliding the fears of organized crime and violence with the much less sophisticated Glasgow gangs (Davies 2007b, p. 513). Crucially, this surge in popular fears was exploited by police and the courts:

Invoking the term gangster provided an effective rhetorical ploy for police officers in court...those labelled gangsters were likely to suffer disproportionately severe punishments, irrespective of the crimes of which they were convicted. (Davies 2007b, p. 520)

Davies' documents the activities of one specific gang in 1930s Glasgow—the Beehive Boys, from the Gorbals in Glasgow's south side. Unlike the majority of gangs at the time, 'which they viewed disparagingly as being merely concerned with non-instrumental violence' (Davies 1998, p. 253; see also Davies 2013, pp. 136–7), the Beehive Boys regarded themselves as 'criminal specialists' (ibid.), involved in organized theft, housebreaking, and robbery: 'The Beehive Boys saw themselves as a new type of gang: capable of ferocious violence, but more interested in the pursuit of profit than in territorial or sectarian skirmishing' (Davies 2013, pp. 136–7).

Davies firmly locates the development of the Beehive Boys from an unsupervised peer group into a more organized gang in the context of the severe unemployment that Glasgow in general, and the Gorbals in particular, experienced during the 1930s (Davies 1998, p. 260). Crucially, too, the Beehive Boys must be understood in the context of working-class life during the period. Davies relates the development of the support and solidarity within the Beehive Boys to the 'vitality of bonds' in the Gorbals at this time, revolving around mutuality and interdependence (Davies 2007a, p. 408). Undoubtedly, the Beehive Boys generated fear and instability within the community—levying fines from residents and shopkeepers to pay bail money (Davies 2007a)—but nonetheless were a communal resource for identity and solidarity during harsh economic times. As Davies notes:

> while it is too crude to depict unemployment as the 'cause' of gang conflicts in interwar Glasgow, the decline of heavy industry does appear to have led to an upsurge in property crime among gang-members. As unemployment increasingly undermined traditional, work-based masculine identities, it became more common for men in their twenties and thirties to play active roles in street gangs. (Davies 1998, p. 268)

In this context, Davies reports that gang membership grew to 5,000 to 7,000 members 'in the city's poorer districts' (Davies 2013, p. 1), with groups better organized, criminally oriented, and able to mobilize large numbers of individuals.[25] Some indeed functioned as social clubs, as Davies relates (Davies 2013, p. 8):

> Larger gangs such as the Billy Boys, San Toy and Kent Star were run by committees, with secretaries and treasurers to administer subscriptions and arrange payments for lawyers, as well as recognised leaders...In this way, gangs reproduced themselves across generations.

While Davies draws connections with street-based groups in other industrial cities of the time, he maintains that Glasgow was different. For him, this resulted from the unique combination of population density, sectarianism, long-term unemployment, poverty, and overcrowding that were inherent in the city at the time (Davies 2013, p. 3). Moreover, he is at pains to locate this hardship in the context of the burgeoning consumer economy in Glasgow, in which economic hardship was made more dispiriting by the 'the new world of leisure symbolised by the glitzy *palais de danse*' (Davies 2013, p. 3).

From Davies' detailed case study, we see the evolution of gang identification from sectarian social clubs, expressing industrial-era masculinities in street-based skirmishes, to more organized,

---

[25] One of the few examples of explicit linkages between gangs and politics occurred in this period. Davies describes the process by which gang members acted as 'stewards' for the Conservative Party (Davies 2013, p. 157). For a broader discussion of the links between gangs, politics, and institutionalized corruption, see Hagedorn (2008).

cohesive units capable of generating systematic illicit earnings. Critically, this evolution must be viewed within the wider context of the extreme poverty of the Depression, as a culturally consistent adaptive response to severely curtailed opportunity. From this period too we see clear evidence of the influence of 'neighbourhood nationalism'—often in the form of politically engaged ministers working to end violent conflicts (Davies 2013)—and the economies of crime and policing playing an influential role in the nature and form of gangs.

1960–70s: The 'New Wave' of Glasgow gangs

While Chief Constable Percy Sillitoe, the self-styled 'hammer of the gangs' (Sillitoe 1956), is credited with the suppression of more organized criminal gangs in the city, Davies argues that it was in fact the Second World War that was their most effective deterrent. Certainly, in the immediate post-war period, the gang phenomenon fell from view—again indicating the cyclical nature of public interest in gangs, and the generational fluctuation in the phenomenon itself. In a recent article, Bartie (2010) notes that Glasgow gangs were not mentioned in the post-war period until 1966—youth violence was instead referred to in terms of 'hooliganism'—until attention began to focus on Easterhouse (Bartie 2010, p. 4). In Easterhouse—as in the other three large post-war housing estates of Drumchapel, Pollok, and Castlemilk—housing had been prioritized above other amenities, resulting in populations of up to 40,000 with no shops, schools, churches, recreation facilities, or other amenities.[26] The resulting combination of socio-spatial marginalization, limited facilities, and a high youthful population led to a spike in public concern over youth gangs in the mid-1960s.

For Checkland, the concentrated social problems that emerged in these estates were inevitable, but was also redolent of the crises in Glasgow's post-war economy (Checkland 1981, p. 65). Half of the population of Easterhouse was under the age of 21, with no resources or amenities, large numbers of young people congregated on street corners and in public spaces (Armstrong and

---

[26] The opinion of many of these peripheral estates is summarised in Billy Connolly's pithy description of Drumchapel as a 'desert with windows'.

Wilson 1973a, p. 67). Established territorial loyalties from previous working-class communities such as the Gorbals became fractured, and the sharp edge of Glasgow's territorial identity came to the fore. The result, for Armstrong and Wilson (1973a, p. 66), was for 'residents of all ages to identify with their own neighbourhood, rather than with the Easterhouse area, the most explicit expression of which has been the "territory-based gang" '. As they continue:

Four schemes or neighbourhoods are readily distinguishable, which until recently were divided by areas of undeveloped waste land...there is little opportunity—or need—for social mixing to take place *between* them...The importance of the built environment and local demography lies in the fact that they structured the *pattern* of youth relationships. (Armstrong and Wilson 1973a, p. 66)

Bartie (2010) charts the development of a classic moral panic over the Easterhouse gang phenomenon, culminating in 1968 in a visit to Easterhouse by popular entertainer Frankie Vaughan to bring together young people from different gangs, and build a youth project in the area. Armstrong and Wilson (1971, 1973a, 1973b) examined this chain of events from the emergent perspective of symbolic interaction and new deviancy theory and found that the representation far outstripped the reality.

While the existence of gangs in the area could not be denied, they were neither as highly organised nor as widespread as the press indicated...One boy had posed as a gang-leader in order to get a free plane trip to Blackpool. (Armstrong and Wilson 1973a, p. 62)

Armstrong and Wilson argue convincingly that the reputation of Easterhouse—and, correspondingly, Glasgow—came about not as a result of the gang behaviour itself, but as a focal point for broader societal concerns of the day. They report that the Assistant Chief Constable of Strathclyde Police, after having conducted a survey of youth violence in Glasgow, declared Easterhouse to be far from the worst area affected (Armstrong and Wilson 1971), yet public anxieties over the lack of amenities and poor social conditions in the new housing estates became concentrated on the issue of Easterhouse gangs. In turn, the issue became heavily politicized in the 1969 council elections, where law and order was a key issue (Armstrong and Wilson 1971). The authors summarize the Easterhouse gang 'problem' in the following terms:

It appears that groups most successful in solving the 'problem' of Easterhouse were those which had the power to publicise and activate their own definitions of the situation—namely the Glasgow administration who faced the problem of their own control ideologies being discredited by the existence of the [Easterhouse] project. (Armstrong and Wilson 1971, p. 18)

It is important to note, however, that gang activities were neither a figment of the imagination nor confined to these stigmatized and stereotyped new schemes. In a format similar to that described by Hagedorn in relation to Milwaukee—whereby gangs emerged from a pre-existing friendship group and from 'break-dancing crews' (Hagedorn 1998b, p. 157)—Armstrong and Wilson describe the development of gang identities from football teams. They quote a 'gang boy' as follows:

It was through playing football that it all started. Used to hang about the corner after a game. After I left school there was nothing to do except hang about, you'd just hang about with the same crowd. If anyone got dug-up [usually a *verbal* provocation] you'd all go down; that was classed as a 'gang fight'. (Armstrong and Wilson 1973a, p. 67; emphasis in original)

In many ways, this 'new wave' of gang identification followed Thrasher's classic model of gang formation (1963)—of street-based youths in overpopulated areas with few facilities, playing out battles for identity and respect. More than this, though, it represents those aspects of habitus that were forged within the unique cultural and economic history of Glasgow, the transference of deep-seated territorial loyalties and violent masculinities to an environment without an established equilibrium of crime and policing.[27] Moreover, this was heavily influenced by the culture and politics of the time—some young men in Easterhouse were also identifying with left-wing politics and 'hippy' culture.

While Easterhouse attracted the most publicity, for Patrick— writing of a similar period of time—'the main gangs are still centred in the old slum areas, and...gang traditions have been transferred to the new estates which proved to be first-rate breeding grounds for gang activity' (Patrick 1973, p. 168). Patrick's brief insight into the activities of the 'Young Team', a group of young

[27] This vacuum was not to last long. The 'Untouchables' policing squad in Easterhouse were notorious for their strong-arm tactics. See Bartie (2010) and Bartie and Fraser (2014) for more detail on this period.

men in a traditional working-class community in the west end of Glasgow, illuminated an entrenched gang culture revolving around violence and reputation. It should be recalled, in this context, that the broader economies of crime and justice play an important role in this development. While the Beehive Boys were operating in a milieu devoid of a broader illegal criminal infrastructure, a second tier of 'Glasgow gangs' started to gather momentum in the 1970s, gaining critical mass as large-scale drug markets came into being in the latter part of the twentieth century (Boyle 1977). While gang identification continued to revolve around a street-based culture of machismo from previous eras, there began to develop an additional tier of criminality in the city that was more sophisticated than found in previous generations. As noted, however, this did not necessarily provide an opportunity for gang evolution as it did in other contexts.

While public concern over gangs began to subside in the early 1970s (Bartie 2010) the issue once more came to prominence in the 2000s. The unique aspects of this upsurge in popular fears in the new millennium and their continuities with the genealogical origins described in this chapter will be revisited in Chapter 8.

Conclusion

Too often in contemporary gang research—in the search for universalized definitions or effective policy transfer—the particular historical, cultural, and spatial configurations of gangs in particular cities are lost or downplayed. Gangs are disembedded from their social context and reimagined as part of a globalized phenomenon with common characteristics. In so doing, the critical role of political economy and cultural history in shaping the preconditions for gang formation is effectively minimized. In keeping with the neoliberal discourse that has come to dominate policy formation in the UK, US, and beyond, gangs are characterized as an individual deficiency rather than a collective response to persistent structural inequality. This chapter has sought to sharpen the approach to the study of gangs advocated in this book by focusing specifically on the role of social change on gang identification in Glasgow—tracing contemporary configurations of gangs back into the past, and the particular characteristics of the city of Glasgow that have emerged, in turn, from its fate over time.

The key variables in the continuation of gangs in Glasgow—persistent inequality, territorial identity, violent masculinities, and neighbourhood nationalisms—are at once comparable to other post-industrial cities, but are also unique, just as gangs themselves might be similar to yet distinct from groups in other similar social contexts. The factors that have prevented the overall evolution from Glasgow's street-based youth into more organized criminal units—economies of crime and justice—similarly constitute vectors around which comparisons can be made: licit and illicit opportunity structures, strength and reach of policing operations, profitability of drugs markets. Although public attention was drawn to gangs during these particular historical periods, evidence suggests a continuity of gang identification in the interceding years. As Davies notes: 'gang rivalries appear to have derived a momentum of their own during the late nineteenth century, irrespective of short-term economic trends' (Davies 1998, p. 252). This suggests that the habitus from which these rivalries are drawn became deeply embedded and reproduced during this time, playing a persistent role in the lives of successive generations of young people.

Gang identification in Glasgow is deeply rooted in the city's history of migration, politics, and sectarian tensions—as well as the social clubs which came to represent these competing interests—but also in social and economic inequality. In Glasgow's most marginalized communities, gangs have formed an ongoing source of status and reputation in a city that was moving away from the industries that once gave life to those areas. The travesty is that the violence caused by this form of territorialism is directed at other, similarly marginalized young people, and not at the social system that perpetuates this form of inequality. The history of gangs in Glasgow tells a story of persistent marginalization, poverty, and violence—but, with a few exceptions, seldom one of political organization or resistance, another issue that runs in deep in Glasgow's history.[28]

---

[28] Davies, for example, reports on the involvement of the Billy Boys in political rallies, as paid security guards (2013).

4

The Best Laid Schemes

The best-laid schemes o' mice an 'men;
Gang aft agley [Go often awry].

Burns, *To a Mouse* (1786)

Scotland's poet laureate, Robert Burns, penned these lines towards the end of the eighteenth century as the star of industrialism was starting to rise. Burns was tapping into, and artfully grounding, ideas that were then prominent in the Scottish Enlightenment; namely, that certain aspects of social life were unplannable and unpredictable, that invisible forces were at work to confound or correct our strategies and goals. This phenomenon can be a rich source of humour—the TV show *You've Been Framed* is premised on exactly this phenomenon—but on a societal level it sounds a cautionary note about the extent that human societies can tame the natural environment, or predict the adaptive responses of individuals to particular circumstances. This idea was to be taken up some 150 years later by Robert K. Merton in his book *Social Theory and Social Structure*, carrying the title 'the unanticipated consequences of social action' (1957). Merton sought to delineate the continually confounding forces involved in efforts of social institutions to plan and exert control over the future: ignorance, error, short-term interests, basic values, and self-defeating prophecies (Merton 1957). Where the Chicago School had looked for causes of social problems at the micro level of interaction, Merton followed a line of philosophy that bored a hole into the heart of the human condition.

This unlikely alliance of Burns and Merton—a wayfaring Scots poet and a pioneering American sociologist—fuses a core of ideas that run through this chapter. In Glasgow, 'schemes' are shorthand for council-housing estates—the public housing estates for which Glasgow is notorious, ironically designed as 'schemes' for social improvement—and the forms of community that have emerged from these environments have in some ways been similarly unanticipated.[1] As was argued in the previous chapter, these schemes have also often 'gone awry' throughout Glasgow's history, the most striking examples being the concentrated social problems that converged in the construction of peripheral post-war housing estates. As a recent report on gang identity in Scotland found, the 'historical roots of today's gangs were generally traced in interviews to the development of housing schemes in the post-war era' (Bannister et al. 2010, p. 16). Given the combination of violent masculinities and territorial identification described in the previous chapter, the segregation imposed by these developments resulted in the rapid development of gang rivalries that persist to this day.

Research, of course, is itself a form of 'purposive social action' that is just as prone to ignorance, error, short-term interests, basic values, and self-defeating prophecies as any other human endeavour. For ethnographic research, however, this very spontaneity and unpredictability can be an asset as well as a curse. Ferrell has described ethnography as being constituted and enlivened by the 'gorgeous mistake' of fortune (Ferrell 2009, pp. 16–17): 'mistakes and misdirections in research, moments of stumbling serendipity, are to be valued—maybe even sought—for their criminological insights'. Just as the history of gangs in Glasgow has been dictated in part by the unintended consequences of housing policy, urban planning, and regeneration, so my best efforts to plan and organize my own study were often derailed by unforeseen circumstance. As Simpson argues:

[h]owever much we might wish to assume the identity of an academic researcher replete with methods, theories and learned degrees, the truth is that once we step into the complex flow of other people's social experience we are novices and bumbling incompetents, largely oblivious to the complex and multiple layering of our informants' lives, identities and histories. (Simpson 2006, p. 125)

---

[1] A 'fly-on-the-wall' BBC series (2010–2011), called *The Scheme*, followed the lives of the inhabitants of a housing scheme in Kilmarnock, near Glasgow. The series was sharply criticized by some media commentators, being labelled as 'poverty porn' for its misleading representation of life in public housing. See Guardian (2010) 'The Scheme: gritty TV or poverty porn?' for further discussion. Available at: <http://www.theguardian.com/tv-and-radio/tvandradioblog/2010/may/28/the-scheme-bbc> [Accessed 9 August 2014].

The chapter will cover each of these areas—the field site of Langview, the study itself, and the unplanned nature of ethnography—by way of introduction to the places, spaces, and faces that make up the remainder of the book. This *dramatis personae* of the characters seeks to illuminate their daily lives and rhythms, while recognizing the particular economic, social, and spatial position that they occupy within the post-industrial city.

Langview

Just as Glasgow was shaping itself into the 'Second City' via the architecture of Alexander 'Greek' Thomson and Charles Rennie Mackintosh—and the elaborate City Chambers in George Square declared the official centre of the city (Oakley 1946, p. 230)—so too was the heart of Langview wrought. The tenemented core was built during the huge upsurge in Glasgow's population during the late nineteenth and early twentieth centuries to house the workers from the manufacturing plants in Langview and neighbouring communities. The period following the Depression brought significant decreases in the population (and the working population) in Langview in particular as well as Glasgow as whole, the result of economic migration, but also of a series of large-scale regeneration policies by the Glasgow City Council. This included the building of the four peripheral housing estates and coincided with the construction of major new transport routes (the M8 and M74) and connected the new towns of East Kilbride, Erskine, and Cumbernauld. For many, these developments caused fundamental ruptures in the tightly knit working-class communities of the past.[2]

More recently, successive waves of regeneration, gentrification, and redevelopment have reshaped the streets of both Langview and Glasgow. As the traditional industries of Glasgow have fallen into decline, so the city has reconfigured around new economies of service and tourism—culminating in Glasgow's status as 'City of Culture' in 1990, 'European City of Architecture' in 1999, and more recently being listed as one of the top ten cities in the world by Lonely Planet (Guardian 2008). Simultaneously the city of Glasgow has comparatively high rates of crime—particularly

---

[2] McKay 'Modern times: 1950s to the present day', *The Glasgow Story*. Available at: <http://www.theglasgowstory.com/storyf.php> [Accessed 28 September 2010].

violent crime—and comprises some of the most deprived areas in Scotland.[3] In Langview, successive waves of de-industrialization, depopulation, and gentrification have resulted in a mixture of housing—traditional sandstone tenements, local authority housing schemes, and, more recently, modern flat developments for the rental market. The area is defined by the Scottish Index of Multiple Deprivation as being within the 5 per cent 'most deprived' areas in Scotland—having rates of unemployment and benefit claimants well above the national average—and has an established reputation, in media and police reports, as being an area with a 'gang problem'. Despite this reputation, however, there has been a recent influx of new residents. Thus, while the area retains a reputation for gang violence it is developing a separate reputation as an area of gentrification. It therefore stands as a microcosm of the processes of de-industrialization, gentrification, and marginalization that have occurred in the city of Glasgow as a whole. Policies have increasingly turned towards neoliberal branding of Glasgow as a post-industrial haven of shopping and tourism, in which streets are being 'cleansed' of the homeless, of street drinkers, and of young people. As MacLeod argues, 'if we search beneath the euphemistic hype and superficial glamour...we gradually unravel some distressing geographies of exclusion' (MacLeod 2002, pp. 612–13).

Official figures place the population of Langview at a little under 7,000. In terms of age demographics, Table 4.1 illustrates the various proportions of different age groups in Langview. As can be seen, there is a significantly higher proportion of young people (aged 16–29) living in the area than the national and city average, although it has a significantly lower proportion of under-16s.[4]

As Table 4.2 illustrates, there is a small proportion of minority ethnic groups, with the largest single group being Pakistani and other South Asian. Although these proportions are greater than the national average, they are below the city average.

---

[3] Scottish Government (2007) *Recorded Crime in Scotland 2006–2007*, Table 7. Available at: <http://www.scotland.gov.uk/Publications/2008/03/06120248/14 [Accessed 29 August 2008]; Scottish Executive (2006) *Scottish Index of Multiple Deprivation: General Report*, p. 6. Available at: <http://www.rics.org/Practiceareas/Property/Regeneration/scottishindex_multipledeprivation2006_enewsnov06.htm> [Accessed 2 May 2008].

[4] No more up-to-date data was available at the time of writing.

Table 4.1 Age demographics of Langview, Glasgow, and Scotland (2002)*

	Langview	Glasgow	Scotland
0–15 years	12.8%	18.4%	19.2%
16–29	26.2%	21.2%	17.5%
30–44	23.2%	23.7%	23.0%
45–60	16.7%	16.2%	19.3%
60 and over	21.1%	20.4%	21.1%

Source: Scottish Census Results Online Warehouse

* Scottish Census Online Warehouse (Undated). Available at: <http://www.scrol.gov.uk/scrol/warehouse/warehouse?actionName=choose-area> [Accessed 1 May 2008].

Table 4.2 Ethnicity of population of Langview, Glasgow, and Scotland (2002)

	Langview	Glasgow	Scotland
White	97.3%	94.5%	98.0%
Indian	0.3%	0.7%	0.3%
Pakistani and other South Asian	1.2%	3.0%	0.8%
Chinese	0.4%	0.7%	0.3%
Other	0.7%	1.0%	0.6%

Source: Scottish Census Results Online Warehouse

Table 4.3 presents the occupational grading of residents of Langview. Residents are most likely to fall into the social grades C1, C2, D, or E, with more than one-third of people of working-age population claiming state benefits or being otherwise unemployed. Indicators for public health in Langview (life expectancy, smoking, hospital admissions) are significantly worse than the national average.[5]

These statistics, however, only give a partial view of the lived experience of Langview. In composing a picture of Langview that alternates between 'hard' and 'soft' interpretation, that explores the liminal spaces that exist between perceived and conceived

[5] NHS Scotland (2004) *Langview: A Community Health and Wellbeing Profile*. Health Scotland: Edinburgh.

Table 4.3 Social grade of working-age population in Langview, Glasgow, and Scotland (as % of local population)

	Langview	Glasgow	Scotland
AB Higher and intermediate managerial/professional	9.8%	14.5%	19.0%
C1 Supervisory, junior managerial/professional	24.8%	23.7%	26.6%
C2 Skilled manual workers	10.5%	10.7%	14.6%
D Semi-skilled and unskilled manual workers	19.2%	17.9%	17.5%
E State benefit, unemployed, lowest grade workers	35.7%	33.2%	22.4%

Source: Scottish Census Results Online Warehouse

space (Soja 1998), it is necessary to shift focus. This 'thirdspace' draws attention to the complex relationship between the subjective experience of space—for example, that of everyday life in Langview—and the perceived meaning of that space—for example, the friends, family, and experiences that are associated.

From the street, Langview appears like countless other inhabited areas of Glasgow. People busy with their daily routine—walking dogs, pushing prams, dragging toddlers. School-aged children swarm the streets, in small knots, dodging traffic. Queues form in the many fast-food outlets, interspersed by lone smokers, grimacing outside pubs. Shops, off-licences, bookmakers, and tanning salons jostle for attention on the high street with boarded-up shops, trendy cafes, and social housing. Walking through the largely residential areas which punctuate the two main thoroughfares, street life quickly fades, replaced by quiet lanes teeming with parked cars and dogshit. Once you leave the tenemented streets, the buildings become a mixture of different ages, styles, and conditions of social housing. Social-housing schemes built for different reasons—in different ways, in different periods, and in different states of repair—stand cheek by jowl with the large, polished blocks of modern housing developments. Factories that once dotted the area have been reinvented as artist spaces and call centres, or have been refurbished as new flats. Some buildings are in a state of total dereliction: windows broken, front locks damaged, storage cupboards open, covered in graffiti, inside and out. The result is a dizzying combination of different spaces, styles, and concepts of housing, a mish-mash of past and present.

On a modern map, the streets of Langview appear uniform. In the centre of the area buildings are regimented tenements, constructed in regular horizontal rectangles. Roads run in grids, with right-angled junctions between each row of flats. Langview appears as any other urban zone—it is difficult for the eye to separate the space from the surrounding area or indeed in Glasgow as a whole. As Lynch notes, however, cities are composed of cognitive maps as well as topographical surveys; in the subjective city, boundaries are defined by psychosocial edges: 'the linear elements not used or considered as paths by the observer...such edges may be barriers, more or less penetrable, which close one region off from another; or they may be seams, lines along which two regions are related and joined together' (Lynch 1960, p. 47). On closer inspection, it is clear that Langview is seen as a distinct and distinctive socio-spatial place. A long arc of railway meets a thickly drawn panel of motorway, a patch of waste ground severs one row of housing from the next. The urban fault lines snaking through the city create natural boundaries and perimeters: roads and railway lines, motorways and canals. Engineered to facilitate greater mobility to and from the city centre, they become immobile borders, no longer linking but separating. For some, the development of new transport links—local, national, and global—has created new opportunities; for others, these developments have placed further boundaries—economic, spatial, and social—on their lives.

Points of entry and exit are carefully monitored. Traffic lights stop the pedestrian abruptly at the main arterial exit points; foot traffic is shepherded towards specific flyovers and railway bridges. CCTV cameras monitor each of these areas, adding to the feeling of border surveillance. The overall effect is that of being hemmed in by modernity. Approaching the motorway that bounds the north edge of Langview, spray-painted names and tags are repeated on railings, police notices, and the path itself as it winds up towards the busy road. Under the flyover, the middle strut is covered in graffiti. It is clear that this is an area of contention—names have been sprayed on top of other names—but there is a rough divide halfway along between the tags. These names—Langview Young Team and Langview Fleet—are in clear conflict with the neighbouring Hillside Mad Sqwad. Crossing the boundary, with cars whistling beneath your feet, there is a palpable sense of unease.

As Sibley argues, moving 'from a familiar space to an alien one which is under the control of somebody else, can provide anxious moments; in some circumstances, it might be fatal, or it might be an exhilarating experience—the thrill of transgression' (Sibley 1995, p. 32). On the ground, the legend 'You Are Now Entering Fleetland' is thickly painted, with a crude arrow.

Entering Fleetland

The original inspiration for my study came from Patrick's (in)famous study, *A Glasgow Gang Observed* (1973). I came across it by chance, in a library, and it made an immediate impact. In its heady, breathless depictions of Glasgow street life, I found an antidote to the detached criminology I had become used to; it cracked a door open to a different lineage of thought and research. By the time it came to designing my own study, however, I had become deeply embedded in the ethnographic traditions of the Chicago and Birmingham Schools; rather than the 12 field outings that underpinned Patrick's study, I was determined to dedicate serious time and effort to understanding what gangs meant to young people today. Unlike the purposive sampling approach to fieldwork favoured by other researchers—drawing on law-enforcement data to identify neighbourhoods to approach (Sanchez-Jankowski 1991; Densley 2013)—I relied on more informal social contacts and open-ended methodological strategies. I was aware that Langview had a 'reputation' for gangs—Langview gangs are listed repeatedly in various official and unofficial records of gangs in Glasgow[6]—but also that it showed signs of change.

I began the study, like many before me, through volunteering at a local youth project (Parker 1974; Robins and Cohen 1978; Back 1996; Alexander 2000; Ilan 2010), referred by a friend who also volunteered there.[7] Langview Youth Project was and is a stalwart organization in the local community, weathering ceaseless financial storms and political wranglings to provide a place for young people to hang out. In a very real sense, the project was at the heart of community life. The project took in a wide range of local

---

[6] The Community Initiative to Reduce Violence, and Violence Reduction Unit 'gang databases' contains these gang names, as do the several unofficial 'gang lists'. See MacCallum (1994) for an example.

[7] For a comprehensive history of ethnographic studies of youth, see Hobbs (2001).

children, families, and young people up to the age of 16, but also beyond, as volunteers, supervisors of young children, staff, and young parents. It is a classic youth project set-up with a pool table, table tennis, games, and computers indoors, and a football pitch, and play area outdoors. The outdoor area of the project was comparable in size and feel to a school playground. My role initially was mainly one of supervision and organization of activities. I was therefore free to mingle and interact with young people, observe interactions and conflicts, gauge social dynamics and hierarchies.

Langview Youth Project (LYP) is located in a lozenge of gridded tenements in the south of Langview, in the midst of a community that falls within the 5 per cent 'most disadvantaged' in Scotland. Nonetheless, as LYP lies between two of the central streets in Langview, in full view of around 60 individual flats, there is a sense of informal community surveillance. LYP also operates as a place for parents to meet and form networks, and is thereby woven closely into community life, gossip, and memory. Given the wide age range attending the project, there is a great deal of overlap, learning, and contestation between different ages. As the nature and form of leisure in Langview has changed over the past four decades, with increasingly fewer cheap and easily accessible options for children and young people available, LYP has emerged as a bulwark in the community—a safe, supervised place away from the fears and insecurities associated with public space.

Many of the young people who participated in the research had been attending LYP since they were very young, and there was a real attachment to the project. After closing time, groups would frequently climb the barriers to use the (locked) facilities. Discussing a new youth project that had recently opened in the area, Willie, Mark, and Gary were staunch in their support of LYP:

> AF: What would yous do if the LYP closed doon?
> WILLIE: Go tae the new place…but right, this might sound weird, but see how they've goat better technology, an computers an aw ae that…Ah prefer the LYP.
> MARK: Aye so dae Ah.
> GARY: See how they've only goat a PS2 an aw that, Ah still prefer the LYP.

For many young people, meeting up at LYP was the default position after school hours, in the evening, and during school holidays during their childhood and early teenage years. In part, this stemmed from the central position (both geographically and meta-phorically) that LYP occupied in the Langview community. The sentiment of one young parent attending LYP with her young son is emblematic: 'Ah've grown up in LYP'. Similarly, when some research participants were given disposable cameras and asked to take pictures of 'things that were important', each included a picture of LYP. The following discussion, based on the photos, demonstrates these points well:

> AF: What about the two pictures of LYP?
> JAMES: It's a great park.
> KEV: LYP's ma life.
> AF: How long you been comin here?
> KEV: Since ever.
> SEAN: Ah've been coming here since Ah wis born. 12 year.

Of the two types of ethnographers identified by Burawoy—'those who return to their communities and those who don't, those who establish enduring human connection and those who negotiate a more instrumental relation' (Burawoy 2009, pp. 268–9)—I fall avowedly into the first category. I continued volunteering well beyond the period of my studies and fulfilled a wide range of roles within the project during this four-year period. Although the project constituted the main site for the study, I was involved across various contexts and in a range of ways in the life of the community: for two years, as a tutor in the local high school; for 10 months, as a street-based youth outreach worker. I also lived in the area for 18 months. Like Whyte (1993, p. 279), I found the research became an intrinsic part of my life.

Where the researcher operates out of a university, just going into the field for a few hours at a time, he can keep his personal social life separate from field activity. If, on the other hand, the researcher is living for an extended period in the community he is studying, his personal life is inextricably linked to the research.

I assisted at open days, events, and trips; socialized with parents and staff from various youth projects; ran field trips, residential events, and discussion groups. I sat on committees, wrote reports and funding applications, gave lifts and arranged transport, got to know people and projects from the surrounding areas. I spent countless hours combing the streets of Langview doing outreach work, tracing and retracing the alleys and lanes; spent hours and hours winning and losing (mostly losing) at football, table tennis, and pool, and innumerable evenings adjudicating arguments, stopping fights, attempting to restore the peace. I huddled in the office over mugs of tea, going over the events of the night, confiding and being confided in by colleagues and friends in the community. I got to *know* Langview; to this day I can see and feel it.[8]

The community spirit present in Parker's classic study of Roundhouse (1974)—and, of course, of Young and Wilmott's study of family and kinship in East London (1957)—was tangible in the project. Like Parker's study, many of the young people in the project would call one another 'cousin', 'auntie', or 'uncle'. After a fashion, I felt welcome and part of community life—friend and confidante to many different and at times conflicting individuals and organizations. As Back reminds us, however, 'community is a discursive construct that is utilized as an ideological resource in situations where inside/outside definitions are discussed' (Back 1996, p. 29). Langview has clearly demarcated boundaries separating it from the neighbouring areas of Swigton and Hillside. Local youth projects in particular could be territorial about 'outside' organizations coming onto 'their patch'. In an incredibly straitened funding landscape, purse-strings were held tight and competition for resources fierce. As in Elias and Scotston's study of Winston Parva, this territorial sentiment was intimately connected with Established–Outsider dynamics of legitimacy and belonging (1994), a finely balanced patchwork of inclusion and exclusion, based on place and length of residence, community involvement, and perception as being 'aw right'. Like Robins and Cohen's analysis in *Knuckle Sandwich* (1978, p. 74), there was an extent to which the territoriality exhibited by young people was a reflection of this broader territorial identity in the community.

Territoriality is, therefore, deeply engrained in most working-class parent cultures, even if its functions are diffused through a number of institutions...But the kids have only one institution to support this function, and a fragile one at that—the 'gang'. The same historical processes which pushed the parent culture inwards on itself pushed working-class youth to its periphery, as the residual legatees of street culture.

---

[8] For this reason, I have included field observations throughout the text. These are quoted verbatim and dated, to retain the immediacy of the observations. For critical discussion of the role of fieldnotes in anthropology, see Geertz (1967, 1990) and Malinowski (1967).

As an outsider to the community, I had a lot of work to do to gain acceptance. The staff tolerated but initially ignored my presence; there was a high turnover of volunteers, and there was nothing to suggest I was any different. Following Polsky's indispensable advice for field research—'keep your ears and eyes open *but keep your mouth shut*' (Polsky 1967, p. 126)—I did what I was told, focusing on activities rather than conversation, kicking a ball rather than chewing the fat. The early period of fieldwork nonetheless was loaded with personal and emotional identity work. Personal experiences inevitably came to the fore—the rough-and-tumble of banter and one-upmanship that made up the masculine culture of young people was not too dissimilar to my own experiences growing up in central Scotland. I was, however, totally unprepared for the crazed tangle of physicality, hierarchy, and verbal interaction that constituted a kick-around at LYP:

There are 25 boys all clamouring for attention, shouting and arguing with one another, with no clear authority figure—rivalries, disputes, politics, discrimination, admiration and power mingle into a kind of unified chant, the dynamics of which are unclear. I am not known, so am treated with some suspicion ... To be honest, I felt like I was at school again, with the same feelings of ineptitude; the crushing indignity of being last picked at football. (Fieldnote, 3 April 2007)

After early shifts in the youth project, I would sit and listen, tired and slack-brained, to the talk of the project office: work politics, community gossip, personal trials. At the same time, I was trying to soak up as much experience as I could in youth work, at which I was a novice. From the first, however, I was conscious of the need to maintain a degree of separation from youth work and research roles. As Polsky noted, nearly 50 years ago: '[a]ny student of deviance who confounds the roles of social worker and sociologist ... is bound to ... have his research flawed by it' (Polsky 1967, p. 141). As I learned the practices and principles of working with young people, I saw that many were consistent with my research goals—privileging young people's voices, creating spaces in which they can lead discussions, encouraging creativity—but that ultimately a purely youth-work role would make analytical insights difficult. I was keen to engage with children and young people in a more natural setting, but due to the difference in age between myself and the young people I was working with, simply 'hanging around' with them on the streets was not an option (Downes 1966).

Moving to the area helped. I found a box-room in a shared flat around 200 metres from the youth project, and started spending a lot of time out and about in the community—in the newsagents, the chip shop, the park—as well as becoming involved in a number of other youth organizations. Foremost among these was a project called Langview Outreach Project (LOP), based less than 50 metres from my flat. LOP engaged with children and young people in public spaces, supplying information on available leisure opportunities as well as more general support and advice. I spent two or three evenings a week for a 10-month period walking the streets of Langview with my street-work partner, John. The nature of street-outreach work is not dissimilar from the work of an ethnographer. As with LYP, I was able to engage with a wide range of children and young people in Langview. The nature of interactions, in public space, meant that I was able to gauge young people's understanding and experiences of the area as well as the group dynamics that occurred there. At the end of each shift, we traced the route we had taken onto a map of the local area, and completed a sheet recording the number of contacts we had made with young people—including age, gender, and nature of interaction—as well as more general ethnographic observations on what had occurred on the streets during the shift. The project manager allowed me to copy these recording sheets for my own research and these formed the foundation for my fieldnotes for each period of fieldwork. The practice of memorizing routes and conversations for these recording sheets also proved invaluable; in both the youth project and outreach project, I would return to my room and type up fieldnotes feverishly while memories were still fresh. Due in part to the outreach training, I became able to recall detailed conversations and movements around the area over prolonged periods.

During the busiest period of fieldwork, I found myself working four to five nights a week, including weekends, with numerous other commitments every day, juggling several work, research, and university responsibilities, which proved both physically demanding and emotionally exhausting. I found myself constantly switching identities, fulfilling different roles, cutting across both the city and the area, often in the space of a few hours.[9] Fox, reflecting

---

[9] For cogent discussions of the role of the 'observer' in participant observation, and the relationship between ethnography and auto-ethnography, see Coffey (1999), Lee-Treweek and Linkogle (2000), Letherby (2000), and Ferrell (2012b).

an extended period of participant observation with drug out-reach workers, describes this experience as 'floating between two worlds' (1991, p. 245):

I had come to feel an undeniable dissonance between the two worlds I was straddling. I was forced to float between two polarized cultures, speak two languages, attend to two divergent sets of concerns. The grav-ity of the problems I witnessed on the streets seemed more worthy of attention than the luxury of academic considerations. (Fox 1991, p. 246)

This feeling of dissonance was an undeniable aspect of my field-work experiences. Many others have written of similar sensations; indeed to be an ethnographer is by its very nature to be a 'pro-fessional stranger' (Agar 1980), 'in two places at the same time' (Pearson 1993, p. ix), both spatially and culturally. As Pearson highlights, ethnographers act as a *bridge* between the experi-ences of actors and audiences, mediating between languages and worlds. Although I had some of the basic cultural knowledge to 'get by'—the area I grew up in, though rural, was not far removed culturally from Langview—there were clear adjustments. I was just about quick enough to catch on to the rapidly moving 'patter' that reverberated round the project; like Parker I recognized that it was important to be 'able to look after yourself in the verbal quick-fire' (Parker 1974, p. 217), but I also found my accent becoming stronger, talking in shorter bursts, swearing more. After smash-ing a pair of glasses heading a football during an early field visit, I swapped these for contact lenses.

As I grew to understand the tensions and opportunities in nego-tiating this unique position, I came to devise a more focused way of generating data for the study. In this sense, much like Parker, 'I grew into, rather than systematically planned, this case study' (Parker 1974, p. 214). In addition to field observations, I carried out a series of 18 tape-recorded discussion groups with different groups of young people, with ages ranging from 13 to 18 years (20 males, 10 females),[10] the majority of whom I had known for at least a year prior to the research being carried out. Most were carried out in LYP, with a smaller number carried out with school-leavers

---

[10] As the study focused on voices of children and young people in Langview, transcriptions are written in the dialect of young people verbatim, with clarifica-tions added in square brackets. Following the example of Damer (1989, p. x), I have not attempted 'the last word in orthographic purity', but rather tried to 'get the *sound* of Glaswegians speaking down with comprehensibility'.

aged 17 to 18 years, from Langview Academy and Langview High School, with whom I worked over as part of the 'widening participation' programme at Glasgow University.[11] The groups were designed in the format of short workshops, drawing principles and practices from the 'new social studies of childhood' (Travlou 2003) and youth-work methodologies (Feinstein and Kuumba 2006). The intention in using these techniques—of mapping, photography, and role-play—was that of creating a platform for debate, allowing space for young people to explore issues from their own perspective.[12]

The groups were by turns rowdy, uncontrolled, spontaneous, and enlightening; individuals dipped in and out of discussion, and the room, at random intervals. The group brought the status politics, group rivalries, and pecking orders from outside the project into the room, resulting in a complex web of insult, collective abandon, and brutal honesty. Although attendance was sporadic—many an evening was spent waiting around to see if anyone turned up, or phoning round houses with reminders—interest remained consistent. While there were some occasions where nobody turned up, it became clear that the young people enjoyed participating in the groups, and they became a talking point within the project. The discussion groups became known as 'that mad group hing', and more young people wanted to join. Through these discussions, I came to know well the group that forms the focus of the study, the Langview Boys.

The Langview Boys

There must be hundreds of neighbourhoods in Britain that talk about their own 'The Boys'. This title usually refers to a recognisable peer group, a network of lads who've grown up together and are seen around together in various combinations. (Parker 1974, p. 64)

My decision to focus on an in-depth study of a particular community was heavily influenced by the tradition of Chicago School

---

[11] These groups were composed of young people from Langview who were going on to college or university, from a school with traditionally low levels of access to, and participation in, further education.

[12] The study received ethical approval from the Board of Directors at Langview Youth Project, and from the Ethics Board of the University of Glasgow. All names of people and places have been altered to protect confidentiality.

participant observation, in particular Whyte's *Street Corner Society* (1943). Like Whyte, I wanted to understand the group dynamics, peer relationships, and collective identities through which young people made sense of the changing world around them.[13] As I became close to one particular group—the Langview Boys—I also saw first-hand the physical and symbolic alteration of Langview in the wake of de-industrialization: local shops closing as large supermarkets opened nearby, factories 'repurposed' as apartment complexes and call centres. I came to see the changes occurring as a result of the rebranded 'new Glasgow' refracted through the environment of Langview, and the impact that was having on young people's everyday lives. I started to become curious about the impact of these broad-based alterations to the city on the opportunities and identities of this particular group of lads.

The Langview Boys were very much the 'likely lads' of Langview, a shifting group of teenage males that constituted a constant presence in the streets surrounding LYP, and a constant source of frustration, concern, and contention within LYP and the community more widely. They comprised a jack-in-the-box of energy, enthusiasm, and spirit, straining to burst out of whatever confines they found themselves in, resulting in anger among some community residents, fear or resentment among others, and awed respect from some younger groups in the area. The majority of the boys lived in the streets immediately surrounding LYP, and most of their time was spent in this small geographical area. Many of their parents were close friends with one another, and the boys spent much of their childhood together—in school, in one another's homes, in LYP, and on the streets of Langview. There was therefore an intensely powerful bond both between the boys and with the area. They knew each other intimately: how to wind one another up, what can be said to whom, how to bring one another down to size. There was an unspoken bond of friendship between them; for most, the group constituted a fundamental influence in guiding both opinion and action. This is not, however, to depict a romanticized portrayal of a uniform, unified, or unproblematic set of

---

[13] The broader focus on the interplay between the development of Langview and the city of Glasgow, and the experiences of young people living through these changes, was also influenced by Thrasher and the broader Chicago School as well as the later revisionist critiques mentioned earlier. In this context, ethnographies of Glasgow (Damer 1989) were an important methodological guide.

group relationships. While there is a keen loyalty to one another, there is nonetheless a fierce rivalry within the group, manifested in insults and contests for hierarchical supremacy.

During the main period of fieldwork the Langview Boys were 14- to 16-years-old, beginning to negotiate the transition from school-to-work but not yet full entrants into the adult economy of work and leisure. Although I maintained contact with the group after the fieldwork ended, the majority of quotations and obser-vations reported in subsequent chapters here are taken from this period and should be read as the comments of school-aged teenag-ers. Unlike the forms of fragile, tensile, and temporary alliances that Winlow and Hall (2006) describe for young adults in the night-time economy, or the 'liquid friendships' described by Smith (O. Smith 2013), the Langview Boys exhibited an overwhelming collectivism. As with Cumbers and colleagues' study of Glasgow youth, 'there was an impressive level of commitment to helping others, rather than the more individualistic ethos which underpins much of the prevailing policy regime' (Cumbers et al. 2009, p. 23).

The boys had grown up together, in every way. Their jokes, rival-ries, and piss-takes were richly layered with a shared collective his-tory, with pecking orders and alliances shifting over time. They were to be found, at more or less any time, roaming Langview. I could rarely go out for a pint of milk without bumping into one or more of them. Hierarchies were continually contested with a friendly, knockabout rivalry that could nonetheless spill over into violence. For example, although many of the boys had scars from stab wounds, the majority had been carried out—accidentally or otherwise—by others in their friendship group. In what follows, I offer a brief sketch of some of the key members of the group, focusing particularly on those whose voices are most prominent in the chapters that follow. The ages quoted represent the boys' ages during the discussion groups from which many of the quotations are drawn.

Kev Carson is 16-years-old, has left school, and, after a stint as an apprentice builder, is currently unemployed. He is tall, stocky, and strong, the charismatic and physical authority of the group. An excellent footballer and all-round athlete, he is feared and respected by the group—and beyond—for his physical size, aggression, and willingness to fight. He was constantly in trouble in LYP, repeatedly excluded for aggressive behaviour, but his wit and mischief also endeared him to many. He was looked on as a leader by others in the group, and as a ringleader by local police and community-members. Towards the end of the fieldwork, however, Kev demonstrated a marked maturity, playing a facilitating role in discussion groups.

Daz Bryant, Kev's close friend and verbal sparring partner, is 16-years-old, has also left school, and after a period of time as an apprentice joiner, is currently unemployed. He is tall, slender, strong, and quick-witted with a ready response or insult to any situation. He is an exceptionally skilful footballer. In activities he is less proficient at, he gains the upper hand via a constant barrage of verbal abuse. He is in perpetual motion—walking and talking, searching for a way of getting one up on whoever is nearest to him. Due to his constant insults, he is feared but not fully respected by others—shown by the many back-handed comments by other members of the group.

Gary Prentice is 15-years-old and still at school. He is tall for his age, lanky, and quietly thoughtful, yet with a fierce temper and competitive streak. Although he was described to me as a 'gang member' by a local community police officer, he described himself not as a member of a gang but 'jist a pedestrian' in Langview. He has lower status than Kev or Daz but holds his own in most of the group's exploits. On the one hand, he is strong and competent on the football pitch but often one of the last to be picked due to his lower status in the group. On the other, he is exceptionally good at computer games and spends much of his spare time playing football and war games on games consoles.

Tommy Mack is 15-years-old and still at school. Tall and gangly, loyal and good natured, he is closest in personality to Gary and the two are good friends. Like Gary, Tommy was described to me by the leader of a local youth project as a 'ringleader', but within the group was mocked for his lack of coordination and slowness on the uptake. Despite this, he is cheeky and takes these insults in good humour.

Mark Duff is 14-years-old, and close friends with Gary and Tommy. Although he no longer lives in Langview, he still goes to school at Langview Academy and is present at LYP as often as any of the others. He is quick witted and good natured, though mocked at times for being slightly overweight. Like Tommy, he is less proficient at most group activities than either Kev or Daz, something he accepts and manages with good grace.

James Smith is 15-years-old and still at school, loud, funny, and mischievous. Shorter and more self-conscious than the others in the group, he is frequently mocked on account of his large ears. As a result, he is extremely sensitive, and quick to take offence. He has two older brothers, both well known in the area, one of whom was in prison for a violent offence during the period of fieldwork.

Willie Jamieson is 14-years-old, still at school, and frequently (and frequently deliberately) confused with his twin brother, Fraz. He is small for his age, wiry and athletic, and plays for a local football team. Although Willie got into a lot of trouble when he was younger, he is mature for his age.

Initially I built up a relationship with the boys through my time at LYP, playing football, pool, computer games, and table tennis, and generally hanging about in the project. I saw them regularly through my work in the local schools, on streetwork, and of course in LYP. This group was also the main focus for the series of discussion groups I ran during the fieldwork. Through these discussions, I became aware of the boys' involvement in gang activity. Several of them identified themselves as being 'Langview Young Team' (LYT), one of the local gangs, whose name has been reported since the 1960s (MacCallum 1994). Their names were spray-painted, with gang tags appended, all over Langview—including the back door to my flat—and the school-based police officer I got to know informed me of their reputation as 'big time gang members'. Later I discovered that police intelligence databases listed several as 'gang members'. Although they did not engage in any form of economically motivated crime—their offending, such as it was, being confined to vandalism, disorder, and graffiti—the majority of the group had engaged in territorial violence. Several had stab wounds and admitted to carrying a knife. Although none had received a serious charge, several had elder brothers in prison for violent offences.

The Boys' activities therefore incorporated elements of Hallsworth and Young's (2004, quoted in Pitts 1998, p. 18) definition of both a 'peer group' ('A small, unorganized, transient grouping occupying the same space with a common history') and a 'gang' ('A relatively durable, predominantly street-based group of young people who see themselves (and are seen by others) as a discernible group for whom crime and violence is integral to the group's identity'). However, the simple categorization of the Boys' behaviour as 'gang' activity belies the complex meanings attached to LYT for the group. Like Parker's Roundhouse Boys, the group were not a 'gang' in the cohesive sense implied by most academic definitions (Parker 1974,

p. 64). Rather than indicating a static identity, the 'gang' name is used interchangeably with the name of the area, used as a shorthand for the attachment to place described. As such, the grouping of the 'Langview Boys' is not synonymous with the local gang, the 'LYT', the latter being a temporary identification that was drawn on in specific situational.

More importantly still, the meaning and form of the gang name altered and reconfigured as the Boys' got older. Getting to know the group over a prolonged period enabled a unique insight into the role of age and social development on gang identification. As Parker, quoting Whyte before him, reflected: '[o]nly as I began to see changes in the group did I realise how extremely important it is to observe a group over an extended period of time' (Parker 1974, p. 224). So, over time I came to see a distinctive pattern emerge, of younger street-based groups seeking to act out 'gang' identities in varying age-graded ways. For younger children, LYT was a form of play—a childish fantasy to be acted out with peers (Katz 1988). For young teenagers, the gang became more closely tied to area identity, and the acting out of group dynamics, status politics, and developing gender identities. As individuals began to age and mature, however, these identities, relationships, and priorities tend to shift and refocus: friendship groups changed, patterns of leisure and recreation altered, and generally more adult activities were sought out. This cyclical pattern, in fact, is not unlike that described by Robins and Cohen:

the street becomes the arena where the Growing Up Game is played, a social space of time and apparent freedom from the more insidious forms of parental censorship and control. Here the peer group assembles itself, to enact its rivalries, and so the game of identities and differences between the sexes and between the generations can begin. In early childhood this takes the form of fantasy games; later, without losing this component, it has taken on a more organized ritual form, and finally becomes elaborated by teenagers into collective narratives or myth, at a time when the game is getting rather more serious. (Robins and Cohen 1978, p. 74)

This process of new groups constantly emerging and attaching meaning to gang activity, of re-enacting specific forms of behaviour in the context of the street culture of the area, gives an insight into the cyclical nature of gang activity in Glasgow's history. As will be discussed in Chapter 8, while this is something of a closed circuit, replicating as it does the behaviours and activities of much older generations, there was also evidence of alterations according to broader social change, particularly in the context of the reshaping of the 'new Glasgow' and the rapid development of consumer technology and privatized leisure (Sweeting and West 2003).

The Langview Boys were not the sole focus of the fieldwork, however. The study sought a range of young people's understanding and experiences of gangs in Langview, predominantly through street- and project-based fieldwork. One downside of this breadth is that I got to know relatively little of young people's home or school lives. Since young people—and in particular the Langview Boys—did not discuss these aspects of their lives, the familial and school-based context of gang identity awaits another study. Nonetheless, alternative voices that speak to the role of the school in inspiring resilience from street-based cultures will be included, through the participation of a group of school-leavers.

The school-leavers

It is important to point out that a majority of young people in Langview do not follow the cyclical pattern of gang identification sketched here. The Langview Boys' behaviour in public space created a sort of gravitational force wherein anyone within its orbit was forced to accede to its rules, a continuum of street-based culture that required a certain degree of proficiency for successful movement through public space (Gunter 2008; Garot 2010). As such, their ubiquity in public space created fears and anxieties among other groups of young people in Langview—resulting in certain spaces become 'no-go' areas for other groups of young people. Percy-Smith and Matthews (2001) describe these areas as 'tyrannical spaces', 'local environments...defined in terms of "no-go areas"', danger and threat. (Percy-Smith and Matthews 2001, p. 49). Like the local residents in Winton's study, 'fear of violence leads to the spatial exclusion of community members, particularly young people, whereby assaults and territorial gang conflicts construct public space as dangerous and therefore restrict the extent to which young people feel positively connected to the community' (Winton 2005, p. 180).

I got to know a relatively large number of individuals and groups who experienced the Langview Boys as threatening and dangerous, and who stayed off the streets as a result. One of the most interesting of these was a group of school-leavers with whom I worked over two four-month periods as part of the widening participation programme at Glasgow University. They—Michael, Robert, Julie, and Pamela—were quite remarkable young people, resilient and articulate yet street-wise and street-smart. Their perspectives offered insights into the lives of young people not present in public space, but also of those who had resisted, or desisted from, street life and gang violence. The perspectives and insights from both groups will be drawn on—in this and following chapters—as a way of emphasizing the difference between children and young people, and illustrating the diversity in the lives of young people in Langview.

By drawing on the experiences of this group—participants in the discussion groups in Langview Academy, and others from LYP and LOP—I hope to communicate a more rounded picture of young people's experiences of growing up in Langview, contributing a critical perspective to so-called 'underdog' analyses of gang identities (Gouldner 1968). Inevitably, however, there are silences in the data, specifically relating to the experiences of young women in Langview, and of the role of ethnicity in structuring young people's identities. While I draw on some perspectives from the school-leavers group, identifiable groups of young women were conspicuous by their absence in LYP and in public space during the period of fieldwork.[14] Similarly, while Langview has a small population of minority ethnic groups, young people from these communities were not present in public space, and only in very small numbers in LYP, for the duration of the research.[15]

---

[14] While this is an intriguing finding in and of itself—particularly given the apparent shift from young women's 'bedroom cultures' in the 1970s (McRobbie and Garber 1976; McRobbie 1980), to a more prominent role in public space in recent studies (Burman and Batchelor 2009)—regrettably uncovering these hidden experiences was not part of the research.

[15] This may similarly relate to the ubiquity of the Langview Boys in the public spaces of the area, and the local forms of 'tough' white masculinity that was layered into their group behaviour. While the Boys evinced a form of 'neighbourhood nationalism' (Back 1996) in LYP, with area of residence coming before any other marker of difference, there also existed complex status games structured by age, gender, class, and ethnicity. In certain cases, this resulted in further marginalization of those deemed weak or vulnerable; reflecting broader social stigmatizations relating to hierarchies of 'whiteness' (Nayak 2007; Webster 2008). For further discussion of the role of ethnicity in the Langview, see Fraser and Piacentini (2013).

Conclusion

Just as earlier chapters have set out a theoretical and empirical foundation for developing a new generation of critical gang scholarship in the UK, this chapter has aimed to contribute to a methodological agenda rooted in ethnographic inquiry, re-engaging with some of the ground-breaking gang scholarship in the US in the 1960s, and the classic Birmingham School studies in the UK in the 1970s, but attuned to the challenges posed to ethnographic authority by the reflexive turn in social research. These alterations have led to a readjustment of the sites and fields of inquiry for academic researchers, and the exploration of new fields of inquiry. However, as has been argued in earlier chapters, the effects of global change are always refracted by the broader social milieu—in this case the city—and made concrete through local experience. As such, there is unquestionably a need for 'local' ethnography alongside 'reaching for the global' (Burawoy 2000) in making sense of the complex and variegated impacts of global change on the everyday lives of individuals.

The chapter has also sought to hone the analytical focus down from the level of the city to the realm of everyday experience—introducing the stage and actors that make up the *dramatis personae* of the remainder of the book. In the chapters that follow, the voices and experiences of the Langview Boys and other local groups will be set against the backdrop of the narrative so far. The everyday routines and rhythms of young people in Langview will be presented within the historical context elaborated in earlier chapters; their territorial identifications, violent masculinities, and neighbourhood nationalisms located within the context of Glasgow's unique pattern of social, cultural and economic development, their gang identifications set against the decline of industrialism and the development of neoliberal post-industrialism, their attachment to place situated within declining leisure spaces in the wake of commercial 'leisure'. In this way, I aim to reach beyond my experiences and observations in the field to a broader-based analysis of the persistence of gang identification in Glasgow, and the challenges this case study provides to universal definitions and claims to homogeneity of 'gangs in the UK'.

Prior to making the shift between history and present, however, I reflect briefly on the ways in which cinematic representations of cities in general, and Glasgow in particular, have reflected the contradictions of contemporary urban life. This 'intermezzo' of cultural analysis is intended to link the theoretical framework presented with the experiential data that will follow, making a case for engaged academic scholarship in which the 'head' of theory and the 'hand' of practice are mediated by the 'heart' of personal ethics.

Intermezzo: Mediating Metropolis

> The mediator between the head and the hands has to be the heart!
>
> *Metropolis*, 1927

Societal ruptures, brought on by the rise and fall of industry, have proven to be a central theme of filmic depictions of the modern city. Fritz Lang's epic dystopic vision of the urban industrialism, *Metropolis* (1927)—appearing the same year as Thrasher's *The Gang*—set a high-water mark for artistic renderings of these ruptures, as well as a path towards their reconciliation. Lang contrasts a highly cultured, leisured class—living in Eden-like serenity on a platform high up above the streets—with the working classes, who fret, toil, and sweat in unending torture in the bowels of the city. Despite repeated efforts to repress the workers' unionism through Machiavellian tactics and *agents provocateur*, the two worlds are bridged by a relationship between a beautiful emissary from the working class, Maria, and a princeling of the leisure class. The final, climactic scene shows the 'head' of the ruling class stretching out towards the 'hand' of the workers, with Maria—the 'heart'—acting as mediator.

The film was a cultural milestone that has in its turn inspired countless film-makers, artists, and musicians with its vision of dystopic urban decay, capitalist destruction, and creeping surveillance. The film takes cities as its inspiration and muse; Lang said that 'the film was born from my first sight of the skyscrapers in New York in October 1924 . . . the buildings seemed to be a vertical sail, scintillating and very light, a luxurious backdrop, suspended in the dark sky to dazzle, distract and hypnotize' (Grant 2003, p. 69). The hypnotic charm of the Manhattan skyline, however, did not distract Lang from the crushing class inequality that underpinned this 'vertical sail'. *Metropolis* tells a powerful story of modernity through the lens of the industrial city and sets an agenda for sociology, art, and politics that resonates still. Since Lang's masterpiece, film depictions of urban environments—like the cities themselves—have become considerably more complex. If the rise of industrialism calcified divisions between rich and poor, the shift to post-industrialism has rendered these class configurations more subtle and opaque. Subsequent imaginings of cities on film have explored a more fluid interpretation of power, constructing the city both as a site for continuing inequality, and as a Petri dish for new forms of social structures that cut across social divisions.

Depictions of Glasgow in film and literature have similarly wrestled with issues of class and creativity, continuity and change, industrialism and post-industrialism. These tensions are perhaps best summarized in Alasdair Gray's epic novel *Lanark: A Life in Four Books* (1981), widely recognized as marking a qualitative shift in fictional representations of Glasgow. As Thaw, a central protagonist, exclaims (Gray 1981, p. 243):

'Glasgow is a magnificent city', said McAlpin. 'Why do we hardly ever notice that?'

'Because nobody imagines living here', said Thaw 'Think of Florence, Paris, London, New York. Nobody visiting them for the first time is a stranger because he's already visited them in paintings, novels, history books and films. But if a city hasn't been used by an artist, not even the inhabitants live there imaginatively'.

Lanark can be read as a call to arms to writers, poets, and artists to throw off the introverted myopia of seeking the ultimate 'truth' of the 'real' working class Glasgow, and instead to understand Glasgow as a postmodern multiplicity of histories and spaces which can be used and interpreted in innovative and creative ways. In *Lanark*, there is no one 'truth' of Glasgow, but instead a commingling of fact, fiction, biography, and fantasy (Smethurst 2000, p. 116; Witschi 1991, p. 58). Crucially, Gray does not ignore previous representations of Glasgow but instead replicates and then challenges their imagery. A semi-autobiographical realist portrayal of working-class life in the city, revolving around the artist Duncan Thaw, is spliced into the separate, though linked, story of Lanark, a stranger in a dystopic, fantastical city known as Unthank. In the latter, Gray connects Unthank (still recognizable as Glasgow) to a wide range of external literary references, self-consciously throwing Glasgow open to a range of reimaginings. As Smethurst argues: 'Lanark does not dismiss earlier representations of Glasgow, but incorporates, transforms, subverts them, and juxtaposes them with other representations, realistic and fantastic, but always connecting with the "real" place' (Smethurst 2000, p. 125).

Like *Lanark*, cinematic depictions of Glasgow have repeatedly explored the tension between the 'old', industrial, working-class Glasgow and the 'new', rebranded post-industrial city, the rich cultural legacy of the city coupled with the need for external sources of inspiration and reference. The films of Ken Loach, Bill Forsyth, Lynne Ramsay, and Peter MacDougall collectively explore a rich seam of social realism, shot through with humour and pathos, in which the everyday grind of life in the city is both painful and enduring. Films such as *Just Another Saturday* (1975), *Comfort and Joy* (1984), *My Name is Joe* (1998), and *Ratcatcher* (1999) have a timeless quality to them, tapping as they do into the long history of community interdependence and everyday struggle in the city. Explorations of gang identification in Glasgow have a similarly nostalgic gloss. Gillies Mackinnon's *Small Faces* (1996) and Peter Mullan's *NEDS: Non Educated Delinquents* (2010), while both being rooted in the past, tell a story of persistent cultures of machismo and territorial violence. Mullan's film, however, is careful to situate these ongoing rivalries in the context of blocked ambition, suppressed emotion, and unrealized potential. Although John McGill, the central character, winds up both 'non-educated' and 'delinquent', the combined weight of an unenlightened education system and an unequivocally drunken (and, it is implied, violent) father lie at the heart of the matter.

While Glasgow now more often stands in for other post-industrial cities—a body-double in the global marketplace of film locations, for films such as *World War Z* (2013)—another strand of film-making has wrestled with the ruptures caused by the 'new Glasgow'. In what might be called a post-industrial *verité* style, these films—as in Gray's *Lanark*—splice together footage from everyday life in Glasgow with more fantastical, postmodern themes. Owing a debt to Tavernier's *Deathwatch* (1980), also filmed in Glasgow, Arnold's *Red Road* and Glazer's *Under the Skin* are perhaps the best examples of this creative tension. In *Red Road* (2006), themes of post-industrial surveillance are explored through the eyes of a CCTV operator, Jackie. Like Glasgow, Jackie is haunted by a difficult past, dealing with the aftermath of a violent rupture in her life in warped and contradictory ways.

In *Under the Skin* (2013), Glasgow plays host to the distended magnetism of Scarlett Johansson, an alien in human form, a wandering spirit who views the city through fresh and strange eyes. Hidden-camera footage of everyday life is interspersed with futuristic sequences of unknown worlds and uncertain purposes. Johansson lands, an urban ethnographer, and through her gaze we see the familiar made unfamiliar; this shift in focus makes normal corner shops look like lunar-scapes, high streets like worm-holes. Yet Johansson, like Maria in *Metropolis*, plays a mediating role, connecting with similarly alienated individuals, providing solace of a seductive yet deadly kind. Both films, interestingly, play with gender roles in depictions of Glasgow. Both have strong female leads, both all-seeing in a way that embodies power. Male characters, by contrast, embody traditional masculinities but are also fragmented, flawed, and isolated, not unlike the fractured view of Glaswegian masculinities envisioned in the novels of James Kelman (1984, 1994, 2009). In *Under the Skin* in particular, men are portrayed as weak, easily led fodder. The ruptures engendered by the shift from industrialism to post-industrialism have caused crises, atomization, and ruptures in masculinities, illustrating both continuity and discontinuity.

In the chapters that follow, these ruptures, continuities, and shifts are similarly tangible. Young men in Langview, like the young men in these film portrayals of the city, are wrestling with the challenges to masculinity brought on by the shift to a service economy, making sense of a changing urban environment in which surveillance, gentrification, and exclusion are as much a part of life as the humour, irreverence, and everyday life that make up the muck and magic of social realist portrayals.[1]

---

[1] For a broader discussion of representations of Glasgow and Scotland on film, see Petrie (2004) and Balkind (2013).

5

Street Habitus

AF: Why is there boundaries there? Where do they come from?
MICHAEL: That's like saying, why does someb'dae fae Britain no' like someb'dae fae Germany. Borders have always been there, fae the start ae time. That's jist how ye define some'hing. Someb'dae comes intae your border, which is yours, you're no gonnae be happy aboot that. Don't know why but...
ROBERT: It's jist an invisible boundary that every'bdae knows. Once you cross that boundary, you know you're in Lang St, you know you're in Swigton. Don't know how it came aboot.

Viewed from above, the city of Glasgow is haphazardly gridded, densely housed, and largely amorphous. Upon closer inspection, however, there are urban fault lines snaking through the cityscape; rivers, canals, roads, and railways dissect the city into a patchwork quilt of neighbourhood spaces. These are the invisible boundaries that Robert mentions above—unseen edges that exist between neighbourhoods, slicing the city up into postage stamps of territory. Like Thrasher's description of Chicago in the 1920s, these subdivided patches constitute a 'mosaic of little worlds which touch but do not interpolate' (Thrasher 1963, p. 6). These territorial boundaries serve a dual role, creating fierce loyalties among peers that share the same neighbourhood space while simultaneously constructing a liminal zone in which local reputations can be forged. These same boundaries, however, can create intense fear and anxiety among the many young people who are not involved in territorial violence, severely restricting their mobility for work and leisure. Territorial gang identity therefore perpetuates a cycle of immobility for already disadvantaged young people.

In Langview, boundaries with neighbouring areas Swigton and Hillside are demarcated by bridges, wasteland, and motorways. These boundaries are known to all young people in the area—as Robert says, these are boundaries that 'every'bdae knows'—and are deeply embedded in the everyday routines and rituals of life in Langview. The fierce attachment that young people demonstrate to the spaces and places of Langview, however, must be viewed in the context of already existing spatial confinement. The Langview Boys, for example, spent the much of their childhoods roaming around, looking for excitement in streets that had become drained of any creative potential. In the process, those streets became deeply entrenched in daily life, forging a unique socio-spatial bond between self identity and neighbourhood. In this chapter, I develop the concept of street habitus to explore the unique processes of territorial attachment, spatial identity, and liminal transgression that recreate this boundedness. In this context, gang activity operates as a way for young people to enact this territorial identity whilst creating a local reputation.

The chapter is set out in five sections. The first describes the process of *street habituation*, in which a deep-seated relationship between self and space is learned and embedded, in the context of limited spatial autonomy in the post-industrial city. The second examines the spatial geographies that bound these habitual movements—territorial boundaries that demarcate insiders and outsiders. In the third, I describe the pattern through which this process is socially reproduced through age-based hierarchies of street-based youth, and the status anxieties brought up by looking up to some people while looking down on others. In the fourth section, these continuities are analysed in the context of the new neoliberal logic that has inflected the streets of Langview as part of the wider process of re-branding in the city of Glasgow. The final section contrasts the experiences of the Langview Boys with a group of school-leavers, for whom the streets are zones of fear and danger, emphasizing the diversity of experiences of space, territory, and gang identification in Langview.

Street habituation

The street represents a space in which young people can have some degree of autonomy to create 'rules of engagement' (Leonard 2006, p. 232) on their own terms. It is an open-ended space in which culture is produced and reproduced, unvarnished by the norms and conventions of either home or school (Soja 1998). It is therefore a space of both opportunity and risk, creativity and danger, a 'parafunctional space' that is recast and reimagined by different groups 'in terms of hidden micro-cultural practices, distinct spatial biographies, relationships (or non-relationships) with surrounding spaces/structures' (Hayward 2012, p. 453). In the context of limited space and resources, young people create 'microgeographies' and 'microcultures' in this environment, gaining spatial autonomy from adult control, and a sense of individual and group identity (Matthews et al. 1998, 2000). 'Ownership' of space is demonstrated, for example, through the construction of 'dens' (Percy-Smith and Matthews 2001), or through use of graffiti (Ley and Cybriwsky 1974). As Childress argues:

[t]eenagers occupy a different space than most of their adult counter-parts: the meaning-laden space of use and belonging; the political space of appropriation; the temporally fluid space of arriving, claiming and departure. Kids make great use of their communities' leftovers—the negative space in the positively planned and owned world....(Childress 2004, p. 204)

As there is no public parks in Langview, when LYP was closed or they were banned, the Langview Boys alternated between patrolling the streets, or 'hanging around' in passageways, 'backs',[1] or spaces under railway bridges. In these environments, the Boys would engage in 'micro-cultural practices' such as reappropriating found objects and the built environment to create exciting games. Light fittings found in bins became jousting sticks, large sticks became lances, smashed-up telephone boxes became the goals in a game of scratch football, doorways became hiding places for throwing eggs at passers-by, shopping trolleys became racing cars.[2] Through this process of covering and re-covering, treading and re-treading, the Langview Boys became *habitualized* to the streets of the neighbourhood, forming a deeply cast attachment. This attachment, crucially, represents a collective fusion of space and self, a group-based attachment in which meaning is pooled and shared.

In this sense, street habitus comes close to Soja's notion of 'third-space', discussed in Chapter 3. This configuration draws attention to the complex relationship between the 'real', lived experience of space—for example, that of everyday life in a housing estate—and

---

[1] Back courts in Glasgow tenements.
[2] For discussion of the creative reinterpretation of 'parafunctional' space in the urban environment, see Hayward (2012, pp. 452–3).

the 'imagined', perceived, meaning of space—for example the friends, relatives, and associations with particular locales. For the Langview Boys, the territory of Langview operated as a kind of 'thirdspace' of collective memory and identity, as well as physical space. The local places and spaces of Langview were vital to the boys, particularly LYP. 'LYP's ma life' was a frequently voiced sentiment. In this way, local places and spaces became fused with self identity, and space an important badge of selfhood, to be defended at all costs. When asked where they are from, for example, the boys don't say 'Ah'm fae Langview' [I'm from Langview]; they say 'Ah'm Langview' [I am Langview]. The streets they inhabited were routine aspects of daily life, known like the back of your hand–instinctively, without thinking or looking, just there. Their navigation of these streets, in Bourdieu's terms, is preconscious—an improvised feel for the game.

Habitus is defined as 'the strategy-generating principle enabling agents to cope with unforeseen and ever-changing situations…a system of lasting and transposable dispositions which, integrating past experiences, functions at every moment as a matrix of perceptions, appreciations and actions and makes possible the achievement of infinitely diversified tasks' (Bourdieu and Wacquant 1992, p. 18). Street habitus, in essence, is an embodied attachment to physical space that results from the delimiting of an individual's social universe. The concept of street habitus represents the deep-seated connection the Langview Boys have with the local area of Langview, formulated and embodied by a childhood spent in a small geographical area searching for excitement and ideas but constrained by a broader set of structural obstacles. Local places and spaces, bound up with individual and collective memory, become fused with self identity and the family, friendships, and relationships which occur there. This form of habituation allows agents to deal with unforeseen circumstances *on the street* and, through the generation of *street capital* (Sandberg and Pederson 2011)—discussed in Chapter 7—develop local reputation and distinction.

This attachment to place can be understood as a defensive response to the uncertain economic conditions of post-industrial Glasgow. As Crow and Maclean (2000, p. 237), drawing on Castells, describe: 'the defence of a place is a powerful element in the construction of what [Castells] calls "communal havens" that offer to provide anchor points for an individual's identity in an uncertain world'. Several studies have pointed to the relationship between economic marginalization and attachment to place as a fundamental source of social identity. As Wacquant notes, 'identification with one's place of residence can assume exacerbated forms that reflect the closure of one's lived universe' (Wacquant 2007, p. 271). Similarly, for Taylor and colleagues (1996, p. 14), drawing on a study of local 'structures of feeling' among adults in Manchester and Sheffield, 'substance of locality' is defined by 'routinised relations, reproduced over time, because of the dependency of actors condemned to geographical immobility'. This is of course exacerbated for young people with limited financial and spatial autonomy, as Loader describes of an older group in Edinburgh:

Denied the purchasing power needed to use, or even to get to, other parts of the city (and most importantly the city centre) unemployed youths are for the most part confined to the communities in which they live...as a result, the 'locality' tends to retain a prominent place in the lives of marginalised young people, both as a site of routine activities and as the basis of their identities. (Loader 1996, pp. 112–13)

Part of the explanation for the persistence of gang identification in Glasgow, therefore, is to be found in the socio-spatial patterning of poverty and inequality in the city. Successive generations of young people are reacting and adapting to similar sets of structural conditions, covering and re-covering the same streets, continuing the same street-based activities. While this inspires a powerful collectivism among young people from the same area—evincing a form of 'neighbourhood nationalism' (Back 1996)—this process also erects clear boundaries between areas, diminishing the potential for inter-community solidarity.

Insiders and outsiders

While the deep-seated connection between the Langview Boys and the streets of Langview is a fundamentally collectivizing process, it is also exclusionary—there are relatively fixed boundaries that delimit the Langview Boys' imagining of the Langview territory. These boundaries, while not obvious to a casual observer, can be experienced as 'invisible walls' (Pickering et al. 2012) demarcating the limits of young people's territorial identification. The border lines between Langview and neighbouring areas represent liminal zones between safe and unsafe, known and unknown territories.

On one level, the line that separates Langview from Swigton is a socially constructed border, arbitrarily defined by the urban landscape. On another level, however, it is an intensely powerful hinterland, embodying complex dialectics of inclusion and exclusion, self and other, friendship and enmity. For James and Kev, continuing the discussion above, these areas are linked directly to conflict, and violence.

> AF: How do you know where the boundaries are?
> JAMES: It's bridges separating them aw.
> AF: Why d'ye think that is?
> KEV: I don't know. Cos the people made them so ye could fight o'er them. Kiddin'oan.
> JAMES: Cos there's a railway. An a motorway...cos there's motorways an aw that.

Sack defines territoriality as 'the attempt by an individual or group to influence, affect, or control objects, people, and relationships by delimiting and asserting control over a geographic space' (Sack 1983, p. 56). In contrast to Sack's definition, however, rather than territoriality resulting from an attempt to control resources, for the Langview Boys area *becomes* a resource; a means of differentiating identity. The creation of boundaries between areas serves as a symbolic means of both differentiating identity and creating a space in which some level of local status can be gained (Bannister and Fraser 2008). While these boundaries are common knowledge to young people in Langview and neighbouring areas, some play a more active role than others in their communication and enforcement. In the following discussion, Kev had taken a picture of the railway line near LYP, which represents the boundary between Langview and Swigton:

> KEV: Aye! We're on the Langview side, and that's the Swigton side. Wait til Ah show you. See that wee fence? That's the Swigton end.
> AF: How do yous know that?
> KEV: We know that, they know that. See when they walk o'er the bridge...see that bridge, see when ye walk doon it, that's you in Swigton, that's you in Langview. There's a wee line saying 'Fleetland', naw 'Welcome to Fleetland', an done a wee arrow. There used tae be.
> JAMES: Remember we writ that.

This symbolic delineation of Langview's boundaries creates an attachment both between the Langview Boys and with the geographical space of Langview, creating a sense of rootedness in space: as the philosopher Simone Weil once said, 'to be rooted is perhaps the most important but least recognised need of the human soul' (quoted in Malkki 1992, p. 24). In defining this symbolic and geographic space, however, an inherent division is constructed between Langview and neighbouring areas—Swigton, Oldtoun, and Hillside. As Sibley argues, '[t]he construction of community and the bounding of social groups are a part of the same problem as the separation of self and other' (Sibley 1995, p. 45). Boundaries create space for transgression—literally experimenting with and exploring the edges of the known social world. In this context, the construction of boundaries between Langview and Swigton creates a liminal space in which children and young people can experiment with individual and collective identities, pushing the boundaries of experience through transgression.

For the Langview Boys, while fostering cohesion *within* a community, the construction of boundaries between areas simultaneously fosters mistrust of those *outside* that community. In constructing one's own area as pure and clean, so the neighbouring area is constructed as 'polluted' (Douglas 1966). In affirming self identity, therefore, the Langview Boys perpetually denigrate bordering communities. These denigrations are woven into the fabric of group conversation, tossed *ad hoc* into ongoing banter in a playful and knockabout manner: 'Have you ever seen a Swigton close? It's aw menchies [graffiti]'; 'Ma sister says that people in the Swigton nick yir shoes'. The gang name in Swigton is the Swigton Young Team, or SYT. When young people from Langview see SYT, however, they shout in unison: 'Steals Yir Trainers'. The tropes which these humorous interludes play into, however, are illustrative of powerful processes of inclusion and exclusion.

Importantly, these denigrations were far from particular to the Langview Boys; they were in evidence among both younger children and older teenagers. In the following excerpt, Pamela reflects on the ways in which these tropes played out in the context of dating relationships. The construction of young people from Swigton as different extended to friends' opinions of her choice of boyfriend:

See, like, if yir a lassie [female], an yir going oot wi someb'dae, when ye were younger, see when ye were going oot wi someb'dae like fae a different scheme, like people in your scheme wid slag [insult] ye fur it. Like, if she wis fae Oldtoun, an she wis going oot wi a guy fae Swigton, they'd be like 'aye, going oot wi a Swigton boay'.

The inside/outside dialectic in evidence in the Langview Boys' group activities, therefore, represents a more general sense of bounded habitus. Implicitly, it is inclusive of everyone who lives within the bounded geographical area, and exclusive of those who live outside it, although this mistrust is particularly pronounced for those in border communities. In the following example, Pamela describes the response of a male friend to her suggestion of attending a party in Swigton; indicating the intersection of area identity and 'subordinate masculinities' (Connell and Messerschmidt 2005):

See someb'dae that Ah know, like see if ye're no fae their [housing] scheme, [he's like that] they're aw gay. Ah'm like, 'go tae this party', an they're like 'naw, it's pure full ae gays, they're poofs, they're gayboys'. Jist because they don't stay in the same place that they dae. It's absolutely ridiculous.

In constructing the Langview community as a symbolic space, the border areas between Langview and Swigton become staging grounds for experimenting with gang identification. In this way, the spraying of 'gang' graffiti around the boundaries of Langview serves a broader socio-cultural purpose of bracketing off the lived environment—and individual identity—from neighbouring communities. Kev describes his rationale for spraying tags:

AF: Why do you write [LYT] after your name?
KEV: Cos that's where ye're fae.

Graffiti in Langview was concentrated around the border areas with Swigton and Hillside—on railings, bins, fences, walls, and hoardings. Graffiti consists of a less intricate web of signs and codes than that described by American gang scholars (Conquergood 1994a), usually the nickname or initials of the tagger, followed by the gang tag or initials. There is some symbolism involved, however; most often the initials (e.g. LYT) are merged to form a single symbol, with date of tag or initials of individuals fitted into the gaps. These graffiti visually unite the group within the symbol of 'LYT'. Most tags also have proclamations of supremacy and/or denigrations of other groups appended. The tag LYT, for example, is normally followed by the phrase 'Number 1' or 'F[uck].T[he].Rest'. These displays, in their way, proclaim the same sentiment as the Latin scripture sculpted into the monument at Glasgow Cross junction, *Nemo me impune lacessit*, 'No-one attacks me with impunity'.

These visual symbols are drawn obsessively on any available surface; during discussion groups, Kev, James, and Sean would sketch tags constantly on pieces of paper; diaries and maps which were handed to me were covered with similar etchings. The boys' email addresses have LYT appended to them (e.g. kevcarson_ LYT_1@...); school jotters, bathroom walls, and desks are similarly inscribed. Daz, Dylan, and Kev are discussing the reasons why tags are sprayed around boundaries:

DAZ: So they know no tae mess.
DYLAN: An try tae dae any'hin. Cos if they dae any'hin, they're deid.
AF: Why's that important? So people won't come in to your area?
KEV: Aye, so they [people from other areas] don't try an mess your area up, writin hunners ae menchies ['mentions' or graffiti tags].

As this excerpt makes clear, however, distinction is central to 'gang' identification. In this sense, distinguishing the borders of the territorial area—the outer limits of street habitus—has the effect of symbolically delimiting a space in which local status can be carved out; as Willie describes: 'Tae get a name for themselves. Tae get a reputation. Tae get "aw look at me, Ah'm the hard-man" '. Local reputation and identity are thus bolstered by reputations for 'gang' activity, with some measure of celebrity attached. In fact, the bracketing of the Langview territory in this way creates space for this form of reputation to be built. For the Langview Boys, territorial identification is therefore overlaid with the performance of a tough, masculine identity akin to Sandberg's (2008) description of 'street capital'. In a social environment characterized by limited opportunities, not only territorial space but also bodily capital is a resource for attaining distinction. In this sense, persistent 'gang' identities in Glasgow must not only be understood in the context of ongoing economic marginalization but also within the context of local culture and status. While the concept of street habitus demonstrates the deep-seated connections between young people and the Langview community, the ways in which these boundaries are negotiated reflect the desire for individual and collective distinction with the context of local forms of 'tough' masculinities (Connell 1995).

Interestingly, however, these divisions were not as fixed or static as might have been expected. Not only were there intense rivalries between individuals from the same area but there were also instances in which young people from neighbouring areas called a truce. Reflecting on his earlier involvement in gang fighting, Michael described how the Langview and Swigton Young Teams 'went pals', hanging around together for periods of time. While the boundary serves on one level as a catalyst for enmity and distrust, it could also be appropriated, subverted, and played with. Its existence could in fact be viewed as playing a role for young people on both sides, expressing unity and solidarity for young people in both Langview and Swigton. Short notes that the status of any one group is *directly dependent* on the existence of a rival; conflict is both the 'major source of status within the gang' (Short 1968) and the major impetus for continued attempts at differentiation.

While young people in Langview develop a deep-seated connection with the local area, bracketing off their territorial environment, there is a tacit sense in which they are aware of the arbitrary nature of these boundaries. They will say, with a resigned smirk, that 'we dinny like people fae Swigton', not because they necessarily believe it but because it has been pre-ordained as such. This indicates the importance of individual and temporal aspects to the formation of a street habitus, as well as the role of social development in the gradual solidification of habits and traits. The following section will elaborate on the street-based age hierarchies through which such boundaries become embedded.

Learning street habitus

Early pioneers of the interactionist method and social learning theory noted that learning occurs through observation, mimicry, and copy-acting—imbibing signs, symbols, and behaviours from peers, family, and teachers (Mead 1934; Piaget 1955). Similarly, for Bourdieu habitus is 'imprinted and encoded in a socialising or learning process which commences during early childhood' (Jenkins 2002, pp. 75–6). The habitus (Bourdieu 1977) is thereby formed in part via social interaction with peers through acting out of relations and testing of boundaries. The processes by which young people grow into adult roles and identities are riven with conflict, doubt, impulse, and apprehension—the habitus is therefore variously developing, melding, and congealing throughout the process of growing up. In Langview, this results in no small part from the mixture of ages in public space and the mimicry of the Langview Boys by younger individuals. The following fieldnote describes an observation in LYP, in which younger children are watching the older boys intently, imitating and replicating:

Winter has arrived with a vengeance; ice coats the pavement. The streets are busy with people walking gingerly, sliding, looking up to see if anyone noticed; only to make eye-contact with someone doing exactly the same. There is an air of lightness to the street—people brought together by the adversity of conditions. At LYP, the outdoor area of the park is has become a perfect sheet of black ice. The Langview Boys are on the pitch, sliding around and having a great time; successive groups of younger boys join in, copying and showing off. This was truly a spontaneous excitement, a natural oasis in the midst of the urban experience; the boys went mad for it. (Fieldnote, 1 December 2008)

This example serves to illustrate the pattern through which street-based behaviours were learned and reproduced in Langview. The street is also, by its very nature, a space that is not private but is shared with other similar groups of young people. As in Thrasher's model, there may be tensions that emerge from competition over space but more commonly these tensions emerged from age-based hierarchies—between the Langview Boys and the 'older wans', or the 'younger wans'. In coming into contact with these other groups, the boys became habituated to the rules of the street and passed them on in turn to the younger group. The Langview Boys themselves looked up to an older group of young men in the area, and spoke nostalgically about the days that they played football with them as younger boys. Similarly, groups of young boys in LYP would talk in hushed tones about Kev and Daz, whispering to me that 'they're pure gangsters'. In this way, the process of reproduction of a street-based culture of bounded territoriality and masculine routes to local status can be glimpsed.

Layered onto these stages of peer association and development are the roles, personae, and identities associated with Langview Young Team. One community police officer, for example, told me he had been approached by a parent asking for advice after finding her son, aged five, playing with toy soldiers. The soldiers were arranged into separate and rival factions and on being asked what he was playing, the boy pointed out the rival factions as 'Langview Young Team', 'Swigton Fleeto', and 'Hillside Tongs'. At this early stage of development, these divisions operated in a realm of imagination and fantasy, but they also represented an embedded sense of individuality and rootedness. Similarly, children's playgroups are an important arena in which meanings, identities, and under-standing of the wider world are learned, enacted, and co-produced. Thrasher describes the imaginative realm of street play in which unappealing spaces can be magically transformed into exciting areas, where 'high-sounding' gang names 'may help compensate for their actual lack of status' (Thrasher 1963, p. 193). In the fol-lowing fieldnote, I recorded observations of a group of children acting out a conflict game near LYP:

When I was walking down to the train station tonight, I walked past some very young children playing in the new flats. The game (conducted behind a metal gate) was to throw stones at one another, in groups of two or three, hiding for cover under two bench-like slabs of stone, set approximately 10 feet apart. In fact, seemingly custom-designed for the purpose. The children could not have been more than 6 or 7. (Fieldnote, 12 May 2008)

As these stereotypes and myths are created and enacted, an increas-ing awareness of the boundaries between Langview and Swigton becomes apparent through observation of the 'big wans' in the area. On being asked where his knowledge of boundaries came from, Michael replied: 'Cos ma pals had aulder brothers, an they'd be a couple ae steps ahead in the whole process'. For younger boys, initial involvement in fights at the boundaries with Swigton were an extension of this form of play behaviour; for these children, gang fights might be described as being 'simply a game of chases like Cowboys and Indians with gang names used' (Kintrea et al. 2008). One night in LYP, for example, I saw first-hand the fine line dividing play and violence, children's gangs and gang identities:

Tonight, there was a group altercation at the bridge separating Langview from Swigton. A group of mixed age boys, one cluster 8 to 10-years-old, one cluster 10 to 12, and one 12 to 14 were congregated near the bridge when a group of 8 to 10-year-olds from the other side came across. There had been verbal exchanges, and dares, and taunts; it culminated in the very young ones swiping each other with long thin pieces of wood (like stripped bamboo). (Fieldnote, 15 October 2007)

In this example, the younger boys are keen to impress and gain the praise of the older boys. In this way, territorial identities and vio-lent resolutions are conducted as successive generations of children seek to play out and perform in front of generations of respected elders. This age gradation is reflected in the following quote from a youth worker in Ironside:

A lot ae it these days, it's the younger wans, seeing their aulder brithers an that fight, so it's basically 'we need tae carry oan the name', that's whit it is wi' a loat ae them up ma way. A loat ae them will jist shout so many names, they don't know who they belong tae, but they jist shout it cos they seen other people daein it before, so that's whit ye need tae do. Wee toaties...8 an 9...running up an down, shouting names and throwing bricks.

Performance of gang activities therefore plays different roles during different stages of social development. Very young children integrate the gang name into play behaviour, in particular pretend or fantasy play. Young males in their early teens, however, draw on territorial boundaries as a space in which to experiment with gang identities without full commitment. In the following excerpt, three of the Langview Boys reminisce over their early experiences at the Langview/Swigton border:

> MARK: Aye we wur talking aboot this last night. We used tae always go tae the bridge, when we were pure young, we used tae always kid oan [joke/play] we were fighting wi' the Swigton.
> AF: The bridge at the LYP?
> MARK: Aye. Every time aw the big wans used tae fight wi' the Swigton...
> GARY: We used tae pure stand at the back, fling bricks an aw that
> MARK: We used tae run down tae half-way, then run back up as if we'd done something.
> AF: Did you like sitting watching the fight?
> GARY: Aye
> AF: Why?
> WILLIE: Entertainment
> GARY: It wis jist pure funny, everyone's pure shoutin at each other, pure callin each other this and that, an we were pure jist sitting watching.

In this way, age and social development intertwine with the development of a street-based habitus, the boundaries of which act as a social arena in which developing masculinities and gang identities are enacted. As will be discussed in Chapter 8, however, the meaning of these boundaries alters and reconfigures at different stages of social development—through play, mimicry, and experimentation—intersecting with developing gender and group identities (Bannister and Fraser 2008).

In the absence of developed opportunity structures in either legitimate or illegitimate activity, gang identification in Glasgow has become an open-ended, repeating pattern of Thrasher's model, a loop that continues to set and reset with each passing generation, waxing and waning over time according to economic and social context. The process is articulated through the repetition of age-based hierarchies on the streets and the jostling for status within peer groups, younger groups looking up to and emulating older groups in repeating cycles. Nonetheless, this is neither an inevitable nor closed process. As will be discussed in Chapter 8, the majority of young people growing up in Langview did not commit to gang identification, and many that did only did so peripherally or experimentally. For this reason, street habituation is perhaps best envisaged—like Gunter's conceptualization of 'on road' youth culture (2008)—on a continuum. Just as there has been continuity and change over the lifetime of the city, so there is continuity and change over the lifetime of the individual. Like Delanty's definition of 'community', gang identification can be regarded as an 'open system of cultural codification' (Delanty 2003) that is used and drawn on by successive generations responding to similar economic circumstances. In this way, gang identity functions like an item of hand-me-down clothing, passed down, and tried on for size, grown into, tweaked to fit, grown out of again and passed on. Crucially, this process operates in dialectical relation to shifts in the economic landscape of the city and is therefore subject to change.

While this process of age-based reproduction allows an insight into the continuity of gang identification in Glasgow—surfacing and resurfacing with successive generations—it is important to emphasize that this process is not hermetically sealed from wider economic and social forces but is mutable. Just as gang identities have altered and reconfigured according to the broader context of the day—at times developing into more economically motivated or politicized groups—so too have gang identities been affected by the processes of neoliberalism that define the post-industrial cityscape.

Neoliberalizing the street

The concept of a stable territory, or 'turf'—understood as a static, geographically delimited and defended space, in which control is exerted over activity and access—has formed a central component in criminological definitions of 'gangs' since the very earliest forays in the field, and remains integral to both popular and academic accounts of youth 'gangs' (Spergel 1990; Klein et al. 2001). Central to these definitions is the idea of an organized, street-based criminal organization, exerting violent territorial supremacy for the purposes of economic gain. As processes of globalization reshape and reconfigure inner-city areas, however, the static nature of this definition has been problematized. Gentrification and displacement have resulted in shifting boundaries and more fluid conceptions of 'turf' (McDonald 2003; Hagedorn and Rauch 2007; Aldridge et al. 2011), while de-industrialization and ghettoization have intensified the spatial immobility of many inhabitants (Wacquant 2008a). While it is clear that gang identification is a predominantly street-based phenomenon (McVie 2010, pp. v–vi), in Scotland socio-structural changes have led to a decline in street-based leisure for young people.

In Glasgow, many of these changes occur in the context of an ongoing programme of neoliberal rebranding strategies employed by Glasgow City Council. Boyle and colleagues trace the intrusion of neoliberal doctrine into Glasgow city politics to the early 1980s, after the brief but shocking loss of Labour control of the City Council to the Conservative Party in 1977 (Boyle et al. 2008, p. 314). For Paton and colleagues (2012), citizenship in this 'new Glasgow' is increasingly defined, at a policy level, as consumer oriented. Efforts at regeneration, epitomized by the Commonwealth Games in 2014, represent market-led efforts to encourage 'flawed consumers' (Bauman 1998) to 'get with the times' of the new economy.[3] In this context, '[d]isadvantaged working-class lives are deemed as problematic, anti-modern and out of step with the revitalized and aspirational world of the new Glasgow, the new Scotland and the new UK' (Paton et al. 2012, p. 1486).

In the context of this wider rebranding in the city of Glasgow, the streets that the Langview Boys know so well are changing; playing fields are being turned into gentrified flats, communal areas watched and policed, bridges and underpasses closed off with spiked fences. Although street-based leisure has a long history

---

[3] The recent BBC Scotland documentary 'Commonwealth City' (2014) demonstrated the powerful impact of efforts at 'regeneration' in Dalmarnock. One resident, being forcibly evicted after an eight-year battle, could be heard to shout: 'All this so arseholes can run about in shorts for two weeks!' (see Whittaker and Batchelor 2014 for further comment).

in Glasgow—as King notes, 'in the period 1750–1914 . . . [w]hen housing was uncomfortable or overcrowded, promenading in the streets became a pleasurable pastime' (King 1987, p. 144)—latterly street-based leisure environments have been increasingly replaced by privatized leisure space (Sweeting and West 2003). Drawing on a longitudinal study of youth leisure in Glasgow between 1987 and 1999, Sweeting and West find that commercialized leisure has increased markedly—with 'very large increases in looking round the shops, playing computer games and going to the cinema, and smaller ones in watching sports matches, seeing pals, and going to discos, clubs, gigs and concerts' (Sweeting and West 2003, p. 16)— while 'going out nowhere' was the only category of leisure to have dropped significantly.

These forms of neoliberal street 'cleansing' have had a direct impact on the Langview Boys' street-based activities. Policing tactics have focused on dispersing groups of young people from public space and areas where young people congregate have been fenced off. In the following example, the project manager of Langview Outreach Project (LOP) had described a concentrated police presence in a specific area of Langview, for a three-month period:

The project manager told me there had been 3,000 incidents recorded in a small area near to Langview over a three month period—38 of which had been for a snowball fight involving youth workers and young people. This is a perfect example of the construction of a crime problem, and the power dynamics involved. Once a problem had been created (part reality, part fiction), the moral barricades had been manned by the local councillor, resulting in an order banning groups of young people from the area. It became a running joke between LOP workers, and the police, that there were no young people around—'you seen any young people tonight?' 'No. If we see any we'll give you a call'. This lasted for 3 months. It was a gang moral panic in miniature. (Fieldnote, 18 February 2009)

These changes to the street occur against a backdrop of gentrification in both Glasgow and Langview. Gentrification is, both physically and conceptually, the site of contest and conflict (Smith 1996, p. 70). Broadly, the concept refers to a range of inclusive and exclusive strategies aimed at 'community improvement', involving the upgrading or redevelopment of housing, facilities, or cultural amenities to attract new, wealthier residents. As opposed to the one-time push to the 'frontier' of undeveloped land, the 'new frontier' is the urban inner-city (Smith 1996, p. xvi). For Smith, gentrification is thus an inherently classed process, excluding those who do not meet the developers' vision of the new community (Smith 1996, p. 39). For Hagedorn, processes of gentrification interlock with neoliberal efforts toward enforcing the security of one group and excluding others, resulting in tension and conflict. In Chicago, for example, as the housing projects that were once the stronghold of organized gangs were destroyed and gang members were rehoused across the other side of the city, new turfs were contested through repeated violent conflicts (Hagedorn 2008, p. 124). In Glasgow, these developments have resulted in 'hidden injuries' amongst traditional working-class communities, whereby older residents are priced out of the new market, resulting in a crisis of identity (Paton 2009).

In Langview, the development of the new flats—and with them the influx of new residents—has resulted in complex dynamics of inclusion and exclusion. These flats are sold as aspirational spaces—advertised with photographs not of Langview but of Glasgow city centre—with no connection to the local area. As with the process of regeneration in Glasgow (Spring 1990), history and context are absent. The design of these new flats, crucially, is also in contrast to the traditional tenements in Langview, encouraging as it does a lack of contact between residents and the communal use of space. In contrast to old tenements, there is nowhere for people to meet and talk and nowhere for young people to play.

One of the spaces most profoundly connected with young people in Langview is the site of the old secondary school; demolished in the 1970s, it was turned into the sole green space site in the area, and quickly became an area in which large groups of young people congregated. In the last decade, however, this parkland had been sold to developers, and new, gentrified flats erected in their place. However, like Anderson's study of Jelly's Place (E. Anderson 2006), in which a group of men continued to meet outside their local bar despite its closure, the former park remains in the collective memory of groups of young people in Langview. The Langview Boys in particular found and used a 'hidden' space within the new flats—a refuse area, under cover. In this area the boys built a den with sofas and furniture culled from skips and bulk refuse, a powerful example of the search for safe 'microgeographies' in the context of a largely adult-controlled world. As the boys discuss, however, this safe haven did not last long:

GARY: Ages ago we hud a den, that's why the polis pulled us up. Up the new flats.

WILLIE: Couches an aw that.

GARY: The polis came an said 'ye better take it away or we're gonnae charge ye, fine ye' or something like that. Then the polis came an took it away.

AF: How did you feel?

GARY: We were pure raging. How long did it take us tae build that, about 2 days?

AF: Were there complaints?

GARY: We only had like one complaint.

This chain of events resulted in the Langview Boys' being cast out onto the same streets surrounding Langview Youth Project, further accentuating the value and importance of the territorial space of Langview.

The police, in particular, are responsible for the creation of 'landscapes of powerlessness' (Matthews et al. 1998). In the following excerpt, the Langview Boys discuss the impact that conflict with police has on their mobility:[4]

GARY: They always pull us up for nae reason. Sometimes the polis are sound, like they jist talk tae ye an that. But see ones that jist come in, like when we're in the new flats, we're jist getting a game of hunt, and be like that 'jist because yous live in a shithole doesnae mean ye kin turn this place intae wan'. And like that's still our local area, if you know what Ah mean. They're like 'where ye's fae', an we're like that 'Lang St', an they go 'well get back doon Lang St then'.

WILLIE: [Pointing at map] There's ma street there. Say we're alang the chippie or some'hing, the polis pull us up. They say 'get back tae your street an get hame' an aw that.

GARY: It's as if you're no allowed to leave your street.

These processes—of 'othering' alongside restricted mobilities—are also fostered by the development of surveilling and policing the Langview Boys and other groups of young people in the area (Zedner 2009). CCTV cameras have been installed throughout Langview; for Kev, this has meant the curtailment of gang fighting:

KEV: So there's no point in fightin them, cos fighting, ye get the jail. Plus, there's too many cameras.

AF: Do you think that has an effect, like, if there's loads of CCTV cameras?

---

[4] For an interesting discussion of the policing of fashion, see Treadwell (2008).

KEV: Aye, cos there's wan alang Lang St an there's wan alang the
bridge, right, an the wans up the flats. Ye can't fight anywhere.

As will be discussed in the next chapter, trends in youth leisure,
bound up with the globalization and redefinition of the city of
Glasgow, has resulted in the narrowing of opportunities for young
people in Langview to have access to public or commercial spaces.
While territorialism has a long history in Glasgow, rooted in persistent social divisions and economic marginalization (Damer
1990a; Davies 1998), these new processes further intensify young
people's attachment to place.

While street habitus continues to be learned and enacted by successive generations of street-based youth, in Langview it appears
that this number may be diminishing. In shifting from public,
street-based leisure to more individual, privatized forms of leisure,
however, the community solidarity and neighbourhood nationalism that have underpinned Glasgow's history may also start to
fragment (Hobbs 2013). Those that continue to engage in street-
based leisure will become increasingly marginalized—or indeed
criminalized—as 'urban outcasts' (Wacquant 2007, 2008a) that
constitute a blemish on the 'new Glasgow'.[5]

It is important to emphasize, however, that there are also emergent
opportunities in the ruptures caused by the shift to post-industrial,
neoliberal space making. One notable advantage is in the opening
up of mobility for 'ordinary' youth in areas with long-standing
territorial rivalries. In Langview, there were many young people
who viewed the Langview Boys as threatening and dangerous, and
avoided public and leisure spaces that they frequented.

Tyrannical spaces

Like Gunter's conceptualization of young people 'on road' in
East London (2008), street habituation operates on a continuum
wherein only a relatively small number of young people are the
most committed adherents. For some, such young people epito-
mize localized forms of respect and distinction—local heroes
whom they wish to emulate. For others, however, such groups represent a source of ongoing fear, resentment and degradation—a

[5] Wacquant suggests this stigma may be attenuated or even be annulled through
geographic mobility (Wacquant 2007, p. 67; see also Rogaly and Taylor 2009).

reason for 'staying in' rather than 'going out'. While street habitus is therefore both relational and contingent, its rules and logic create 'no-go' areas for certain groups of young people. Percy-Smith and Matthews (2001) describe these areas as 'tyrannical spaces':

some children, through their propinquity within neighbourhood spaces, clash and collide to such an extent that their experiences of a locality become severely blighted. For these unfortunate young people local environments are tyrannical spaces, defined in terms of 'no-go areas', danger and threat. (Percy-Smith and Matthews 2001, p. 49)

In Glasgow, both quantitative and qualitative research has found a similar dynamic at play in relation to young people's use of public space, particularly in relation to a perceived threat from youth gangs. A Glasgow Youth Survey, for example, reported that 25 per cent of young people did not feel safe in their area, and that young people living in housing schemes or areas with problems with youth 'gangs', felt particularly intimidated (MORI Scotland 2003, pp. 15–16). Similarly, qualitative research on territoriality in Scotland has uncovered a perception among young people of heightened risk in these areas and a corresponding fear of public space. Consequently, young people report a restriction on mobility both within their local areas and beyond which affects both friendship networks and leisure opportunities (Bannister and Fraser 2008, pp. 102–3; Frondigoun et al. 2008, pp. 43–50). Young people employ various risk-avoidance techniques, staying within 'safe' areas, remaining in groups, and returning at 'safe' times (Seaman et al. 2005, pp. 51–4).

Research has also identified the 'double-edged sword' of these avoidance strategies. When hanging around in groups, young people found that they may attract attention from the police or local residents who perceive them to be a 'gang'. Turner and colleagues highlight the 'need to distinguish between individuals "ganging together" to keep safe and "gang behaviour"' (Turner et al. 2006, p. 463). Winton, describing the use of public space in areas of Guatemala with a reputation for gangs, highlights the amplification of these 'no-go' areas by the construction of youth gangs as particularly dangerous and threatening:

fear of violence leads to the spatial exclusion of community members, particularly young people, whereby assaults and territorial gang conflicts construct public space as dangerous and therefore restrict the extent to which young people feel positively connected to the community'. (Winton 2005, p. 180)

In a mapping exercise with the Langview Boys—in which I asked the boys to place stickers on a map of Langview illustrating their homes, their friends' homes, and the places where they spent time—it was notable how clustered the stickers were around the space of a few streets. Significantly, however, all of the stickers illustrating 'no-go' areas were clustered around the areas immediately over the boundaries with Swigton and Hillside. The Langview Boys felt confident roaming within Langview, spending the majority of their time within this relatively small geographical area. In discussion with other groups of young people in LYP or during periods of streetwork, however, it was clear that this freedom within Langview was not felt by all—in certain cases as a consequence of the Langview Boys' ubiquity. Young people I met during the course of my streetwork indicated their fear of various spaces in Langview, with fears of older groups overlaid with other trepidations of 'stranger danger', unknown areas, and groups from different areas:

Tonight I spoke to a 12-year-old male, known to me from LYP, who has spoken to me previously about threats against him and his family by another family in the area, which now it seems has resulted in two older members of the offending family appearing at his family home, armed with knives, and shouting that they were going to 'chop you up into wee bits'. As a result, the male felt unable to walk the streets. Another girl (11) talked of her fear of going to the top end of the area due to a threat from older girl. (Fieldnote, 18 June 2008)

Like the young people in MacDonald and Shildrick's study in the north-east of England (2007), it was clear that young people within this hidden majority operated with 'subjective, mental maps of their area that sub-divided it into separate locales, each with their own reputations (i.e. greater or lesser associations with crime and risks to personal safety)' (MacDonald and Shildrick 2007, p. 345; see also Kintrea et al. 2008). One of the school-leavers, Susan, describes her feelings of apprehension in crossing the boundary between Langview and Swigton:

AF: What do you think of living in Langview?
SUSAN: I think it's all right. It's just the Swigton is a wee bit dodgy sometimes, coming o'er the bridge, when I'm walkin back at night...
AF: You mean the bridge between Langview and Swigton?

SUSAN: Aye. Cos see sometimes when ye've been at school, like ye've been at school for study, an it's pure dark, it's quite dodgy walking o'er there yerself. It is! It's scary but...

AF: Aye, cos it's all undercover as well, you feel like you're walking down this dark tunnel...

SUSAN: Aye, ye think ye can hear footsteps behind ye, it's pure scary and that. But Langview Ah think's fine. Ah don't bother.

These interlocking fears and insecurities indicate some of the reasons for the relative emptiness of the streets of Langview at certain points. During streetwork, for example, there would be long periods each night in which few contacts were made with groups of young people, despite, as highlighted in the first part of this chapter, the comparatively high number of children and young people living in the area. In this context, others among the school-leavers describe again a quite different experience of public space in Langview. For the young women in the following discussion, negative body image, a preference for the sanctity of the home, or lack of parental consent resulted in their 'staying in':

AF: I mean, what about the rest of you? Why did you not want to go and hang about on the streets [and drink, get into trouble]...

MEL: My ma wouldnae let me, so...

PAMELA: Ah wisnae allowed, but Ah jist done it anyway.

CAROLINE: Ah didnae like hinging about the streets cos Ah wis fat and got cold...and didn't like walking about the streets! Ah wis just lazy. Ah just wanted to stay in and watch telly.

SUSAN: Ah never wanted tae dae that. An my ma an da would have pure killed me, but it jist wisnae what Ah wanted tae dae. It didnae bother me.

AF: At that age, when you were 14, 15, were you in a minority? Were most people out on the streets every Friday and Saturday night?

[ALL]: Aye

SUSAN: People would say stuff tae ye, mair the boays, like 'oooh', pure 'ye never go oot' an whatever, an it's jist like...it didnae bother me.

While the Langview Boys spent much of their childhoods in the public spaces and streets of Langview—and remained ubiquitous in these spaces during the period of fieldwork—there were large numbers of young people absent from these spaces. As a result of fear, informal social control, preference, or available leisure outside the area, these individuals exhibited a less marked emotional attachment to the streets of Langview—expressing a desire to move away at the earliest opportunity.

These complex geographies of immobility point to the diversity of experiences of young people in Langview. While the Langview Boys, and other street-based youth, evince a deep-seated connection with the locale—learned and reproduced through age-based hierarchies—there are many others for whom the streets are 'no-go' zones of fear and anxiety. While neoliberal processes of gentrification, street-cleansing, and surveillance have narrowed the opportunities for public leisure—further marginalizing street-based youth—these processes may also improve mobility for the other groups of young people in these communities.

Conclusion

As the opportunities, spaces, and futures available to young people in Glasgow have been reconfigured, so locale has retained a powerful role. This street habitus reflects a cultural adaptation to economic marginalization and spatial immobility; rather than these local spaces being employed as an economic resource, space itself becomes a resource for identity (Pickering et al. 2012). 'Gang' behaviour, in both symbolic and violent forms, represents perhaps the most potent symbol of this localism. Identification with a local 'gang' becomes the confluence of area identity: a root of identity, status, and excitement in an uncertain and unsteady world. In constructing Langview as a geographically delimited area, young people are simultaneously creating a boundary within which local status and identity can be carved out, a physical and symbolic staging ground for experimentation, boundary testing, and 'edge-work'. Filtered through the prism of local forms of 'tough' masculinity, the border becomes a space in which to test individual and collective mettle. This pattern indicates a repeating pattern of street-based leisure that underpins the persistence of certain habits, traits, and dispositions at a local level.

In the midst of current debate and conflict relating to youth 'gangs' in the UK, the stereotype of the American street-gang—an organized, cohesive, violent criminal unit, dominating a specific territory for economic gain—looms large. Following this trajectory, there has been an increasing tendency in UK gang discourse to collapse the phenomenon into a single narrative of 'gangs in the UK', with the distinctive historical trajectories and meanings of gangs in different cities subsumed into a singular construction. This chapter has sought to make the case for situating understanding of 'gangs' within specific cultural contexts, and the corresponding need to respond to 'gangs' in a way that is sensitized to their particular meaning and impact in that environment. Unlike popular stereotypes of gangs, which construct gangs as a fixed and static entity, gang identities in Langview were fluid and context-specific.

6

'Learning to Leisure'

AF: Why did you do it? [set off a fire-hydrant]
JAMES: Cos he said he wis gonnae batter [attack] me. Kiddin' oan.
   Fir a buzz.
AF: How d'ye mean?
JAMES: Cos they wanted me tae dae it, so Ah done it. Jist fir a buzz.

A constant refrain of the children and young people I met in Langview—be it in LYP, on the street, in school, or elsewhere—was 'this is pure borin'. On further prompting, this was frequently followed by 'there's nuthin tae dae', or 'there's nivir any'hin tae dae'. The implication was not literal—in every case, there were options—but rather that everything there was to do had been done a hundred times before, and was therefore completely drained of any novelty, value, or creative potential. The streets had been walked a thousand times; the youth projects, shops, and public spaces visited and revisited until there was nothing left to excite any interest. In this context, the phrase 'fir the buzz'—for the excitement, for a laugh, for the sheer hell of it—is pivotal. When leisure time is spent in a constant round of dull monotony, exciting moments of spontaneity take on special significance. Whether it is pushing the edges of rules and acceptable behaviour in a youth project, testing security guards and police in commercial venues, or creating edgy excitement in public space, the group engage in activities 'fir the buzz'; as a means of creating energy and spontaneity in a landscape of boredom.

Much like the alterations to street-based leisure described in the previous chapter, leisure opportunities in Langview have reconfigured around the privatized, commercialized logic of the 'new Glasgow'. Where various forms of leisure were once easily and cheaply available in local areas, these spaces have largely been replaced by out-of-town entertainment and shopping complexes, each containing the same multinational shops and restaurants.

In addition, new digital leisure spaces have become mainstream, providing new opportunities for private, home-based communication and excitement. It might be imagined that youth leisure would move in-step with these changes, replacing old forms of leisure with new, and acceding to these new field arrangements. However, the Langview Boys demonstrated a clear desire not only for continuity in their leisure pursuits—finding ways of reproducing leisure habits in this new environment—but also in creating 'fir the buzz' excitement in the new cathedrals of consumerism. Their leisure activities therefore did not represent a clear or definable 'break' with previous generations, but a dialectical process of old and new, learning and reimagining. In a process similar to that described by Jefferson (1997) and Nayak (2003), the leisure activities of the Langview Boys can be read as a means of co-producing cultural meaning in the context of these changes. The re-enactment of leisure behaviours from previous generations can be viewed as a way of creating meaning in a world where the future is uncertain and precarious—adaptive responses to the conditions of late modernity within the 'glacial forces' of habitus (Appadurai 1996, p. 6).

The chapter is structured in two parts. The first examines the various leisure pursuits of the Langview Boys, emphasizing the importance of 'fir the buzz' excitement in both public and private leisure spaces. Despite some new configurations, these activities demonstrate a clear sense of continuity with previous generations of leisure activity, despite changes to Glasgow's economy that encourage alternative forms of leisure pursuits. The second locates these leisure habits within the broad-based alterations to work and leisure for young people in the 'new Glasgow', arguing that the rupture caused by the shift to a post-industrial economy has resulted in both continuity and change in youthful identities.

Fir the buzz: Leisure and the Langview Boys

Leisure, for the Langview Boys, consisted of a fluid cycle of activities between home, public space, commercial venues, and local youth projects. The Boys switched and flowed between different leisure activities, pin-balling from one to another—structured and unstructured, local and non-local, free and paid—in an endless cycle of boredom relief. The Boys' use of public space was a perpetual repetition of group activities in the same public spaces—constantly searching for new excitements, dares, and risks through which to test individual distinction and reaffirm group cohesion—in which boredom and 'doing nothing' (Corrigan 1979) were central motifs. Cohen, drawing on Goffman (1959), refers to these diversions as 'character contests':

These are ways of seeing who will have the honour and character to rise above the situation. Action gets restructured around the familiar settings of streets, sports ground, the weekend by the sea, railway station. The settings are given new meanings by being made stages for these games. (Cohen 1973, p. 53)

In these circumstances, gang identification emerges as a means of puncturing the daily routine with a transgressive 'thrill' of violence or boundary crossing (Katz 1988). While elsewhere post-industrialism has created fragmentation, atomization and dissolving of community (Hobbs 2013), the Langview Boys—young as they were—evinced a marked sense of continuity in social relations. While changes are clear, these are neither as epochal nor as rapid as might be expected. In the following sections, the continuities and changes in leisure habits—one instance of more broad-based ruptures to the foundations of social and economic life in the city—will be analysed through six key arenas in which the Langview Boys spent their free time: hanging about, football, fighting, 'malling', cinema, and gaming.

Hanging about

The Langview Boys spent a great deal of their time in public space, bored and restless, seeking diversions from the mundane everyday. Willie describes the Boys' evening routine:

See tae be honest, right, we go hame fae school, we get our dinner an that, we go tae LYP at 6, we go oot fae LYP we get a game ae hunt roon the streets.

When LYP is closed—during evenings and weekends—the Langview Boys spent much of their time, together or in smaller knots, patrolling the streets of Langview, in search of creative diversion of any kind. As Willie mentions, the street game 'hunt' was a popular activity. 'Hunt' is basically hide-and-seek on a broader canvas, with added risk and excitement; played in the dark, in nooks and crannies in the cityscape.[1] Emphasizing both

---

[1] 'Hunt' (also called 'manhunt' or, interestingly, 'gang up') can involve either one 'seeker' or one 'hider', with the rest playing the opposite role. For further analysis of street games, see Robins and Cohen (1978) or Opie and Opie (1969).

group solidarity and individual distinction, the game represents well the relationship between play, excitement, and space within the Langview Boys' group activities in public space. The game is played in the area surrounding the boys' homes—within the space of a few streets—and is thus geographically bounded, with inside/outside groupings woven into its fabric. For the Langview Boys, the street was the most common site of leisure—a free, open, and public space where they felt at home.

Nonetheless, the Boys were unquestionably in the minority in enacting street-based leisure. During streetwork shifts, there were long periods of time—particularly during the winter months—when there were very few young people on the streets. In fact, much like the Langview Boys, we walked the streets of Langview in a seemingly endless round—stopping at the same places, having the same conversations, looking for some sort of excitement. This represents a marked alteration from previous generations, for whom the street was the primary source of leisure (King 1987). As Patrick argues of 1960s Glasgow:

Life with the gang was not all violence, sex and petty delinquency. Far from it. One of the foremost sensations that remains with me is the feeling of unending boredom, of crushing tedium, of listening hour after hour at street corners to desultory conversation and indiscriminate grumbling. Standing with one's back against a wall, with one's hands in one's pockets, in the late afternoon and in the early hours of the morning, was *the* gang activity. (Patrick 1973, p. 80)

Similarly, Jephcott's study of youth leisure in the 1960s revealed that a majority of free time was spent 'hanging out' in public space, cafes and pubs, alongside group-based, organized leisure. Dancing, cinema, and cafes feature most prominently—though for many the majority of leisure time was spent at home, watching TV (Jephcott 1967, p. 59). Table 6.1 summarizes some of these key findings.

These findings, crucially, point to some of the structural causes for the recent decline in street-based leisure among young people in Glasgow (Sweeting and West 2003). Popular leisure has, by and large, become delocalized, privatized, and commercialized (Rojek 1995). The most popular activities listed in Jephcott's survey (1967) were easily and cheaply available in the Langview of the 1960s. Several local cinemas, a large nearby dance hall, and extensive playing fields constituted the

Table 6.1 Participation in leisure activities in 15 to 19-year-olds, by gender (%) (1967)

	All	Male	Female
Dancing	69	62	76
Cinema	82	83	81
Café	51.5	57	46
Pub	11	16	6
Skating	6.5	6	7
Bowling	3	3	3
Spectator sport	4.5	8	1
Read magazines	68	55	81

Source: Jephcott (1967)

main leisure attractions for young people in the area, and work was to be had in the numerous factories in the immediate area. The cinemas, after various incarnations as bingo halls, dance halls, and pubs have fallen into disrepair; the space of the local dance hall, reopened as a supermarket, is now occupied by a car-park and a modern flat development—as are the playing fields. The factories have been converted into chic artists' spaces and outsourced call centres; or flattened to make way for apartment blocks. Only one café from the 1960s remains—one of the few in the area where young people spend any length of time. The others have either closed down, or replaced by the 'global nowheresvilles' (Bauman 2002) of globalized café and fast-food chains.

In this context, new technologies and consumer spaces have arisen to meet the needs of young people's free time. Nonetheless, as Table 6.2 demonstrates, while consumption of new technologies—phones, gaming, and internet—have risen in influence, traditional activities such as cinema-going remain popular. Notably, a sizeable majority of young people in the 2003 survey wanted more cinemas, bowling and leisure activities in their local area (MORI Scotland 2005).

These survey findings demonstrate, on one hand, the changing nature of leisure time for young people in Glasgow, with localized, public leisure increasingly replaced with commercialized, private

Table 6.2 Weekly leisure activities among 15 to 20-year-olds, by age (%) (2003)*

	15	16	17–18	19–20
Listen to music	90	75	92	91
Watch TV/videos/DVDs	87	61	86	85
Go to friend's houses	85	58	77	72
Text friends	80	55	–	–
Talk on the telephone	75	49	–	–
Surf the net	70	68	71	79
Go to the cinema	64	24	55	58
Play computer games	61	55	–	–
Go shopping	64	50	51	52
Read books or magazines	55	37	–	–
Go to a pub/bar	–	–	66	83

Source: MORI Scotland (2005)

*NB. Some different questions were posed to 15- and 16-year-olds than 17 to 20-year-olds.

leisure. Notably, the proportion of young people frequenting pubs and bars has increased dramatically—from only 11 per cent of 15 to 19-year-olds in 1967, to 66 per cent of 17 to 18-year-olds in 2003. For Winlow and Hall, this upswing in night-time leisure reflects a broader shift toward consumerism in youth leisure. The authors paint a vivid picture of young men and women 'living for the weekend' (Winlow and Hall 2009b); carrying out the drudgery of service-sector work in order to fund the temporary release of alcohol, drug and violence-fuelled revelry in the night-time economy. The Langview Boys had begun to incorporate street-based drinking in their weekend leisure habits—Kev talked of 'planking a 3L' [a three litre bottle of cider] in bushes near the LYP for later consumption—but alcohol-based leisure was not yet part of their leisure lives.

Despite these changes, young people in the later survey also demonstrate a clear desire for the non-commercial, public leisure activities of previous generations. This suggests that the rupture caused by the shift from industrial to post-industrial economy has resulted in both continuity and change in young people's leisure habits. Crucially, this shift has the effect of marginalizing street-based leisure—and those that continue to enact street-based leisure—in favour of commercialized leisure spaces. In this context, the Langview Boys enact a rebellious street habitus that contrasts with many of the leisure pursuits available.

Football

Football was by far the most popular and dominant form of leisure activity for the Langview Boys. Playing, spectating at games, watching on telly, supporting; the boys lived and breathed football. Uniting individual distinction with collective identity, one-upmanship with physicality, brinksmanship with excitement, masculinities with competition—football embodies the very spirit of the Langview Boys' leisure lives. The football pitch was a key staging area where reputations were staked and claimed on a daily basis. In line with broader changes to leisure, however, the number of football pitches available was changing; increasingly there were fewer and fewer municipal facilities. Despite these alterations to the field, however, their playing habits persisted—the Boys would, for example, climb the fences into paid facilities after-hours.

In terms of playing, the Boys were far more interested in relatively unstructured, free-flowing matches than in training or tactics. While many of the group had phenomenal natural ability, only a small handful played for a formal team. Kev, for example, started playing for a team but quickly found the discipline and regularity of training too much to handle. Efforts at training in LYP had varying success, with the Boys' often grudgingly attending in order to get on the team for matches. In the following fieldnote, the Boys were subtly subverting the training by making semi-secret gang signs—both from LYT and other groups from neighbouring areas—to one another, further demonstrating the connection between football and territorial identity:

During the (all-male) training, it was fairly regimented, but I noticed numerous small and large-scale efforts to subvert the authority of the situation; Fraz when stretching made the LYT sign (one forearm vertical, with a clenched fist, the other horizontal, with a fist meeting the elbow); Frankie made some sign for the SYT; James mocked a T for Hillside Tongs. (Fieldnote, 11 February 2008)

This represents a subtle but clear example of group identity being densely woven into both public and leisure space in Langview. The phrase young people use to refer to gangs—'team'—is further evidence of this bond (see also Conquergood 1994a, p. 26). In the following fieldnote, a group of boys from Swigton had come to LYP for a game of football. In the context of group competition, involving some children aged 9 and 10, these rivalries quickly gave way to violent conflict:

The 'Swigton v Langview' game from the previous week was reconvened. Tonight the rivalry was in full flow; one Swigton boy in particular, Chris, was pushing and swearing and bullying his way round everyone on the opposite team; at one point one of the bolder Langview boys (aged 10) retorted 'who are you talking to'; Chris immediately squared up to him. This kind of thing was occurring left, right, and centre—there was one point where Chris was pushing around a younger boy from Langview, and several of the Langview boys started shouting 'fight back, fight back'. (Fieldnote, 3 June 2008)

This, of course, is not new. If ever there was an activity that defined the unique blend of social divisions, masculinities and physical prowess that defines Glaswegian identity, it is football. As Damer notes, 'football is the sporting expression of the city's hard masculine edge, and contains all the ritual displays of skill, courage, competition and controlled violence which the local version of machismo demand' (1990a, p. 200). It was in the boom years of Glasgow's economy that spectator sports—particularly football matches between the city's 'Old Firm' of Celtic and Rangers—became popularized, 'offering spectators vicarious release from the profound insecurities of industrial depression' (Maver 2000, p. 276). Football matches 'arose to meet the needs of large urban populations with limited time and money and a new legal right to a free Saturday afternoon' (Jephcott 1967, p. 14), as a release from the pressure of the working-week.

Like the Boys' subversion of formal expectations of training, however, spectating at professional football matches were also approached as an opportunity 'fir the buzz'. Like the boys in Corrigan's study, going to the game '*includes* watching the football...but is a collection of experiences that are not simply watching a game of soccer...[to] go with your mates...is to take part in a collective and creative experience' (Corrigan 1995, p. 74). The Langview Boys had developed a raft of strategies to gain entry to the ground without paying—from squeezing through the turnstiles with those with tickets, to distracting security guards while others got through—and had found a part of the stadium where they could stand as a group and still see the game. The whole experience—whether getting in or not—was described in carnivalesque terms, as an experience of creative spontaneity.[2] The following fieldnote describes a discussion with the boys about their spectating at a football match (see also Deuchar and Holligan 2010):

The boys said it was good to be a football fan 'fir the buzz' you get from being in the crowd—singing, dancing, cheering. For the duration of the match, as the boys acted out, you are jumping around as at a carnival, forgetting everything else—not on the edge of life and death, but on the edge of something. Despite the multinational forces which now shape the phenomenal wealth of football teams and players—for the boys, all that exists is an opportunity for carnival, and a means of getting one over on your mates. (Fieldnote, 23 September 2008)

The final aspect of football that formed an important part of the Langview Boys everyday lives was supporting a team. In Glasgow, this means in effect a choice between one of the 'Old Firm' of Celtic and Rangers. Like the young men in Deuchar and Holligan's study (2010), however, all the boys agreed that the best thing about supporting Rangers or Celtic was the 'slagging'—or insults—you could give people over their team. It was an opportunity to get one over on your mates, a way of gaining symbolic one-upmanship in the constant tussle for status.

Interestingly, though many of the Boys supported Celtic, in a discussion about the Old Firm it transpired that almost all present had in fact supported Rangers at some point in their lives. As Kev and Scott discuss, this significant change came about as a result of a change in significant male presences in the household:

AF: Why is there such a rivalry between Celtic and Rangers if it's that easy to change between which one you support?
KEV: It's no easy tae change. Ah'd never change.
AF: But both of yous have changed.
SCOTT: Aye when Ah wis aboot two Ah supported Celtic. Because ma da. When Ah stayed wi' ma ma, it wis her boyfriend.

This was incredibly surprising. Anyone familiar with the intense loyalty of the Old Firm fans, and the passionate rivalry, would

---

[2] For critical discussion of the relationship between carnival, youth, and social control, see Presdee (2000).

find this hard to believe. While this may have only been true for the Boys, the sense was that, up to a point, it didn't matter which side you were on, as long as you had a side and stuck to it. Like the imagined boundary between Langview and Swigton, this social division was a tacit way of ensuring a constant source of banter and rivalry; a socially constructed barrier against boredom. The greatest derision was reserved for those who either changed sides regularly—'glory-hunters'—or who wouldn't commit to either. Rather than representing any form of sectarian or religious identity, for the Langview Boys supporting an Old Firm team meant creating a space for rivalry among friends, while reaffirming the masculine identity of male role models.

Fighting

While territorial fighting was not a regular activity for the Boys during the period I worked with them, it was nonetheless a daily subject of conversation. Conversations about who got 'do'ed' [beaten-up] at the weekend, whether a single punch constituted a 'doin', or about large-scale fights from previous years, were part of the Boys' shared narrative. As Corrigan argues, 'within the context of "doing nothing" on a street corner, fights are an important and exciting occasion…an easy and an interesting event' (Corrigan 1979, pp. 131–2). Julie, one of the school-leavers, describes the spectacle of violence in public space by drawing a comparison with the frenzied excitement surrounding a fight in her school: 'It's like, see in this school, see when there's a fight, it's like pure 'yaas', everybody's pure jumping up oan chairs'.

In areas of Glasgow characterized by extremely limited leisure opportunities, fighting has long represented a source of excitement and rivalry. John Carnochan, head of Scotland's Violence Reduction Unit,[3] uses the phrase 'recreational violence' to describe these ritualistic fights. Pearl Jephcott, drawing explicit parallels between fights and 'boys from a "superior" background…rock-climbing' (Jephcott 1967, p. 98), found in 1960s Glasgow that:

[a]nother set of those involved in Trouble, and a much larger one numerically, were the boys who looked on it as a pleasurable break in an

---

[3] Guardian (2011) 'Glasgow gangs chose route to peace in face of tough crackdown'. Available at: <http://www.theguardian.com/uk/2011/aug/11/glasgow-gangs-peace-crackdown> [Accessed 8 August 2014].

otherwise tame existence. There was an exciting element of unpredictability about Trouble. 'Once a fight starts *anything* can happen'. This
attitude to fighting, combined with the opportunity to prove one's guts,
suggested that it was not so far removed from play in the original sense of
the word. (Jephcott 1967, p. 139)

As was discussed in Chapter 2, territorial gang fights have more than
a hundred years of history in Glasgow, most often taking place in
communities experiencing considerable economic disadvantage. As
Jephcott notes, for some young people in these contexts fighting can
represent an exciting break in the absence of alternative opportunities. However, it must be remembered that these incidents can cause
real and lasting damage to those on the receiving end. According to
Strathclyde Police, both victims and offenders share similar traits,
tending to be 'very young (mostly in the 14–18 age group), male,
white and to come from under-privileged backgrounds' (Squires et al.
2008, p. 86). Robert, one of the school-leavers, describes an incident
when he was ambushed by a group of young men from Swigton:

ROBERT: Aye. Ah had tae walk by it, every night, when Ah wis coming hame fae the shop, or the LYP even. I even got jumped one
night.
AF: What happened?
ROBERT: Ah wis jist, walking home fae the LYP, the bottom way, tae
ma street, an then three ae them came up an asked where Ah wis
fae. An I didnae answer them, Ah wis only in first year [of high
school: aged 12–13] or something, an Ah just kept walkin, an then
the three ae them jist grabbed us and jist started punching intae
us. An Ah couldnae dae nothing obviously, cos there wis three ae
them. An then jist a couple ae wummen jist walked by an split it
up, an then they jist ran away.

In a very real sense, therefore, the boundaries of Langview become
staging grounds for physical transgression, for the bolstering of
reputations and self-identity; and sites of danger and fear. In this
context, gang identities emerge as a way creating opportunities
'fir the buzz' on an otherwise dull evening, in turn limiting the
mobility of other young people in the community. In the following
discussion, one of the school-leavers, Michael, describes the development of a gang fight from the context of 'standin aboot':

AF: How do fights happen? How do they get organised, and how do
they happen, right there an then?
MICHAEL: Dunno, jist get a group ae the boays, an jist go tae the
bridge, an ye'd shout down the bridge, like 'ye want a fight' or

something like that. An if there wis a couple ae them standin aboot they'd say 'we'll go an get a team'. An it wid jist happen fae there.

Occurring as they do on the edges of the neighbourhood, accompanied by risk of severe injury, this form of violence speaks to Stephen Lyng's conceptualization of 'edgework' (1990, 2000). Adapted from the work of infamous gonzo journalist Hunter S. Thompson, 'edgework' refers to human action that tests the edges of human skill and experience, such as extreme sports, activities, and occupations, which are engaged in as an escape from the routinization of work and life (Lyng 1990, pp. 871–3). These activities represent efforts to puncture the routine of everyday life—reclaiming a sense of self and identity through highly individual examples of adrenaline and excitement.

As several commentators have pointed out, however, the forms of transgressive edgework available to economically marginalized young people are more limited than the 'hang gliding, rock climbing, motorcycle racing/car racing, and downhill ski racing...fire fighting, test piloting, combat soldiering, movie stunt work, and police work' (Lyng 1990, p. 857) to which Lyng refers. Batchelor (2007) discusses this disparity pointedly:

Socially excluded and socio-economically disadvantaged young people, for example, have little connection with the world of work and typically lack access to pre-arranged excitements such as skydiving or base jumping. Rather, they spend much of their time 'bored', hanging about street corners with their peers'. (Batchelor 2007, p. 144)

Gang fighting, as a spectacle and activity, represents an 'edgy', free, and accessible source of excitement. Liam, for example, describes the gang fighting he sees every weekend in another area of Glasgow:

LIAM: Every weekend.
AF: An are the polis out every weekend after folk?
LIAM: There's always polis about. Up an doon the road an that, up the park. But they nivir catch anyb'dae, cos they aw wear big red jaickets. When everyb'dae's fighting, someone'll jist shout 'edgy' [danger] and everyb'dae jist runs.

The symbolism of the word 'edgy' is important here. For these groups of 'socially excluded and socio-economically disadvantaged young people', crime and transgression—like Willis' and Corrigan's boys—are one of a small number of avenues for controlling the 'edge' (Katz 1988). As Willis noted of violence: 'Fights, as accidents and other crises, stand you painfully in "the now". Boredom and petty detail disappear' (Willis 1977, p. 34). For young people—in a liminal 'waiting room' between childhood and adulthood (Miller 2005)—edgework therefore represents the *construction* of situations in which individual distinction can be carved out in the context of group-based activities.

Importantly, however, such fights can also be thought of as a form of street-based leisure, reproducing territorial identities and routes to local status that have existed in Glasgow for generations. As has been argued, however, these streets are changing. In this context, new leisure spaces have opened up. The Langview Boys' engagement with these spaces, crucially, demonstrates a similar sense of continuity and change; the slow-boat of street habitus being confronted by changing waters.

'Malling'

One of the most significant alterations to the leisure lives of young people since the 1960s survey, quoted above, is the introduction of 'shopping' as a category of entertainment. The Langview Boys now frequently go 'doon the shoaps' as a way of spending time during evenings or weekends. Since the late 1960s, however, local high streets have been increasingly hollowed out in favour of large shopping centres outside of the neighbourhood. Langview is no exception. While there remain a small number of local shops, the shopping mall has come to represent a site of both subsistence and entertainment for the Boys. This increase in importance of commercial spaces for youth leisure represents a fundamental alteration in the field of activity for children and young people in Langview. The trend towards delocalization in youth leisure, bound up with the globalization and redefinition of the city of Glasgow, results in the narrowing of opportunities for young people in Langview in public space. As will be seen, however, 'malling' does not just involve straightforward consumption, but the creation of transgressive excitement.[4]

This shift in work and leisure is symbolized powerfully in the changes to one of the former industrial centres of Glasgow, the

---

[4] Though 'malling' is not a term the Boys would use, I think it captures well the spirit of their activities; not least because the Boys would use the term 'mauling' to describe a beating in a play fight.

Parkhead Forge. The Forge was one of many large-scale hubs of industrial production that used to pattern the city of Glasgow. Employing over 20,000 at its peak in the early twentieth century, and covering a site of some 25 acres,[5] the Forge was integral to Glasgow's shipbuilding economy; forging steel and iron plates for the 'Clyde-built' shipyards of Govan. The Forge finally closed its gates in 1976; in effect closing the door to Glasgow's industrial past, leaving generations of skilled workers out in the cold. In a powerful piece of symbolism, as the City Council set about an aggressive strategy of neoliberal place marketing and regeneration (MacLeod 2002; Paton et al. 2012), the site reopened as the Forge Shopping Centre in the late 1980s. In both a physical and metaphoric sense, shopping was feted as a replacement for industry (Charlesworth 2000). The workers were no longer left out in the cold, but beckoned into the airless warmth of consumerism. As Spring notes:

> The Parkhead Forge is gone, the walls crumbling, the vast wooden shuttering demolished, the massive gates forever closed...today...on the site of the Parkhead Forge...is the Forge shopping centre, retaining the name and the industrial connotations from the original site...as if to buy a packet of cornflakes or dried prunes were social history in the making. (Spring 1990, p. 104)

In their search for edgework experiences, these new commercial spaces play a dual role for the Langview Boys—as centres for boredom relief through consumption, and as spaces bound by rules and constraints that can be subverted and played with. Commercial spaces are viewed in the same light as public spaces, but with an added edge of control, authority, and supervision in the form of surveillance and security. As Presdee argues: 'Young people, cut off from normal consumer power, invade the space of those with consumer power...the "space invaders" of the 1990s, lost in a world of dislocation and excitement; a space where they should not be' (Presdee 1994, p. 182).[6] As Gary and Mark describe:

---

[5] The Glasgow Story (undated). Available at: <http://www.theglasgowstory. com/image.php?inum=TGSA00847> [Accessed 25 June 2014].

[6] Though this was true for the Langview Boys, it is not necessarily true elsewhere. Hayward argues that Presdee's reading is in fact outdated—'the shopping mall now epitomises a world of conformity and mundanity' (Hayward 2004, p. 189), with

GARY: We aw got a chase in Princes Square [high-end shopping mall],
   we aw got a game ae hunt an that so we could get a chase aff the
   security guard.
AF: Did yous get a chase?
GARY: Naw, no really. They tried tae run, bit they jist did walkin.
WILLIE: See the couches? The couches you sit in. See Daz, he wis
   pushin Frankie oan wan ae they wee couches, an see they esca-
   lators, the wans that go doon, he pushed him oan that oan the
   couch. We wur aw laughin an that.

The Boys' discussed doing this kind of thing repeatedly, in a
number of different locations, but Princes Square is particularly
symbolic of the 'new Glasgow' that has little place for young people like the Langview Boys. Princes Square, in the city centre of
Glasgow, stands as a cogent example of the tensions involved in
the 'new Glasgow'. For Spring, Princes Square is the 'epitome of
Postmodern consumer culture' (1990, p. 59):

> The mall is not, of course, for practical shopping, but for recreation—
> shopping is a new culturally rich, leisure experience. Princes Square is
> characterised by its extravagance. Built from the skeleton of an old gal-
> leried warehouse, it has been adorned with mahogany and beech, brass,
> marble and glass, arranged in fanciful designs. (Spring 1990, p. 59)

Whilst it may be a stretch to present The Langview Boys' use of Princes
Square as a playground as a deliberate effort to subvert the 'new
Glasgow' that has marginalized their leisure, their behaviour
undoubtedly offers a striking example of the consequences of
changes in youth leisure over the past 40 years.

Cinema

Long-standing popular entertainments such as dance halls and
penny-theatres were popular throughout the nineteenth century
in Glasgow (Maver 2000, p. 101–4), and the twentieth century
saw the emergence of a vast network of localized cinemas.[7] While a

---

surveillance swamping non-conformity and subversion. Recently, online retail and
reorganization of suburban space has caused the closure of a large number of US
shopping malls. Journalists have been talking of the 'death of the American shopping mall'. See Guardian (2014): <http://www.theguardian.com/cities/2014/
jun/19/-sp-death-of-the-american-shopping-mall> [Accessed 25 June 2014].

[7] For a comprehensive database of traditional cinemas in Scotland, and the
stories of their closure, see <http://www.scottishcinemas.org.uk/>.

trip to the cinema remains a semi-regular activity in the Langview Boys' leisure lives, this no longer takes place locally—Langview once boasted several local cinemas—but in a trip to the same out-of-town shopping multiplex. Such complexes contain a wide range of commercialized entertainments concentrated in one spot, yet connected to the global flows of consumerism rather than the immediate locale; encapsulating the contemporary logic of consumption and boredom relief:

Boredom is one complaint the consumer world has no room for and the consumer culture has set out to eradicate it... To alleviate boredom one needs money—a great deal of money—if one wishes to stave off the spectre of boredom once and for all, to reach the state of happiness (Bauman 1998, p. 39).

For Bauman, relief from boredom to a 'state of happiness' is illusory—a fleeting experience—traded in during the moment of consumption. The logic of consumption thereby not only encourages, but actively creates boredom, while excluding many from attaining the leisure careers sold as antidotes.

Nonetheless, the approach of the Langview Boys to cinema-going suggests a resistance to this neoliberal logic, and an effort to recreate 'fir the buzz' excitement within these contexts. For example, the Boys 'sneaky in' to the cinemas, combining edgework with the re-appropriation of leisure space. In the following excerpt, the boys discuss an exciting chase scene, retold with requisite cinematic effect:

GARY: We got chased off the security this weekend
WILLIE: Aye, in the pictures [cinema], there wis aboot, at least twenty people chasing us or something cos we tried tae sneak in.
GARY: The other side started chasing us, she started radioing in and aw that. An see the fire exit...
WILLIE: What the workers use tae get intae the screen, tae go through the mad staff exit bit, that's whit we were walking through... when we go in the lift we huv tae cover up the mad security camera bit...

Importantly, as with their attendance at football matches, when the Boys talk of cinema-going, it is less the action on-screen that is of interest, but the action off-screen; throwing popcorn, dodging security, having a laugh. In a similar way to the experience at a football match, the sensation was of consumerism shot through with transgression. While the Boys demonstrated a rebellious attitude to these new sites of consumption, they also evinced a clear desire to revisit sites of leisure for previous generations. In the following discussion, the Langview Boys discuss revisiting an old, disused cinema in the area. Here, they recount one episode of breaking in, with Scooby Doo-like spookiness:

AF: Have you all been in there like?
MARK: Aye, we've aw been in
GARY: Aye
AF: What, just sneak in? Cos it's all shut up and that.
MARK: Aye, it's aw shut up
GARY: It's like a pure horror movie, man. Ye walk in with the torch, it's pure pitch black. Aw ye kin see is jist, yir, immediate path with yir torch.
MARK: Ye know that movie 'Most Haunted'? It's like that.
GARY: Ye cannae see any'hing. Like you're jist lookin aboot wi' the torch.

As the leisure landscape of post-industrial Glasgow has changed—with leisure opportunities increasingly delocalized, privatized and securitized—the Langview Boys re-create 'edgy' forms of entertainment wherever they are to be found. These can be broadly categorized into two areas: the creation of 'edgy' excitement in new leisure spaces, or revisiting/re-enacting leisure pastimes from previous generations. These continuities suggest a deeply entrenched leisure habitus that has not acceded to the post-industrial landscape of the 'new Glasgow'.

Gaming

As the findings of the Glasgow Youth Survey (2005) described earlier attest, a substantial portion of young people's leisure time is spent playing computer games, browsing or communicating via the internet, or using mobile phones. The comparison in this regard to leisure of the 1960s—or indeed the 1980s—could not be more striking. Technology has moved on apace—for many, reconfiguring the form and nature of interaction and identity. This reliance on consumer technology to relieve boredom has resulted in continual fads and fashions in technology and gaming; and an unquenchable desire for new and different forms of consumption. To take an example, on one occasion in LYP, I suggested to one 11-year-old that he played computer games while he waited his turn on the table-tennis table. To this, he expressed disgust—'who plays that anymair'—as the technology had since been updated.

Nonetheless, it is worth noting here that smartphone technology was relatively new during the period of fieldwork, and social media was restricted to 'Bebo' and 'Profileheaven', both relatively low-tech forerunners of sites like Facebook.

Of the photographs the Langview Boys took at home, as part of the discussion groups, the majority were taken in bedrooms—televisions, computer games, and football posters featured prominently—away from adult supervision and control. The opportunities available in 'bedroom leisure' have altered fundamentally in the last two decades, with televisions, DVD players, computer games consoles, and stereos proliferating to an unprecedented degree. Computer gaming makes up a significant portion of some of the Langview Boys' leisure time—as the following fieldnote, from a chat with Gary, reveals:

Asked Gary how long he spends playing the computer each day, and he was very precise in his reply: 'Ah get in fae school aboot 4, and play computer til aboot 6, then come tae LYP til half 8, then go hame an play again til aboot 12. So Ah guess aboot 5 hours a day'. (Fieldnote, 27 January 2009)

In some ways, these technologies were used to facilitate 'old' forms of interaction and bullying. A number of young people I spoke with talked about 'getting a slagging on Bebo' (a social networking website)—having vicious insults posted on their public profile. In one case, a 12-year-old from LYP had been getting regular 'slaggings' on Bebo from a specific individual. Similarly, young people have been quick to capitalize upon the possibilities and opportunities of new technologies—particularly mobile phones and social networking websites—to communicate in new social spaces.[8] As Daz mentions:

DAZ: See all the casuals [football hooligans]? Ah've goat them oan ma Bebo. Aw the fitbaw casuals.
AF: What, you've got them as you're friends?
DAZ: Ah've everybody. Casuals. Aw them.

---

[8] Despite the evident extension of processes of self-presentation and imagined selfhood into their online lives, police have increasingly used these images, videos, and information to construct young people as gang members, resulting in enforcement activities against suspected gang members (Fraser and Atkinson 2014).

In a similar way, computer gaming, both individually and collectively, has become increasingly integrated into the daily physical lives and interactions of the Langview Boys. Gaming has become a spectator sport in LYP, with up to 10 boys watching the action, mesmerized:

Daz sits, staring smugly at the playback of Pro-Evolution Soccer 6 on the Playstation II, switching the angles and zooming in to see the ball flying into the net from the best possible vantage point. In the usual run of things, this kind of gloating replay is actively discouraged by both participants and spectators; distracting and time-consuming as they are for all. There being limited time for all to play, there is a democratic expectation that time will not be wasted. In this instance, however, the goal was unusually spectacular, and the unwritten rules allow for some degree of gloating. 'Who's yir da?' he shouts at James. (Fieldnote, 7 August 2009)

But for young people in Langview, new technology does not necessarily mean new lifestyle. In a landscape whereby group interaction in physical space is increasingly difficult and contested, and options for affordable and enjoyable group leisure are few and far between, new technologies are increasingly used to foster traditional forms of individual and group identity.

During the period of fieldwork, social networking sites, mobile phones, and instant messaging represented new ways of maintaining contact with friends, and were used in much the same way as physical interaction. A vivid example of this trend came from a conversation about computer gaming with Gary:

Gary talked tonight about the games he normally played—war games, and football games—and in particular about the X-Box 360, which allows players (with an internet connection) to play one another. He said that he often spent evenings in his own house, playing with up to 10 of his friends, all in their own houses, either on the same team or against one another. Friendships are still localised, but they are conducted remotely. (Fieldnote, 27 January 2009)

The continuities between past and present could not be more striking. Purged of space to play eleven-a-side football, harangued by the police for inhabiting the gentrified spaces of the 'new Glasgow', tracked on the streets with CCTV, the Boys nevertheless find ways of recreating collective leisure. This is a powerful demonstration of the cultural continuities that constitute the heart of the Langview Boys' leisure activities; of habits reproduced and recreated in new economic contexts.

Youth, work, and leisure in the 'new Glasgow'

Changes in the youth labour market over the past three decades have resulted in a decline in predictable school-to-work transitions for young people across Europe, with a stable manufacturing and construction industry giving way to more insecure and precarious employment in the service industry (MacDonald and Marsh 2005; Furlong and Cartmel 2007). As the labour market has seen an increasing demand for educated workers, however, so the youth labour market has become increasingly hostile for those left behind by demand for higher education. For many across Europe, school-to-work transitions are marked by casual, part-time, or temporary employment (Quintini et al. 2007; Furlong and Cartmel 2004), with these problems disproportionately impacting on those with fewer educational qualifications. Jones, summarizing a diverse range of contemporary research on youth transitions, concludes that 'young people are becoming more and more sharply divided, between those who have and those who have not' (Jones 2002, p. vi).

These large-scale reorientations in the labour market over the course of the twentieth century have been matched, of course, with rapid shifts in the field of leisure. Where leisure was once conceived as the antidote to work—a period of structured release to refresh the worker for the next day's toil—the balance has shifted in the opposite direction, with work viewed instrumentally as a way of attaining funds for leisure (Winlow and Hall 2006). As Rojek notes, 'most workers relate to paid labour as the means to finance leisure activities rather than the means to forge self worth, distinction and the pursuit of power' (Rojek 2005, p. 315). This shift has seen UK leisure spending increase 'five-fold in real terms since the 1950s; that is, at more than three times the rate of the overall growth in spending' (Roberts 2012, p. 332). As work for young people has become increasingly precarious and casual (Cumbers et al. 2009), so leisure has delocalized, commercialized, and privatized, creating a fragmented archipelago of leisure options for young people.

Young people in Langview do not enjoy the certainty of labour in the large steel-works and production plants that once dominated the city's skyline. While Jephcott could state with confidence, in 1967, that 'the great majority [of young people] make the vital transition from school-to-work at 15' (Jephcott 1967, p. 3), young people are no longer 'getting on' with the skills and opportunities they have; rather, they are simply 'getting by' (MacDonald et al. 2005, p. 884). Glasgow has the highest rates of youth unemployment in Scotland, and some of the highest number of young people 'not in employment, education or training' in the UK (Hudson et al. 2012). In this context, in a very real sense, leisure has replaced labour as a defining feature of young people's future life trajectories. As Cumbers et al. found in a study of youth employment in Glasgow, though 'the transition to a more service-based economy has resulted in new jobs, the quality of employment and training offered to young people in the contemporary economy is generally of a much lower quality—in terms of pay, job security and job satisfaction—than those lost in traditional manufacturing activities' (Cumbers et al. 2009, p. 2). Similarly, a study I undertook of young adults' work trajectories in Langview (Fraser 2009) found the types of work available to them to be unsatisfying and unfulfilling, but found it difficult to break the cycle owing to money constraints. Jennifer, for example, spoke with fatalism of her job prospects:

sometimes you just think, because of where I stay [live/come from], I'm not going to get there so there's no point in even trying sometimes, so you just go into a job to get money. When you've not got a job, it's hard to expect people to go and get good careers when they've not got much when they're not working, and how can you expect people to go out and look for a good career and they struggle for a couple of years before they get the reward for it. And I just think, no wonder people go into jobs they don't really like, just because they need the money because they can't survive.

The resignation shown by Jennifer reflects a broader sense of aspirations limited by economic realities; of ambitions clipped by experience. A survey of young people in Glasgow revealed that while 86 per cent of respondents 'want to earn a lot of money', only 36 per cent actually expected it to happen (MORI Scotland 2003).

The limiting of ambition in evidence here speaks to Bourdieu's concept of doxa. Doxa is the outer limits of habitus—the 'world we know'. Forces of inequality, domination, and exploitation can become, over time, embedded and acculturated in such a way that they are no longer recognized as such. In this way, systems of inequality are reproduced, in a process Bourdieu terms *symbolic violence*, which is 'exercised upon a social agent with his or her complicity' (Bourdieu and Wacquant 1992, p. 167). In Bourdieu's terms, through this process the world as we know it becomes 'misrecognized' as the way the world must be, and our behaviours (or habitus) aligned to reflect this status quo. Doxa is therefore 'the coincidence of the objective structures and the internalized structures which provides the illusion of immediate understanding, characteristic of practical experience of the familiar universe, and which at the same time excludes from that experience any inquiry as to its own conditions of possibility' (Bourdieu 1990, p. 20). This conceptualization indicates the cultural patterns through which structural marginality are reproduced.

In this context, a range of scholars have argued that consumerism has stepped in to fill the void left by work. For Young, those most excluded economically are simultaneously the most included in consumer culture—swallowed up by consumption, but vomited back by the economy in a process of 'social bulimia': '[t]hey are barred from the racetrack of the meritocratic society yet remain glued to the television sets and media which alluringly portray the glittering prizes of a wealthy society' (J. Young 1999, p. 12). In this anomic cultural context, young people marginalized from the world of work seek out transgressive means of attaining self-actualization:

What we are witnessing today is a crisis of being in a society where self-fulfilment, expression and immediacy are paramount values, yet the possibilities of realising such dreams are strictly curtailed by the increasing bureaucratisation of work (its so-called McDonaldization) and the commodification of leisure. Crime and transgression in this new context can be seen as the breaking through of restraints, a realisation of immediacy and a reassertion of identity and ontology. (Hayward and Young 2004, p. 267)

Structural shifts in Glasgow's economy, shaped by the vicissitudes of the global market, have had profound impacts on young people's work opportunities, and leisure habits. As predictable school-to-work transitions have evaporated, consumerism has filled the void; for many, leisure has replaced work as a defining feature of identity. In this context, traditional, street-based leisure is increasingly giving way to new forms of sociability—facilitated by social media, the internet, and mobile technology. Nonetheless, there are significant continuities as well as changes. Under these circumstances, habitus is 'potentially subject to modification...this occurs when explanations of a habitus no longer make sense' (Webb et al. 2002, p. 41). The responses of young people in Langview to alterations to work and leisure, however, indicate only minor modifications—adapting to the new conditions under the old rules of habitus.

'Learning to leisure'

Classic studies from the Birmingham School demonstrated the cultural means through which structures of power, domination and inequality were reproduced. Paul Willis, for example, detailed the ways in which strategies of resistance amongst working-class 'lads'—from systems of authority, and middle-class 'ear'oles' [snobs]—prepared them for the manual shop-floor culture they were soon to enter (Willis 1977). An important component of this rebellious attitude was a constant search for excitement—anarchistic breaks from monotony were minor victories that were experienced as liberation. One of the lads, Joey, answers the question of 'what is the opposite of boredom?' with the following: 'Excitement... Defying the law, breaking the law like, drinking like' (Willis 1977, pp. 33–4). For Joey, deviance acted as a way of reclaiming determination in a cultural environment experienced as repressive. Rather than liberating, however, these activities reproduced hierarchical class-cultures. Paul Corrigan, in *Schooling the Smash Street Kids* (1979), describes a similar phenomenon. The 'Smash Street Kids', a group of working class boys in Sunderland, discuss the 'weird ideas' that emerge from the 'talking, joking and carrying on' which constitute 'doing nothing' (Corrigan 1979, pp. 103–4):

> Do you ever go out and knock around with the lads?
> ALBERT: Sometimes when I feel like it.
> What do you do?
> ALBERT: Sometimes we get into mischief.
> Mischief?
> ALBERT: Well somebody gets a weird idea into their head, and they start to carry it out, and others join in.
> Weird idea?
> ALBERT: Things... like going around smashing milk bottles.

For Corrigan, 'weird ideas are then are born out of boredom and the expectation of future and continuing boredom... a good idea must contain the seeds of continuing change as well as excitement and involvement' (Corrigan 1979, p. 104). The double-bind of these transgressive acts, however, are the ways in which they serve to reproduce systems of structural inequality and powerlessness. For Willis, the rebellious humour and class-based antagonisms of the high school translate into a clear demarcation between the 'lads' and the 'ear'oles' in the workplace. The lads wound up in physically demanding and poorly remunerated manual work, while the ear'oles were carried forward into senior management in the same factories. The class-based subculture that the lads formed in school, for Willis, prepared them for this socioeconomic division of labour—detailing, in cultural terms, 'how working class kids get working-class jobs' (Willis 1977). As Chambliss (1973/2011) found in relation to the 'Saints' and the 'Roughnecks', privileged youngsters frequently act out similar forms of transgression, but have accumulated greater cultural capital with which to escape censure.

The rebellious attitude to boredom (Conrad 1997; Barbalet 1999) that the Langview Boys demonstrate echoes a similar attitude to that found among the 'lads' in Willis' and Corrigan's earlier studies. Seemingly insignificant events acquired disproportionate importance, and seemingly meaningless activity found justification. The Langview Boys' 'weird ideas' involved, for example, throwing eggs at passers-by from a hidden space near the main street, or pushing a shopping trolley to the top of the hill, and taking turns to ride it at breakneck speed towards the main road. Similarly, the names of the Langview Boys are everywhere in Langview—on abandoned walls, street signs, paths, bins, and railings—but it is not a planned or coordinated activity; more a 'weird idea' that emerges in the moment. James, for example, spoke about how he sprayed his name all over the area "cos Ah'm crazy'.

The edgework that forms the substance of the boys' group behaviour translates to a constant testing of the norms, rules, and procedures of LYP, resulting in a perpetual cycle of exclusions and re-entry. In the following example, the football pitch had been closed for refurbishment and was out-of-bounds—as the testing of the boundaries of project rules gave way to group enmity towards the project:

A vicious circle began whereby every time someone was caught they were excluded for another week—some of them for up to four weeks. As a knock-on effect, the punishment value of excluding them from the project lost its weight, and they collectively turned to give a 'fuck you' to the project; egging one another on to sneak in, having competitions to see who could get barred for the longest, knocking on windows and doors and running away, throwing rubbish over the fence, and eventually throwing stones at the project; all of this while continually sneaking in. The end result of this was the exclusion of 16 boys. (Fieldnote, 25 November 2008)

This form of edgework was also a core aspect of younger boys' behaviour in the project, particularly when the older boys were present. These in-group processes of interaction and domination are without doubt heightened in dealings outwith the group—the ability to manipulate the 'younger ones' was a feather in the cap of the Langview Boys. For 'younger ones' with little status amongst their peers, the esteem for the 'older ones' is amplified greatly, creating opportunities for exploitation. The boys frequently monopolized their chosen activities—table tennis, football, computer games—leaving younger groups to fight for participation. This is one means through which leisure habits are reproduced:

The park is quiet tonight; the ghost of the exclusions continues to hang quietly in the background. Though some of the older boys drift in and out of the project in bunches, they do not stay. The younger boys have begun to realise their new-found freedom; they can rule the roost. As a result, the younger group act up, shouting and running and carrying on beyond the bounds of the norm. This, in turn, allows younger groups access to table tennis and pool; items previously monopolised by the oldest group. (Fieldnote, 1 December 2008)

In the temporary vacuum left by the Langview Boys' absence, younger groups took advantage of the new-found space; their competitions and rivalries, however, closely mimicked the Boys' themselves.

In this context, the continuities in the Langview Boy's leisure habits represent a cultural response to structural marginalization; a way of maintaining a sense of self in the face of alterations to the social environment, reproduced through age hierarchies among predominantly street-based youth. However, the rebellious attitude taken by the Langview Boys to leisure spaces—engaging in 'fir the buzz' activities that subvert the hegemonic form of structured consumption—had the effect of creating a collective identity that conflicted with the new economic landscape. What felt like creative rebellion in fact resulted in further marginalization. Unlike Willis' lads, however, they are not preparing for the shop-floor, but for an uncertain post-industrial landscape in which consumption has replaced work as a fundamental source of identity.

Elsewhere, this commingling of global consumerism and post-industrialism has created a toxic blend of individualism and violence among young adults in other post-industrial cities

(Winlow and Hall 2006; Hall et al. 2008). The Langview Boys, however—not yet entrants into the night-time economy of city-centre bars and clubbing—evinced a clear-cut desire for localized, group-based leisure rather than atomized hedonism.

Conclusion

This chapter described and analysed the leisure habits of children and young people in Langview, focusing on the Langview Boys as a microcosm of these experiences. As a result of spatial immobility, constraint and repetition, boredom is a constant threat. To counteract boredom, the boys seek creative excitement in various 'fir the buzz' activities—pushing the boundaries of rules, acceptable behaviour, and laws to reclaim identity and control in each environment. Despite alterations in the cultural, social, and economic landscape in Langview and Glasgow, however, these leisure habits exhibit some similarities with previous generations. Though processes of globalization have reshaped leisure opportunities for young people in Langview, the effect of these alterations has not been as profound as could be expected. On one hand, these processes have further limited the leisure spaces available to children and young people, resulting in more time spent in public space, and the corresponding continuation of young people's street habitus. On the other, commercial leisure has come to occupy a prominent place, resulting in the transplanting of the street habitus to commercial venues and virtual worlds.

The continuities in evidence between the Langview Boys leisure lives and that of previous generations suggest that the Boys' *street habitus* is deeply cast and resistant to short-term alteration, despite alterations to the leisure fields in Glasgow. The rebellious attitude the Boys embodied in their leisure activities—not dissimilar from the subcultural rebellions of 'the lads' in Willis' (1977) study of Hammertown—privileges group-based excitement and boredom relief. In this context, gang fights emerge as a free source of excitement that 'fit' with the leisure habits of the past. Nonetheless, while the 'lads' in Willis' study were 'learning to labour', the jobs that were once available to young people in Glasgow have become increasingly precarious and casual; creating an uncertain economic future for the Boys. In this context, though they may be 'learning to leisure', there are fundamental challenges to traditional models of masculinities that they must confront.

7

Damaged Hardmen

MICHAEL: You want tae make a name for yourself. Ye don't want
tae be jist anyb'dae. Ye don't jist want tae be wan ae these faces in
a crowd.
ROBERT: It's aw about reputation. Aw gang fighting. There's nothing
in it anyway, except for reputation. Jist so some people will say
'he's crazy' an that.

Like many other post-industrial cities, Glasgow's economy has
reconfigured away from traditional industries of manufacture and
ship-building towards a service economy based on tourism, leisure, and retail, from a reputation as an industrial powerhouse
to that of being the call centre capital of Europe. Despite these
shifts, however, most of the Langview Boys still wanted to work
in labouring jobs. Apprenticeships in trades were sought after and
work in construction much prized. Such jobs, however, have by
and large disappeared. Discussing this issue, the comments of
a local councillor on a BBC documentary[1] are emblematic: 'It's
unfortunate, but under this climate, there's a lot of people can't get
jobs on building sites... we've got to try and convince them there
are opportunities, maybe in call centres, retail, leisure, where there
is growth'. This has posed clear questions to traditional models of
industrial masculinity in Glasgow. As Connell asks, under 'such
conditions, what happens to the making of masculinity?' (1995,
p. 94). One answer, for young men in Langview, was to reach back
towards traditional 'hardman' masculine identities. In a precarious economic environment, as Michael and Robert discuss, this is
a route to status that avoids individuals being 'jist another face in
a crowd'.

---

[1] BBC (2010) *Revealed: Glasgow's Gang Wars.*

While fieldwork stopped before their full entry into the labour market, I could see the Langview Boys beginning to wrestle with this conflict between the local, street-based culture they had grown up with and the vicissitudes of a precarious work environment in the post-industrial city. This disjuncture will inevitably have an impact on their sense of self. As Bourdieu notes, 'where dispositions encounter conditions (including fields) different from those in which they were constructed and assembled, there is a *dialectical confrontation* between habitus, as structured structure, and objective structures' (Bourdieu 2005, p. 46). Such a confrontation can result in adaptation to reconfigured field conditions, drawing on available forms of capital in order to make a living in the new economic environment. As Winlow (2001) has documented, some working-class men in post-industrial Sunderland have made 'hardman' capital profitable in the night-time economy of drugs and private security. For others, however, this confrontation will be experienced as a rejection, with individuals' finding themselves increasingly excluded, frustrated, and marginalized. In this context, gang identity represents a root of, and route to, masculinity in an uncertain economic environment. As Nayak notes:

In a culture where the supposedly 'feminized' attributes of 'deference and docility'...are in demand, it would appear that certain white working-class males may be out of step...Post-industrial masculinities must now adapt, risk unemployment or, as we shall find, indulge in underground activity and criminal hyper-masculine displays...(Nayak 2006, p. 817)

In this chapter, I explore the 'making of masculinity' among the Langview Boys, examining the patterns through which local cultures of machismo are learned and embedded. The first section elaborates the five key attributes of masculinity among the Langview Boys which structure social relations within the group and form a core strut in the formation of a masculine habitus. For the Boys, street masculinity operates in a relational context in which certain forms of masculinity are prized while others are derided. The second section examines the conflict between this habitus and the new economic environment of post-industrial Glasgow examining the continuities and changes caused by a 'tormented habitus'.

Locating street masculinities

As Bourdieu has argued, 'masculinity is stitched into the habitus' (Bourdieu 1997, p. 199); habitus is both 'gendered and gendering' (Behnke and Meuser 2001, p. 155). In the process of socialization through which habitus is formed, gendered attitudes and beliefs are also imprinted, forming a 'layer of embodied experience that is not immediately amenable to self-fashioning' (Thorpe 2010, p. 194). This preconscious aspect of a gendered habitus has been cited as a key factor in the reproduction of male violence. As Baird (2012, p. 32) notes, 'masculine *habitus* helps explain the...intergenerational transmission of masculine comportment' that underpins male violence. Nonetheless, while there are clear homologies of habitus between street masculinities in diverse geographical contexts—from Philadelphia (Bourgois 1996) to Oslo (Sandberg and Pederson 2011), Central America (Brenneman 2012) to Dublin (Ilan 2013)—it is important to recognize that certain forms of masculinity are locally constituted by unique configurations of history, culture, and gendered relations. Local cultures of machismo intersect with global processes of economic and socio-spatial exclusion. As Connell and Messerschmidt (2005, p. 836) argue:

[m]asculinity is not a fixed entity embedded in the body of personality of individuals. Masculinities are configurations of practice that are accomplished in social action and, therefore, can differ according to the gender relations in a particular social setting.

As such, it is necessary to understand the formation and reproduction of masculinities at a local level.

In this section, I examine five 'ways of being' for the Langview Boys—being a 'gemmie', taking a slagging, being 'best at stuff', being 'in the know', and being 'wan ae the boays'—that represent a localized form of street masculinity. These masculinities are premised on perpetual, group-based tussles over status and reputation, and efforts to gain, or regain, a higher place in the pecking order. Together, they represent the 'homosocial dimension of the male habitus' (Streicher 2011, p. 24) in which fighting, competition, and hierarchy are instrumental in the development of masculine identity. While these 'fratriarchal masculinities' (Thorpe 2010) create a route to status among the group, however, they also create inherent precariousness deeply instilling a street-based formation of masculinity that allows little space for difference.[2]

Being a 'gemmie'

AF: So there's always one person you respect more than everyone else.

DAZ: Aye. Gemmer, bolder.

AF: What's does a gemmie mean?

DAZ: You wouldnae run.

KEV: Jist someb'dae ye wouldnae mess wi'. See in every scheme, there's always wan.

JAMES: In every single scheme, there's always wan person who everyb'dae 'hinks is the gemmiest an aw that.

As Kev, Daz, and James discuss, in every area there was one individual who they respected and feared above all others, a local legend who epitomized and embodied the masculine 'ways of being' in the area. Being a 'gemmie' referred to an attitude of fearlessness, of violent defiance, and of fighting your corner against all odds, an ability to hold one's own in every situation, a form of symbolic or 'street' (Sandberg 2008; Ilan 2013) capital that denotes a street-wise disposition. Although none of the Langview Boys laid claim to being 'the gemmiest' in Langview, many of the tussles for status described in the previous chapter can be read in these terms, as the constant creation of new, risky challenges in which the boys could assert their 'hardman' credentials. For the Boys, there was a recognition that physical conflict was necessary in retaining 'face' in encounters of differential status.[3]

---

[2] These aspects of group life are similar to Miller's (1958) 'focal concerns' of young men in a working-class community in the US—trouble, toughness, smartness, excitement, fate, and autonomy. However, where Miller posits these attributes as particular to the anachronistic 'lower-class culture', I emphasize their embeddedness in the history and culture of Glasgow more generally (for further discussion see Hagedorn 1998a). In a recent study, for example, the Glasgow police force were 'still dominated by a persistent and hegemonic "cop culture"' (Fraser and Atkinson 2014, p. 155) that was not too dissimilar from these 'ways of being'. For a re-evaluation of Miller's 'focal concerns' theory in the light of female gang members, see Brotherton (1996).

[3] This dynamic was not confined to young men, but has direct parallels with Batchelor's (2007, p. 180) research with incarcerated females, in which 'the young women expressed the importance of being *seen* to "stand up for yourself", repeating the mantra: "Better a sair face than a red face"'.

WILLIE: See like Kev and Daz, they'd do us [beat us up in a fight]. But we still wouldnae back doon. Ah'd rather take a doin.

MARK: Cos if you know someb'dae's gonnae batter ye, ye jist need tae try an fight back....

GARY: ... defend yirsel...

MARK: ... cos ye cannae jist sit there....

GARY: Aye see if ye jist sit there, you're gonnae get an even worser doin than ye would before. Ye have tae stand up for yourself.

For Willie, Mark, and Gary, despite being smaller in size, 'being a gemmie' required a physical response to threats, fighting back against attacks to prevent future threats. Importantly, this is also an attitude of defiance. 'Being a gemmie' doesn't require physical size or strength but instead demands bravura and willingness to take on a challenge. In the following fieldnote, for example, the game 'hardest nut' creates a space in which the strongest male gained status, despite being smaller in size.

Tonight, the boys were playing a game of 'hardest nut'—simply, going forehead to forehead, like rutting stags, and pushing until one backed down. The best at it shouted it from the roof-tops, particularly as his diminutive stature rendered him generally less able in other situations. (Fieldnote, 15 May 2007)

This form of 'gemmie' masculinity runs deep in Glasgow's history. William McIlvanney, summarizing this embeddedness, argues that 'standing up for yourself, sometimes against improbable odds, became a Glaswegian convention' (McIlvanney 1987, p. 18). The 'gemmie' sensibilities of the Langview Boys, therefore, must be understood in the context of the historical pattern of masculinity in working-class communities in Glasgow.

Johnston and McIvor (2004), in their study of risk and masculinities in Glasgow's mining communities, uncovered a similar culture of 'gemmie' risk taking in both work and leisure. Through oral history interviews with miners, the authors reveal a competitive environment in which young men were desensitized to danger. Young boys would play risky games, such as the 'big sui', jumping gaps between wash-houses in the back of tenement flats. In this context, 'actual bodily harm was risked for the sake of peer group status' in a pattern that was shown to have real and lasting physical impacts on individual health (Johnston and McIvor 2004, p. 2). This same attitude to risk and reputation is also evident in Patrick's study of youth gang violence in 1960s Maryhill. Patrick describes a 'gemmie' as embodying a 'devil-may-care' attitude to risk and danger, particularly in the form of violence (Patrick 1973, p. 189). For the participants in Patrick's study, a 'gemmie' was 'someone who is prepared to fight, whatever the odds, even if defeat or physical punishment is inevitable' (Patrick 1973, p. 85).

Where this form of risk taking and competitive masculinity once prepared young men for industrial labour, these connections have increasingly evaporated. As Cumbers and colleagues found: 'the erosion of traditional skilled forms of manual work and the rise of different types of work—based on "soft" skills is posing a number of challenges for particular social groups, especially young men, for whom the pathways into skilled manual labour have all but disappeared' (Cumbers et al. 2009, p. 4). In this sense, the continuation of old-world models of masculinity are explicable as reconstructions of a deeply cast habituation. The continuity of gangs in Glasgow, therefore, should be read in part through the lens of reproductive cultures of machismo, in which 'being a gemmie' represents a central means through which masculinity is attained.

Taking a slagging

Taking (and giving) a 'slagging' is basically the means of gaining verbal one-upmanship in any social encounter—either through insults, or verbal manipulation—and operates as a means of effecting both group solidarity and individual distinction. Humour is quintessentially a group activity, deriving its nature and form from shared social meaning (Zijderveld 1983, p. 3). Humorous verbal sparring, on one level, involves a strong sense of group cohesion (Sanders 2004). Repeated reference to common insults—the size of Gary's nose, James being overweight, someone's mum being seen as attractive—draw a laugh from all those present. Like the factory workers described by Collinson, there is an unmistakable sense that the ability to 'take a slagging' is a key component in the masculine camaraderie that characterizes the group. Being able to 'take a slagging' marks out an individual as worthy of some respect: 'only "real men" would be able to laugh at themselves by accepting highly insulting nicknames' (Collinson 1988, p. 185). On another level, however, these episodes represented a constant source of potential shame and embarrassment for the group.

While gender can be viewed as a temporally fluid and contextually flexible set of performances—shaping and reshaping according to different circumstances—these forms of practice occur in the context of a hierarchy of gendered relations (Connell 2002). Masculinities are relational, occurring in the context of a hierarchical field of gendered activity in which some attributes are prized while others are derided: 'the relationships are constructed through practices that exclude and include, that intimidate and exploit, and so on' (Connell 1995, p. 37). 'The patter' among the boys defines and regulates the edges of normative malehood by deriding those who embody subordinated types of masculinity (Bourdieu 2001, p. 24), leaving little space for alternative constructions.

In many ways, 'slagging' plays a similar role to what Matza refers to as 'sounding', 'a probing of one's depth, taking the form of insult' (Matza 1964, p. 53). The metaphor of 'sounding' is particularly apt with regard to the Langview Boys, as many of the insults are retracted as soon as proffered. The device most commonly used to achieve this goal is that of veiled humour. Frequently, a barbed remark or comment will be followed by the phrase 'kiddin oan' (meaning 'only joking'), thereby testing the edge of what is acceptable to say without fear of reprisal. This, too, is done knowingly. In one discussion group, asked about the constant stream of insults, Gary replied that 'we jist say these things tae each other, we dinnae take it tae heart'. The constant stream of insult and retraction induces cohesion, as there is tacit group agreement of 'acceptable standards' of trading insults, the minimum level of conduct discussed below as part of being 'wan ae the boays'. As Gabriel notes, 'this may lead to a continuous state of insult-trading which may be contained within certain parameters (as with football crowds)' (Gabriel 1998, p. 1347).

This fusion of masculinity, humour, and 'patter' has formed an important element in Glasgow's history. This repartee is part of the broader Glaswegian culture of comic 'banter' and verbal quickfire that nurtured the talents of comedians like Billy Connolly. McIlvanney has described it as a unique cultural formation that has emerged from the economic circumstances of Glasgow: 'an old Glaswegian art form: the transformation of your circumstances with humour and pride' (McIlvanney 1987, p. 20). As Johnston and McIvor note, however, this humour can also have a protective function—young men working in Glasgow's former industries were socialized into a macho pecking order involving black humour (Johnston and McIvor 2004) that discouraged workers from being seen to take risk seriously. Nonetheless, it is an unforgiving verbal culture that creates a constant precariousness with regard to status.

Within the Langview Boys' group, those with higher status frequently pick on those with lesser standing, creating a powerful tension within the group as tempers fray and snap in turn. As a consequence, there was often a very fine line between insult and joke, play and violence, resulting in a constant need to reaffirm masculine identity, and a constant edge to playful banter (Collinson 1988, p. 19). 'Slagging' acted as a test for non-group members but also as a cruel tool of oppression for those not in the group. As Gabriel argues, 'some insults can be read as *tests* ... establishing inclusion and exclusion, or classification rites establishing status and power hierarchies or tests of loyalty, establishing coalitions and alliances' (Gabriel 1998, p. 1349).

Joke, insult, play, and violence are therefore finely graded and balanced precariously in group interaction. While jokes create group solidarity and construct group cohesion, the potential for violence is ever present. In Collinson's study of factory humour, even some of its most ardent adherents were emotionally wounded: 'joking was often misinterpreted... the result was that its victim would "snap"' (Collinson 1988, p. 193). In the following fieldnote, precisely such a 'snapping' is in evidence, as a pattern of insult results in a violent encounter between two of the Langview Boys.

As I was walking back into the room, Tommy was punching Connor full in the face. I took both of them out of the room and sat them down separately, and spoke to them about what had happened. I had heard some murmurings of this earlier, but essentially the night before Tommy had been round at one of the other boy's houses playing the computer, and had embarrassed himself. He had been getting mocked mercilessly for the previous 24 hours, and had eventually just snapped, and lashed out at whoever was nearest; which turned out to be Connor. Daz and the others had also, however, been goading Connor into fighting with Tommy for a while—Connor is taller than most of the boys, but two years younger than the oldest, and gets manipulated by some of the older ones. So the punch was between two boys towards the bottom of the group pecking order; in essence fighting for who was at the bottom. (Fieldnote, 22 April 2008)

The relational nature of violence in this context exposes the pecking orders within the group in which those at the top can peck, but not be pecked (Phillips 2003; Mullins 2006). While the ability both to 'give' and 'take' a slagging was part of this group dynamic, the equilibrium was constantly oscillating and frequently shifting according to the context in which the Boys found themselves. In each new environment, the Boys created new ways of proving their individual worth.

Being 'the best at stuff'

Being 'the best at stuff' refers to the ability to turn your hand to any and every sport, activity, or game that you are presented with: there is little or no desire to *learn* to be good at a sport, but rather the ideal is to be *instantly* good at something. Raw athleticism and natural talent—effortless skill and unblinking competence—are therefore the most likely attributes to gain status. As with the hierarchies of knowledge mentioned below, the sports and activities most highly prized are those which accord most closely with a local masculine habitus. In this context, football—representing as it does toughness, aggression, loyalty, and distinction—is a crucial arena. Like the boys in Epstein and colleagues' study, football and fighting represent a central axis around which status and masculinity cohere.

For these boys, being a 'real man' is established through their prowess in both activities [football and fighting], and they gain popularity and status both with other boys and with girls through them. Football and fighting become a measure of success as boys/men and a more important achievement than academic success, while relative failure or lack of interest in them becomes a marker of stigmatized effeminacy. (Epstein et al. 2001, p. 159)

These ways of being a 'real man'—being strong, skillful, effortless—are embodied on the football pitch, and the boys' ability on the football pitch is important to the overall pecking order within the group. As with Whyte's analysis of the Norton's and bowling, in which the highest status members were also those that were most proficient (Whyte 1943), those with highest status among the Langview Boys were frequently those that were most proficient at football. Those with lower status receive passes on the football pitch less frequently, and those with higher status more. The status games and regulation of masculinity that occur on the football pitch thus also play a crucial role in the learning and enactment of the physical means of 'being a man'.

The football pitch also operates as a key social arena for the learning and enactment of masculinity for groups of younger males. The football pitch in LYP was dominated by the Langview Boys, requiring younger boys who wished to play to 'measure up' against the rough physicality and verbal insults which inhered in the Boys' play (Eveslage and Delaney 1998). While games could, if well managed, result in the challenging of age and gender hierarchies, these balances were often precarious.

Four of the Langview Boys challenged the younger ones (about 18 of them) to a game; this both sides relished. The older ones got a chance to show off, and the younger ones got a chance to vent their frustrations at being younger and smaller. Tempers were running high, and the younger ones began venting their pent-up frustration at being younger, smaller, and picked-on by taking wee digs at the older ones. The boldest among them starting cursing them, and putting in aggressive tackles; the older ones stopped putting up with it, and started hitting them back with insults and physical challenges. The end result of this was the boy being upended on the floor, cursing like a trooper. I asked him to calm down—his first response was 'Nae fucking wonder, he fucking snapped me'. After discussing it indoors with Boab, it became clear that the whole incident is reflective of the frequent injustices levelled on the younger group by the older ones. In a situation whereby there was strength in numbers, they felt empowered to seek retribution. (Fieldnote, 3 June 2008)

In this way, these configurations of masculinity are learned and enacted by younger males, demonstrating the means through which patterns of masculinity continue through time.

Those who are less skillful at football—both younger and older—constantly challenge the rest of the group by presenting new arenas for becoming the 'best at stuff'—table tennis, pool, computer games—requiring higher-status individuals to constantly assert and reassert their masculine dominance in each of these games. This perpetual one-upmanship results in a pressure to perform, and continually pushes at the boundaries of risk and status. Within this dynamic, however, there was a common standard of skill in all activities; the contest was not for competence, however, but for *distinction*. In this context, much of the physical interaction between the boys consists of 'play fighting'. These contests of masculinity and domination include play fights, wrestling, and other 'body reflexive practices' (Connell 1995, quoted in Epstein et al. 2001, p. 168), in which being 'the best at stuff' is reduced to basic strength and aggression: '[s]ymbolic exchanges fusing violence with play' (Kehily and Nayak 1997, p. 72).

This form of contact—friendly exchanges, within the boundaries of acceptable masculine conduct—can be viewed as a culturally acceptable means of contact, but also as a means of distinguishing and solidifying status hierarchies and masculinity (Back 1996, p. 78).[4] As Bourdieu argues, however, this constant tussle creates inherent tensions and anxieties:

> a 'real' man is someone who feels the need to rise to the challenge of the opportunities available to him to increase his honour by pursuing glory and distinction in the public sphere. Exaltation of masculine values has its dark negative side in the fears and anxieties aroused by femininity...Everything thus combines to make the impossible ideal of virility the source of an immense vulnerability. It is this vulnerability which paradoxically leads to sometimes frantic investment in all the masculine games of violence, such as sports in modern societies. (Bourdieu 2001, p. 51)

Having status in the group, be it through physical gameness, verbal skill, or athletic competence, was a constant struggle.[5] Through this struggle, however, a distinctive masculine habitus became imprinted in which certain behaviours are simply not tolerated, creating a perpetual set of fears and anxieties, and continual efforts to reassert masculinities in different ways.

Being 'in the know'

While formal education was not valued, street wisdom was highly prized. Any information that had a direct, or indirect, bearing on the Langview Boys was highly desirable. Once gained, it was held close, and delivered back to the group for maximum kudos;

---

[4] In fact, the etymological root of the word 'play' is the Latin term 'pleg'; which translates as a 'blow; game, sport, usually skirmish, fight' (Jephcott 1967, p. 98).

[5] While there are similarities between being the 'best at stuff' and the importance placed on sporting prowess in the Adlers' (1998b) ethnographic study of 'pre-teenagers' in the US, there are also important crucial differences. For the Adlers, sporting competence 'was so critical that individuals who were proficient in sport attained both peer recognition and upward mobility' (1998b, p. 39). While sporting competence is important to the Langview Boys, it seldom operates in isolation from other attributes—those who are exceptionally good at sport, but can't 'take a slagging', for example, will be given grudging respect in their area of expertise, but will be given no quarter in other activities.

for example, names of those being excluded from the project or included in the LYP football team, local gossip, or up-to-date information regarding key areas of interest, such as football. Forms of knowledge, much like forms of masculinity, were hierarchical; where certain forms of knowledge were prized, others were dismissed. In this context, the knowledge most sought after—the most mysterious and the most treasured—was that relating to gangs. Individuals who held reputations as gang members were discussed in awed tones and the group were keen in discussions to demonstrate their knowledge about gangs in the area. In one discussion group, when asked to associate words with the term 'territory', the group jostled to display their knowledge of gang names elsewhere in Glasgow. Similarly, in examining a map of Glasgow, the group were keen to display their street knowledge of gang territories across the city.

The importance attached to being 'in the know' also extended to the activities of the group. There was an intense desire to be involved in, and have knowledge of, everything that has relevance to the group. Conversely, there was a keen sense of anxiety if access to anything is denied. This group dynamic became the reason for the Boys to climb the fence back into LYP after closing, to vandalize, to drink alcohol, to participate in every activity and so on, so as not to miss out on anything that might have a bearing on status in the group. Recently the phrase *FOMO*—fear of missing out—has entered the popular lexicon; it describes this dynamic well. Layered into these knowledge divides is a richly textured shared knowledge—of group activities, community histories, and local scandals—which constitute a core of meaning in group interaction. Unquestionably, it is the shared aspect of the boys' biographies that creates this unquenchable thirst for local knowledge as one method among many of creating distinction in Langview.

Crucially, however, group dynamics and 'pecking orders' (Phillips 2003) also formed a central element in claims to knowledge. The value placed on certain knowledge claims was often relative to the status of the individual making the claim rather than to any external source of proof; while high-status group members could make unchallenged assertions, lower-status members had knowledge claims frequently challenged and derided. For example, when Gary started talking about the history of gangs in Glasgow—starting as 'wee stone fights o'er the Clyde'—he was universally mimicked and mocked despite the fact that what he said was based on an identifiable source (a website I had seen). On the other hand, when Kev informed the group that the world was going to end that day, as a result of a 'black-hole machine' being switched on and 'sucking in the sea', the idea was taken up and discussed excitedly. The story was in fact an obscure retelling of the unveiling of the Large Hadron Collider in Switzerland.

'Being in the know' was therefore contingent not only on the value placed on the information by the group but on the level of respect garnered by the individual who relayed it. In an environment where everyone knows everyone else's business, any piece of new information would be leveraged for kudos. Telling everything to the rest of the group was also, of course, expected to be 'wan ae the boays'.

Being 'wan ae the boays'

Being 'wan ae the boays' refers to loyalty to the group—being 'up for' anything that is suggested. This is also strongly linked with area identity; the boys have grown up together, and the power of peer relationships is intimately bound up with their place and space in Langview. Being 'wan ae the boays' denotes a minimum level of conduct in group activities: for example, level of dress (up-to-date football tops, tracksuits, and trainers), proficiency at sport (good enough to be competitive in chosen activity), available income (able to afford group activities), and verbal interaction (ability to give and take a slagging). Deviation from these standards results in informal group controls in the form of ritualized insults. Being 'wan ae the boays' also means remaining loyal to the group and everything the group is involved in. One of the boys spoke reverentially of a young man from Langview who now plays for an English Premiership football club but 'still climbs in the LYP for a game' when he's home.

The dynamics surrounding being 'wan ae the boays', moreover, gives an insight into the precarious and insecure nature of masculinities within the group. Like 'being in the know', remaining loyal to the group necessitates a constant need for validation in all group interactions. As Bourdieu notes:

[l]ike honour...manliness must be validated by other men...and certified by recognition of membership of the group of 'real men'...Some forms of 'courage'...spring, paradoxically, from the *fear* of losing the respect or admiration of the group, of 'losing face' in front of one's 'mates'

and being relegated to the typically female category of 'wimps', 'girlies', 'fairies' etc. (Bourdieu 2001, p. 52)

Being 'wan ae the boays' also necessitates an implicit acceptance of the models of acceptable masculinities within the group. Younger or weaker boys are viewed through the lens of 'subordinated masculinities'. In this sense, the group is closed to those that are not seen as 'wan ae the boys'. While creating space for individual distinction, there is nonetheless a powerful collective bonding created by risky situations. As Mark, Willie, and Gary discuss:

> MARK: See if someb'dae tried tae do [attack] us, Ah wouldnae be scared cos Ah know aw ma pals would back me up.
>
> AF: Have you ever had to put that to the test though?
>
> GARY: One time up Hillside. Ah didnae want tae fight, but James got caught...they aw started running doon...and when we looked around we couldnae find James. An that's when Ah thought 'they've caught James'. Then Ah done that 'let's fucking go!' Me, Willie, Daz and Dylan...
>
> WILLIE: When we thought oor pal got caught, that's when we all came round...see when that adrenaline's kicking through ye...
>
> GARY: We were all bottling it at the time, but see when we thought oor pal got caught, that's when we thought 'naw, we're no taking this, we want tae back up our pal here'.

The narrative the Boys created relived the emotional fear of the incident, reimagining the visceral response as an experience of collective solidarity, reaffirming the bonds of loyalty and friendship. Moments such as this both draw from and solidify a masculine habitus that is shared by the group. In competing for individual distinction, group cohesion is instilled; in Thrasher's evocative phrase, the group were 'integrated through conflict' (1963).

Being 'wan ae the boays' therefore solidified the 'fratriarchal masculinities' (Thorpe 2010) within the group, imprinting a set of gender norms that replicate some long-standing aspects of masculine identity in Glasgow. Where once these masculinities were coupled with forms of capital—both physical and symbolic—that were productive in the industrial economy, however, this connection has largely been severed in the shift to a service economy. As a result, these 'ways of being' are increasingly disconnected with the broader economic field in the post-industrial city. This has caused significant challenges to young men entering the job market in the 'new Glasgow'.

The hardman in the call centre

As cities across the UK and US have shifted toward post-industrial service economies, young people have experienced a 'fundamental transformation in the relationships between waged work, gender and class' (McDowell 2003, p. 59). Under such conditions, Bourdieu has written of the existence of a 'tormented habitus', or *habitus clivé*, 'bearing in the form of tensions and contradictions the mark of the contradictory conditions of formation of which they are a product' (Bourdieu 2000, p. 64; Bennett 2007). When confronted with new conditions in which habitus does not make sense, individuals might experience a schismatic tension, experienced as 'horrific and barbaric' or 'absurd and comic' (Webb et al. 2002, p. 39). This tension may give rise to a retreat to known habits and traits, or alterations that may still give rise to uncertainty. Under certain circumstances, the 'disjunction between habitus and the field...may lead to a critical consciousness and the attendant possibility of social change' (McNay 2001, p. 146).

The challenges to masculinities posed by the shift to post-industrialism have resulted in a complex range of continuities and discontinuities. Bourgois, for example, argues that unemployment and corresponding challenges to traditional 'bread-winner' masculinity form an important backdrop to the enactment of violence.

Fewer and fewer men are able to find stable, unionized jobs that pay them a family wage with family benefits as factories relocate overseas in search of inexpensive labour. Unable to provide economically for their conjugal unit, they lose the material legitimation for demanding autocratic 'respect' and domineering control over their wives and children. (Bourgois 1995, p. 413)

In the UK, as youth unemployment has increased and stable long-term employment diminished, cultures of drinking, drugs, illicit leisure pursuits, and crime have flourished as alternative routes to masculine expression (Collison 1996; Hall et al. 2008). Processes of economic and social change have resulted, for some, in the consolidation of traditional models of masculinity as bulwarks against social change (Jefferson 1997; MacDonald and Shildrick 2007). In this context, spatial immobility has confined these expressions to the immediate locale (Alexander 2000):

Male redundancy has created cultures of prolonged adolescence in which young male identities remain locked into the locality of estate, shops and school. In their struggle to assert their independence, young men adopt a culture of risk-taking…Violence, criminality, drug taking and alcohol consumption become the means to gaining prestige. (Rutherford 1988, p. 7)

In this context, Nayak has written of the ways in which a group of young men in post-industrial Newcastle 'were negotiating various life-paths that would *preserve* rather than eradicate their subcultural allegiance to football, drinking and going out' (Nayak 2003, p. 151). In the face of challenges to their habituated sense of self, this group weaved together old and new cultural traits into new, hybrid forms. As Nayak argues:

the cultural re-imagining of Geordie masculinities reconfigures the relationship to production within the fields of leisure and consumption. In doing so it offers a reassuring, masculine means of preserving local identities and managing change in what appear to be uncertain, risky times. This would suggest that in an increasingly globalised and 'shrinking' world, place-based identities continue to be of significance. (Nayak 2003, p. 156)

While the Langview Boys were still at school during the research, and therefore they were only beginning to be confronted with the contradictions between the 'gemmie' sensibility and the service economy, older participants demonstrated one of the future paths they could tread. A separate study I conducted with 18- to 25-year-olds in Langview (Fraser 2009) found that this group—variously unemployed, in some form of training, or employed in the service sector—experienced a 'churn' between different forms of low-paid jobs, unstable or insecure agency work, and unemployment (MacDonald et al. 2001; Shildrick and MacDonald 2007). Steven, for example, had been unemployed for the last six months. Now 20-years-old, he left school at 15 with no qualifications to attend a local college course in cookery. He left this course after six months and began a bakery apprenticeship at a supermarket. He was made redundant from this job and began a long series of different jobs peppered with periods of unemployment. His work in a call centre was short lived, due to a long wait for a pay cheque. Instead, he had hoped to get an apprenticeship in construction or joinery, but at the time there was no stable work in those industries. The aftermath of the recession had seen a significant downturn in the work available.

STEVEN: Used tae dae construction, brick-cladding but cos the recession and that's kicked in, nae work at aw the noo. Ah've been trying the agencies, they've nae work either.

AF: What are you best at?

STEVEN: Labouring work, construction work, paintin and decoratin...Ah've done a lots ae hings, carpet-fitting an aw...Ah've been wi a lot ae agencies an aw. Manual work, movin materials, takin deliveries, stuff like that.

Like the young people in Gunter and Watt's (2009) study, Steven articulated a clear desire for work in traditional industries. Ironically, the few major construction projects available for Steven were in the construction of one of the large out-of-town shopping centres that stand on those former industrial sites. Once construction was complete, however, the agencies who arranged the work stopped returning his calls. For young men in London, however, there were still some pathways to traditional industries.

The relative buoyancy of London' s construction industry means that a well-trodden transition is still available to young males who possess a positive attitude to dirty, hard graft, and who can also access key neighbourhood employment networks and subculture. Grafter culture demonstrates continuities with traditional...masculine, working-class transitions...as well as East London particularities of ' ducking and diving' ...The major difference, however, between the 1970s and 2000s is that the employment base of grafter culture in London is largely restricted to what amounts to the niche construction industry, since its other, larger pole, manufacturing, has so contracted. (Gunter and Watt 2009, p. 526)

Steven's experience is representative of a broader pattern of *dialectical confrontation* (Bourdieu 2005) between the forms of masculinity embodied by the Langview Boys, and the dispositions required by work in the service sector. Call centre work, in particular, requires a degree of deference—both to management and customers—that is antithetical to the 'gemmie' sensibilities that the Langview Boys valued and exhibited. This creates a clear tension within the individual, who is riven between his inculcated disposition and a new 'way of being' that is economically productive but culturally inconsistent. While the rebellious subculture evinced by 'the lads' in Willis' study prepared them for the—albeit subservient—work on the shop floor, rebellion does not fit with work in the global consumer marketplace.

Taylor and Bain (2003), in an ethnographic study of call centres in Scotland, found that subversive humour, trade unionism,
and rebellious subcultures—all of which run deep in Glasgow's
history—were given short shrift by corporate management. As the
authors argue, 'humour contributed to the development of vigor-
ous countercultures…which conflicted with corporate aims and
priorities…the particular combinations of managerial culture,
attitudes to trade unionism and dissent, and the nature of oppo-
sitional groupings helped impart a different character to humour
between the two call centres' (Taylor and Bain 2003, p. 1487).

In this section, I will describe some of the ways in which young
people in Langview were responding to the shift to a service
economy, in some cases by reaching back to traditional models of
masculinity through gang identification, in others demonstrating
the seeds of change. For some young men in Glasgow, a similar
shift has resulted in adaptation; for many others, however, it has
resulted in a fractured and fragmented path into employment and
the re-enactment of gang identities as a root of identity amid a
changing world.

Gang identity and post-industrial masculinities

As gang research in the UK has gathered momentum, critics have
drawn attention to a developing 'malestream' in approaches to the
phenomenon.[6] In a media environment in which young women
remain constructed as 'tomboys', 'sex-objects', and 'she-male
gangsters' (Young 2009), Batchelor calls for a deeper engagement with the experiences of young women, setting out an agenda
for research that draws on the complex meanings and motivations for female violence. These contributions create a powerful case for the inclusion of sociological perspectives on gender
in the development of knowledge on the UK gang phenomenon.
Such an approach 'allows for recognition that there are multiple
masculinities and femininities, shaped by structural positioning'

---

[6] Batchelor (2009, 2011), for example, points out that the vast majority of
UK-based gang research has been carried out by male researchers with male
respondents, silencing the voices of young women in a way that closely adheres to
the development of gendered approaches to gangs in the US. For critical discussion of young women in gangs in the US, see Chesney-Lind and Hagedorn (1999),
Miller (2001), and Nurge (2003).

(Miller 2002, p. 438), emphasizing the contingent and intersectional nature of structured agency (Miller 2001). In developing a nuanced approach to gang and gender, therefore, it is important to engage with concepts of both masculinities *and* femininities.

For Alexander, writing in a UK context, gang identities may be conceived of as 'the building of a defensive culture of masculine survival against social marginalization' (Mac An Ghaill 1994, p. 187), as a means of attaining masculine distinction in contexts where traditional routes to masculinity are blocked (Miller 2000, 2001; Messerschmidt 2002). For young men in Langview, in the context of an uncertain future, the performance of gang identities represented the acting out of an idealized form of masculinity through which individual reputations were established and maintained. In the following example, Michael discusses the pressures towards establishing a reputation for young teenagers, and the pull this exerts towards gang fighting.

> AF: Did you enjoy it [gang fighting] at the time though? Were there good things aboot it?
> MICHAEL: Obviously ye think it's fun, an ye think ye're some sort ae hard man, cos ye kin run aboot in a group an pick on people that are stonnin theirsel [standing on their own] an that.

Local reputation, and identity, are bolstered by gang identification, with some measure of celebrity attached. This distinction becomes a feather in the cap of young men in the area, afforded respect and submission by younger boys. Gang identification therefore helps create both a superior individual *and* group identity—LYT are Number 1, Fuck The Rest. In this way, too, masculinity is emphasized through the construction of those in neighbouring communities as individuals who embody subordinate masculinities.

> AF: Why do you think people want to gang fight?
> KEV: Tae keep your gang's name up on the leaderboard.
> AF: The leaderboard?
> DYLAN: There's no a leaderboard.
> KEV: Aye there is. LYT's number wan.
> DAZ: So people are scared ae ye.
> AF: Why do you want people to be scared of ye?
> DAZ: So people don't come in an start hinking they can sit, and walk aboot...
> KEV: That they kin be the big man in your scheme

In an economic environment in which traditional masculinities are threatened, gang fighting represents a route to status and masculinity that 'fits' with young people's street habitus. In another group discussion, Dylan and Kev discuss the 'talk of the town' after Dylan attacked a male from a bordering community.

> DYLAN: Ah hud a big log an Ah threw it at his legs an he fell. Decked it a heavy belter [fell over hard].
> AF: Did that make you feel good though?
> DYLAN: Aye. (laughs)
> KEV: He's still feeling good the noo.
> AF: Did everyone talk aboot it afterwards?
> DYLAN: Aye. Saying ma name.
> KEV: He wis the big man.

This masculine bravado in 'gang talk' serves to confirm, consolidate, and legitimize the violent aspect of gang identity. Reputation—in Bourdieu's (1984) terms, cultural capital or *distinction*—becomes embodied and realized through talk; it is talk that normalizes and neutralizes negative emotions. The role of the 'big man' in this way serves to unite the group both through reference to the local area and gang identity.

In this context, as young men begin to develop an awareness of young women, gang identities merge with developing gender and sexual identities, and performance of gang violence becomes an activity charged with emotional energy. For the Langview Boys, there was an important connection between developing masculinities, reputation, and sexual identity. The following fieldnote describes a night at LYP in which a young woman came to the project to watch the Langview Boys play football.

One of the most interesting events of tonight was that of Sarah-Jane watching the boys perform on the football pitch. She chose to come into LYP alone, and watch the boys from outside the pitch. They were all extremely aware of being watched. James in particular would go over to where she was and make small comments to her, and put his hand up against the wire while she did the same. Kev made repeated comments to her, but from afar; Daz repeatedly took the ball in that direction, but didn't really communicate with her. They all obviously wanted to show off, and were more ball-greedy than usual, but also more testy/tetchy than usual. (Fieldnote, 18 May 2008)

In a similar way, in the following discussion, two young women from the school-leavers group, Pamela and Julie (both aged 17) reflect on their teenage years spent in public areas watching their male friends act out these developing identities. The discussion is based on a normal weekend night when they were 14- or 15-years-old and fights were taking place:

JULIE: An there's always lassies involved.
AF: In what way?
JULIE: They're always just fightin cos ae lassies. Always.
AF: An are there boys as well watching on the sidelines or is it mainly girls standing on the sidelines, or eh...
PAMELA: It's maistly jist lassies.
JULIE: It's maistly jist lassies. That's when the boays think they're bold, cos they're tryin tae show aff, cos they've got an audience.
PAMELA: Aye, an they try tae show aff.

While some young men will 'grow out' of gang identities—as will be discussed in Chapter 8—for other this forms a more fixed aspect of masculine self-identity. This continuity can be read as a key factor in the persistence of gangs in Glasgow—of young men acting out the same street-based culture as previous generations, responding to similar processes of socio-spatial marginalization. Nonetheless, just as gang identification has waxed and waned over the course of the twentieth century, so broader social, economic, and cultural shifts have made an impact on the habits and dispositions of young people in Glasgow. The following section will document some examples of the impact of social change on young people's gang identities.

Masculinities and social change

'Gender-appropriate' behaviour is deeply encoded in individual dispositions and embedded in local cultures while feeding and perpetuating a broader system of gendered relations and inequalities at a societal level. Gender is therefore historically and culturally situated, occurring in the broader context of age, ethnicity, and class subject positions. McIvor (2010), discussing the history of working-class masculinities in Glasgow, suggests that the particular embodiment of the Glasgow 'hardman' was forged in the heavy industries in the early part of the twentieth century, whereby hard physical labour necessitated a desensitized and hardened configuration of what it meant to be a man. In this context, sport, leisure pursuits, and drinking—associated with the independence that comes with earning a wage—became allied with this hardened masculinity, with office work viewed as effeminate and subordinate. While this form of street-based masculinity has its roots in the industrial era, it has been passed on through the generations via age-based hierarchies, in the context of persistent inequality in the city.[7]

Nonetheless, masculinity—like habitus—is not a fixed or static aspect of social identity. Performance of masculinity may alter and realign during social development, and at successive points through history. As such, masculinities—and, correspondingly, gang identities—must be understood within the broader context of social changes that refract through the lens of the city. Much like Bourdieu's concept of habitus, these gendered attitudes are learned and embodied during various stages of social development—through play, experiment, and mimicry—thereby creating the possibility of continuing local configurations of masculinities. As Connell points out:

hegemonic masculinity is a concept which may function in a number of ways in analyses of violence. Used with awareness of historical context—and not as a catch-all formula—it may help explain the cultural embedding and specific shape of violence in communities where physical aggression is expected or admired among men. (Connell 2002, p. 93)

In the microcosm of LYP, the Langview Boys' were the eldest, most well-known, and highest-status grouping, thereby eliciting both fear and adulation amongst younger groupings of boys. This is important to the boys; as Kev says, of a photograph of some of the younger boys in LYP:

AF: Do they all know ye?
KEV: Aye. They all praise me. They all bow down to me.

As a result of this deference, the Langview Boys would frequently insult, mock, and 'test' younger boys along similar lines to those which would be used within their own group. Younger groups of boys were generally subordinated—physically, verbally, symbolically—and rarely afforded any clemency. It is clear that this was how the Langview Boys themselves were treated by their

---

[7] Glaswegian actors, footballers, and politicians are often renowned for—or constructed as—having had a hard working-class upbringing, often involving some flirtation with gangs or violence. The film maker Doug Aubrey has commented that is now *de rigeur* for Glasgow actors to make reference to their involvement in street gangs—the whiff of menace that this invokes plays well in terms of media constructions of the city, and results in repeated parts for Glasgow 'hardmen' in mainstream popular culture.

elders in previous years, and therefore how these cultural ideas are learned and transmitted; the boys talk about the 'older ones' in the area, including their own elder brothers, in awed tones. Through insults, humour, and denigration, along with fighting, competition, and violence, the Langview Boys were 'tested' by older groups in the area and they in turn 'tested' out younger groups, forming a repetitive loop in which locally dominant forms of masculinity were reproduced and alternative forms of masculinity subordinated. These vertical relations are in turn regulated horizontally through the peer group, and gender becomes embedded within the preconscious of habitus. In this context, gang identification represented a clear route to attaining masculinity and respect in the keenly contested arena of popular opinion.

Nonetheless, I observed some seeds of different models of masculinities emerging. In the following fieldnote, a group of younger males (aged 9–10 years) in the project—described by some in LYP as the 'new set' of the Langview Boys—struggle with balancing masculine identities with an activity perceived by them to be feminine: dancing.

There is a DVD of *Grease* showing, in preparation for a short production that some of the girls are putting on, with a dance teacher coming in weekly to help out. A few of the younger boys (aged 10) are interested, but are obviously caught between wanting to participate and not wanting to be seen to be seen as 'girly'. The boys were struggling with being seen to be enjoying it too much in front of one another, and ended up acting hard, making a joke of it, laughing, being disruptive, and being asked to leave. (Fieldnote, 20 October 2008)

Interestingly, in previous generations dancing was seen as a masculine activity. In studies of youth in 1960s Glasgow, dancing in the 'palais' dance halls was a popular activity (Jephcott 1967), and prowess in dancing undoubtedly a way of being 'best at stuff'. In the famous Glasgow folk-song, 'Cod Liver Oil and the Orange Juice', a 'hardman' goes to a local dance hall in search of a partner. As these dance halls have closed down, however, and alternative forms of leisure developed, dancing as a masculine 'way of being' has fallen out of fashion. In LYP, dancing is now perceived to be something 'for lassies'.

Nonetheless—like *Billy Elliot* swapping his football boots for ballet pumps—in successive weeks, several of the boys returned to the class, quietly enjoying 'doing masculinity' differently. Masculine

habitus, crucially, is therefore subject to change according to alterations in the broader gendered field, and it is clear that some young
people are altering in line with these new field conditions. Similarly,
as young men begin to develop an awareness of young women, gang
identities merge with developing gender and sexual identities and
relationships can help formulate alternative routes to a different
type of masculinity. Pamela and Julie, for example, would try and
prevent fights, and stopped their boyfriends from participating.

> JULIE: That's how Ah always greet [cry], cos Ah try an split it up.
> AF: I mean, were you the only person that felt like that though? Or
>   were other people, were they happy to, cheering on an stuff?
> JULIE: Well, a lot of them … aye. They thought it wis pure good.

Like Pamela and Julie, however, many of the young men that were
their peers stopped hanging about on the streets—and stopped
their involvement in gang fighting—as they reached the age of 16
or 17. Gang fighting, for some, was viewed as something for 'wee
wans', aged around 13 to 15.

These examples—slight as they may be—are evidence that the
disjuncture between young people's street habitus and the conditions of post-industrial Glasgow have evinced change as well as
continuity. While gang identification has a long history in Glasgow,
the phenomenon also alters according to extant social conditions.
The following chapter will further elaborate this account of continuity and change.

Conclusion

In this chapter, the competing group dynamics, status politics, and
pecking orders which make up the Langview Boys' group identity
were contrasted with the economic realities of the service economy. These ways of creating and co-producing meaning—'being
a gemmie', taking a slagging, being 'best at stuff', being 'in the
know', and being 'wan ae the boays'—cohere around a specific
configuration of masculinity in which physical toughness, verbal
aptitude, and group loyalty are highly prized. These attributes
of masculinity are regulated and policed through various physical, verbal, and symbolic techniques—humour, insult, play, and
violence—continually challenging and contesting the masculinities of group members. In this context, gang identities emerge as an
idealized form of masculinity which embodies these ways of 'being

a man'. However, these 'ways of being' create a constant sense of precariousness within the group and a perpetual effort for each individual to prove themselves in front of others.

The second part of the chapter contrasted these models of masculinities—which run deep in Glasgow's history—with the needs of employment in the service economy. This shift has resulted in a dialectical confrontation between young people's street habitus and the broader economic field in post-industrial Glasgow. This rupture between habitus and field has created a complex range of continuities and discontinuities in young people's activities. Some have adapted to these new configurations in a way that continues previous traditions—as with the trade unionism shown in Taylor and Bain's (2003) study. Others, however, have chafed against the new casual work environment and experienced of further marginalization. In this way, through adaptation to new economic environments in the context of previous cultural histories, gang identification alters and reconfigures with successive generations while retaining clear-cut continuities with the past.

8

Generations of Gangs

Ah used tae fight, an Ah used tae have a name, but now Ah don't enjoy that. Cos that's jist putting a label oan ye. It's jist no good. When ye take a step back an look at it, like at how stupid it is...[you ask] how kin this be enjoyable, how kin this be your life?

Michael

Although gangs have a long history in Glasgow, only during particular periods has the issue become an object of popular outrage and political attention. While reports of gangs have operated cyclically, with certain periods—notably the 1930s, 1960s, and the 2000s—producing more interest and publicity, various sources suggest that gang identification persisted before, during, and after these periods: from reports of a gang 'reign of terror' in 1916 (Patrick 1973, p. 123) to discussion of police 'gang lists' in the immediate post-war period (Mack 1958), and from the history of Jewish youth involvement in territorial violence in 1920s Govan (Taylor 2013) to longitudinal data illustrating continuity in gang identities between 1974 and 2008 (McKinlay et al. 2009). Throughout this long period of time, gangs have been reported in working-class communities in Glasgow marked by a lack of amenities, frequently accompanied by high levels of overcrowding and high populations of young people.

This suggests a clear lineage of gang identification that exists independent of public, political, or academic attention. In this chapter, drawing together arguments from previous chapters with data that speak to this 'closed loop' of gangs in Glasgow, I piece together an analysis of the persistence of gangs in Glasgow. In communities with limited leisure opportunities, young people grow up spending a great deal of time in public space, and they form a deep-seated connection with their local area. In the context of developing masculinities, the boundaries between these areas become staging areas for the acting out of 'gemmie' sensibilities, with the intention of gaining a local reputation. These patterns of behaviour are informally regulated by age-based hierarchies through which young men seek to continually impress older groups while denigrating younger groups. Nonetheless, as the quote from Michael suggests, gang identity is frequently outgrown, a rite of passage that prepares young people to be street-wise in a fragmented post-industrial landscape, but that may also serve to further alienate them from prospects of stable work.

The chapter is set out in two main sections. The first elaborates a model through which gang identification is learned and socially reproduced through age-based hierarchies, based primarily on data from Langview. This section examines the process through which young people in Langview 'grow into' and 'grow out of' gang identities, and reflects some of the consequences—both positive and negative—for young people's engagement in this group-based behaviour. The second, drawing on oral histories, traces this model of reproduction back through previous generations of gangs, arguing that gang identity has become an 'open system of cultural codification' (Delanty 2003) that is used and experimented with by successive generations. I discuss the continuities and changes in this form of violent territorialism in the post-industrial era, drawing connections with gangs in other cities in the UK and elaborating a framework through which to make sense of persistence of gangs amid broad-based social change.

Gang identity and social reproduction

Groups of young men, engaging in crime or violent conflict, are reported in spaces of 'advanced marginality' (Wacquant 2008a) throughout the world (Dowdney 2007). In some contexts this is a relatively new development but in many more these forms of youthful identification have long historical antecedents, with marked continuities over time and space. Glasgow represents a striking example of this persistence, demonstrating marked continuities that set it apart from urban histories of gangs in other cities. While there may be apparent similarities between groups, these may mask critical differences in different geographical contexts. In seeking to understand the 'glocal' or global/local (Robertson

1995) nature of gangs, therefore, it is necessary to analyse the *process* through which gang identification persists. In this section, I sketch the intersections between age, social development, and gang identification for young people in Langview, drawing particular attention to the cyclical nature of age-based hierarchies as a means of understanding the persistence of these forms of behaviour over time.

Growing into gangs

As was described in Chapter 5, for very young children 'the gang' was integrated into play behaviour—LYT was a name given to toy soldiers and play fights over territory closely resembled a game of 'chases'—in a pattern that created deep ties between young people and their local area. This street habitus represented an embodied response to structural immobility and the ongoing likelihood of economic disadvantage. As these children grew older, however, the boundaries between Langview and neighbouring areas became an exciting space for watching fights between older brothers or their peers and rival groups, a space in which local reputations were staked and claimed. As the group grew older still, these boundaries became places in which to enact their own 'edgework' activities. As Sibley notes, '[c]rossing boundaries, from a familiar space to an alien one which is under the control of somebody else, can provide anxious moments; in some circumstances, it might be fatal, or it might be an exhilarating experience' (Sibley 1995, p. 32). Michael, one of the school-leavers, describes his route into gang fighting with friends he had known since early childhood.

> AF: Did you get involved in some of the fighting then, over the bridge?
> MICHAEL: Aye, Ah used tae when Ah wis younger.
> AF: Why do you think you got involved in it at the time?
> MICHAEL: Ah think it wis jist, aw ma pals were daein it. Ah'd known aw ma pals fae when we were all in cots. Like we'd jist go tae the LYP, an ye'd jist like grow up wi them an then that wis jist what happened.

Similarly, Pamela and Julie defined 'a gang' as being based entirely on friendship groups and area of residence: 'Jist pals really. Jist people that stay in the same scheme that talk, and that back each other up'.

A range of studies has similarly highlighted the many ways in which children and young people experiment with gang identification. Anderson, for example, describes how the 'code of the street' is learned and internalized by 'children...mingling on the neighborhood streets and figuring out their identities' (E. Anderson 1999, p. 68). For Conquergood, the streets similarly represent 'a liminal space for neighbourhood youths to experiment and play with gang symbolism and traditions without a full commitment' (Conquergood 1994a, p. 37). In such environments, street culture may be played with, subverted, or challenged (Garot 2007), but it is learned through age-based hierarchies of influential individuals. The Langview Boys 'grew into' gang identity through an intersection of social development, collective identity, and street masculinities. In the following example, Gary and Willie are discussing an episode when they were 13 years old, taking the initiative for the first time to invade the space of a border community, Hillside. After learning the street habitus, watching fights, and 'playing gangs', the boys decide to seek out a reputation.

> GARY: We were aw like, 'who kin reach the furthest intae Hillside'? Then we decided tae try an get them aw runnin, it wis dead icy, an we thought they'd pure slip on the ice an faw [fall].
> AF: Why do you think you were doin that?
> GARY: Cos we wur jist daft wee boays at the time.
> WILLIE: Tryin tae get a name for ourselves.
> GARY: Aye, cos we aw used tae...aye aboot a year ago, two year ago, we used tae think we were the pure LYT an aw that. But see compared to people from, like, Hillside an aw that, we wur pure wee guys.

In this example, the Boys are experimenting with the boundaries between Langview and Hillside, 'tryin tae get a name' through enacting localized street masculinity. In this case, however, the Boys realize their own naïveté in testing the boundary in this way. Their fantasy world of the gang—'we used *tae think* we wur the pure LYT'—was brought face to face with the reality of the team from Hillside, young men in their late teens and early 20s. Nonetheless, this event had the effect of consolidating the group and played a role in the Boys' collective social development.

In the process, geographical space is transformed into self-identity and projected onto a performance of gang fighting. In 'protecting' the area, therefore, an individual is protecting all that they hold dear, kith and kin. As Sibley argues, '[w]e cannot understand the role of space in the reproduction of social relations without recognising that the relatively powerless still have enough power to "carve out spaces of control" in respect of their day-to-day lives' (Sibley 1995, p. 76). In the following excerpt, Kev and James discuss the performance of physical violence:

AF: What makes a gang then?

KEV: See, people from Swigton try tae come in Lang St tae walk aboot, they jist start fightin wi' them. But they don't gang fight any mair.

AF: They would though, if boys from the Swigton tried to walk in?

JAMES: Aye. They don't like people walking through Lang St.

AF: Why not?

KEV: Cos it's their community.

The process of 'growing into gangs', therefore, forms part of broader set of social processes involving attachment to place, collective solidarity, and community loyalty. While gang fights create fears and anxieties for both young people and adults in the community, they must also be understood as being rooted in the territorial identity and masculinities that have deep roots in Glasgow.

In this sense, the Langview Boys' behaviour is much like the 'gangs in embryo' described by Thrasher (1963); of street-based friendship groups, in search of excitement and reputation. As well as a collective identity and solidifying existing friendships, territorial violence also represents a staging ground for individual distinction. For the Langview Boys, gang identity in both real and symbolic terms offers a route toward cultural capital which 'fits' with the street habitus of young people growing up in the area. It is also, however, explicitly edgework, allowing participants to 'test the edges' of space and self physically and psychologically and step into the murky and denigrated world beyond. As Lyng argues, 'criminal edgework is a much more relevant and accessible means to re-enchantment than the pursuit of leisure edgework or postmodern consumption opportunities available to more privileged social groups' (Lyng 2005, p. 29). The boundaries between Langview and Swigton, therefore, operate as both symbolic and physical 'edges' through which masculinities can be risked, tested, and co-produced, and local reputations created, bolstered, and reinforced. In the following discussion, Dylan and Kev discuss the 'buzz' of a gang fight.

AF: Are there any good things about fighting?
DYLAN: What's it cault? Adrenaline.
KEV: Rush. Coming right through ye an yer just, you're up for it, an ye crack someb'dae an rush o'er their heid.

Gang fights, whether planned or unplanned, are unpredictable and fleeting events—'fight or flight' stand-offs involving differing degrees of experience and expertise in violence. The moment of conflict is random and involves a potent mixture of masculinity, excitement, and status. In a social environment defined by spatial immobility, limited leisure opportunities, and an uncertain economic future, this form of ritualized violence offers a temporary release where such concerns are pushed into the background.

Growing out of gangs

As Kev's earlier comment 'they don't gang fight anymair' suggests, however, this form of violent territorialism is often age limited. The 'older wans' of the LYT spent less time on the street and looked on gang fighting as something for younger boys. In seeking to move 'beyond the gang' as a fixed and static entity, toward an understanding of the complex and contingent role that gang identities play in young people's social development, there are distinctive parallels with criminological approaches to 'desistance from crime' (Maruna 2001; Thornberry et al. 2003). As Vigil notes, most young people 'mature out through a process of gradual disaffiliation and breaking away from the gang' (Vigil 1988, pp. 106–7). For some, gang identities become a more fixed aspect of identity, fusing violent masculinity and local reputation with group status and attachment to a given area. For others, following similar processes as those involved in more general patterns of 'desistance' (Smith and Bradshaw 2005; Thornberry et al. 2003), gang identities are simply outgrown like a hand-me-down that no longer fitted.

Michael, one of the school-leavers, had been involved in gang violence for a prolonged period in his early teens, establishing a local reputation—and a police record—in the process. He described the use of bricks, bottles, machetes, and knives, resulting in serious injury in some cases, getting 'hit in the eye wi a bottle, hit in the heid wi bricks an that...caught an like punched an stuff like that'. As the quotation at the beginning of the chapter indicates, however, at the time of the research Michael had stopped his involvement and was beginning to reflect on the circularity and pointlessness of gang involvement, taking 'a step back' and looking at 'how stupid it is'. In the following excerpt, Michael expands on this idea:

when you're wee boys, an you're aw at primary, and you're fighting against other wee guys fae aw the different areas, an then as soon as it hits secondary, we aw end up in this building here [the school]. An yir sittin in class next tae guys. You're like that 'kin Ah get a bit ae help wi number four' an that, an then later oan he's hitting ye over the heid wi' a brick. It's jist stuff like that, it's crazy.

Later, Michael discussed the ways in which gang identities continued in the places of young adulthood, in particular pubs and clubs in the city centre. He described one incident of meeting a previous rival in a nightclub: 'He wis like that—you hit me in the heid wi' a brick once. An I wis like "Aye". An he wis like "how you doin!?" shaking ma hand an aw that'. In this incident, Michael and an ex-rival, having both 'grown out' of gang fights, share a moment verging on nostalgia about their shared experiences. For Michael, however, 'leaving the gang' didn't mean leaving the community— he was still living in the area during the period of fieldwork—but leaving behind that particular aspect of his life.

Several of the other school-leavers discussed this period of their lives without regret but as an experience that prepared them for adult life: becoming street- and worldly wise. Pamela and Julie, separately, had spent much of their early teens hanging around border areas between Langview and Swigton and elsewhere as part of a large group, drinking, and watching gang fights between young men from these areas. In the following discussion, they describe an 'average Friday night' when they were 14 or 15 years old:

JULIE: Ye walk up the street, go tae the shops, go o'er tae the hill, aw the boays fight, and then ye come hame. [laughs nervously]
PAMELA: Every Saturday, like, when Ah used tae hang aboot the streets every Saturday, without a doubt, they wid fight. Like ye jist knew it was gonnae happen at some point during the night.

For Pamela and Julie, the experience of time spent in public space witnessing gang violence was a relatively normal part of growing up. Nonetheless, both were intending to go on to university and—like Michael—had left this part of their lives behind. Reflecting on this change in their lives, they discussed the importance of changing friendship groups in making this shift. Crucially, however, they did not look on their involvement in street life in a negative way, but as a positive element in their self-definition, as they now understood something more of life.

> AF: Are you still in touch with people that you were friends with then? (pause)
> PAMELA: If ye pass them in the street ye say hello.
> JULIE: Aye ye say hello.
> PAMELA: But that's it.
> AF: An how did you feel in yourself? I mean, did you always know that it was the wrong thing to do, and that you'd be alright in the long run, that you had bigger fish to fry sort of thing?
> JULIE: Ah liked daein it.
> PAMELA: So dae Ah. Ah don't regret daein it. It's not affected me. Ah'm gaun tae uni an aw that, an pure getting on in life, but Ah've still experienced it. An had a good laugh.
> JULIE: It makes ye mair streetwise. It's like, if ye don't dae it, ye don't actually underston whit's actually happenin, an hink hings are much easier. An a loat ae them think, like, 'they're aw wee neds', like she said before, it's 'neds, just neds'. But it's no. It's jist the way they are. An that's aw right.

Pamela and Julie have *grown through* these experiences, forming new friendships and refashioning their identities, and while others may not have the same experience, this temporal development is important to a social understanding of gangs.

Trapped in a legend

While some young people are able to successfully 'grow out' of gangs and move on to alternative sources of identity, for others the reputations gained through gang fighting are not straightforward to live down. Like scars, reputations do not always easily fade. As Pickering and colleagues (2012) found in their recent research on territoriality in the UK, the development of ' "street respect", that is something that had to be won, typically by fighting, with the aim of forming a "hard" reputation that extended beyond the home territory' (Pickering et al. 2012, p. 951) could be difficult to live down. As Pamela and Julie describe, what began as group-based excitement can quickly escalate into a long-standing reputation.

> JULIE: Cos they're aw pals, an if somebdae batters your pal, like, right in front ae ye

PAMELA: Ye'll have something tae say about it

JULIE: Like ye dae something, ye widnae stand an watch yir pal getting battered. An then ye just gie yersel a name. An then they get a name fur themsel an they think they're pure invincible.

As Phillips notes, the status gained from 'getting a name' can be a double-edged sword, involving enhanced reputation but also 'reluctant fighting to protect a reputation' (Phillips 2003, p. 717). While in other times and places Kev was 'top dog' among the Langview Boys—and the individual with the greatest degree of scope for acting outside group norms[1]—in other ways he was also the individual most bound by them. In the following fieldnote, Kev had received an abusive telephone call from young people from Swigton, and left to challenge them to a fight.

There has been a situation developing between boys from Langview and Swigton over the past few weeks, culminating in an abusive phone call to Kev. As a result of this, Kev left the project, puffed full of bravado, alone, and attacked two males, punching and kicking both of them repeatedly. The youth worker present beforehand expressed surprise that one minute before the attack, Kev was sitting chatting away, the picture of good cheer. After the call, they had never seen Kev so angry. (Fieldnote, 9 November 2008)

In this incident, Kev's high status level in the group dictated in no small part that he act in the way he did. As a charismatic authority figure within the Langview Boys, Kev could not be seen to 'back down' from an insult, resulting in a violent encounter.

Once a reputation has been established it is difficult to erase from collective memory. Steph, another of the school-leavers, described the way in which her dad's friends referred back to his youthful reputation: 'Even now...ma da goes tae the pub wi people he's known since he wis wee...an his pals are like that "your da's mental"'. Similarly, a police officer described to me an incident whereby a man in his 30s was stabbed in a cinema by a man he had fought against in his teens. For some of Michael's friends, gang identities in their early teens led to more consolidated violent masculinities and increasingly risky behaviour.

---

[1] For example, Kev talked about the idea of 'love' in discussion groups, and of wanting bright pink football boots, both of which would have evoked derision had they been admitted by others.

It never goes away, cos you're still in the area, an even when Ah'm with ma new pals, Ah'd still see ma auld pals, an there'd still be like the odd occasions where situations [challenges to fight] would come up. An it widnae be your fault, jist the situations would come up.

Critically, these reputations can have a profound impact on young people's employment prospects, limiting mobility around the city. In the following discussion, Kev discusses an incident in which he was challenged by an older group from another part of the city, resulting in the humiliation of having to give up an item of clothing.

> AF: If somebody said to ye, where ye from, what you up to, would you
> say 'Ah'm from Langview'?
> KEV: Ye jist get heavy para [paranoid], an shut up...that happened
> tae me, when Ah wis in the toon, he said 'where ye fae?' Ah said
> 'Langview'. They said they were fae Woodtown, an took ma hat
> aff me.
> AF: What did you do?
> KEV: Just stood there.

Cumbers and colleagues found a similar impact on mobility in work opportunities for young people resulting from the 'territorial limitations of local gang culture within many of Glasgow's poorer neighbourhoods'. The authors point to a 'recurring theme among all our respondents—young people themselves, union officials, training officers and agency workers—was the extent to which spatial confinement prevents many young men in particular taking up training opportunities' (Cumbers et al. 2009, p. 15). Bobby, aged 21, was interviewed for the youth employment project (Fraser 2009) and talked about the difficulties he found in travelling through the city for work:

Certain buses, people won't go on. Like the Number 17 bus has got a big reputation, cos it goes through literally all the territories. So people don't feel comfortable going on that bus, cos they know it's got to go through somewhere that they know that they'll get attacked. So they avoid doing jobs in town, or far from where they live, cos they know it's going to be hard for them, or not worthwhile.

Crucially, this limit to mobility was particularly pronounced for young people who had established a local reputation and many other young people in communities where gang fighting is well established had to contend with similar restrictions. Gang fighting, while emerging from persistent inequality and spatial restriction, has the effect of further limiting the opportunities of already disadvantaged youth. The cyclical nature of this territorial disadvantage indicates a pattern in the persistence of gang identity in Glasgow; a repetitive age-based hierarchy that interlocks with localized forms of masculinity at different stages of social development. Nonetheless, as was discussed in Chapter 3, gang identification has waxed and waned over Glasgow's history, indicating the prospect for change. In the following section, I aim to piece together an account of continuity and change in the Glasgow gang phenomenon, drawing particular attention to the nature and form of gang identity in post-industrial Glasgow.

Generations of gang identity

[T]here have been few consistent attempts to theorize the novel aspects of gang activity in the post-Fordist age...researchers have...not adequately explained why certain aspects of street gangs have remained relatively unchanged despite a continuously changing urban social order. (Venkatesh 2003, pp. 3–4)

Since the rich outpouring of sociological theory in the post-war era, efforts to capture the complex flows and eddies of the contemporary gang phenomenon have become increasingly few and far between. As a result, there are some significant holes in our understanding about the global topography of gangs including the role of history and social change, diversity and difference, age and social development, structure and agency. This space is often filled by fearful imaginings of the 'global gang' (Hallsworth and Young 2008), involving pathologizing stereotypes of gangs *per se* as a static, criminal entity with common characteristics and patterns of development. As has been argued, however, for young people in Langview 'the gang' had complex meanings and motivations, which reconfigured at different stages of social development. Nonetheless, as was seen in Chapter 3, territorial gang identity has a long history in Glasgow, stretching back over 100 years. In order to develop a critical foundation from which to challenge these fearful narratives, it is crucial to focus attention on the *process* through which these gang identities have reproduced over time. In the following section, I aim to integrate theories of gang persistence with Bourdieu's concept of habitus to develop a framework through which to make sense of continuity and change in gang identity in Glasgow, before sketching the contours of gangs in post-industrial Glasgow.

Theorizing persistence

In the US, Hagedorn draws on the vocabulary of economic sociology to explore the persistence of gangs in Chicago. For Hagedorn (2007), gangs have arisen through a process of *institutionalization*, playing an ongoing, functional role in severely disadvantaged communities where state-based order is weak. In some areas, gangs have become a functional aspect of the social ecology of disadvantaged neighbourhoods, playing a social and political role in the informal economy, 'an institutionalized bricolage of illicit enterprise, social athletic club, patron to the poor, employment agency for youth, substitute family, and nationalist, community or militant organization' (Hagedorn 2007, p. 23). Sanchez-Jankowski (1991) paints a similar picture of persistent gang activity in urban areas of the US, but emphasizes the self-determination of gangs in self-perpetuating as organizations. Through role allocation, provision for members, and strategic planning, gangs persist through pursuing an aggressive quasi-business model. In both these accounts, however, there is a strong economic motive for young people to identify with the local gang, in which drug sales represent an economic opportunity in the absence of other forms of work (Bourgois 1996).

Brotherton, however, suggests an alternate construction of gang identity—as a subculture resistant to structures of oppression. Taking an opposing stance to both positivist efforts to universalize gang definitions and critical efforts to conceptualize change, Brotherton suggests that gangs can themselves become social actors capable of changing their conditions of existence:

For these scholars, gangs are a key socializing milieu or even quasi-institution that produce a habitus wherein members develop the dispositions and/or reproduce the social conditions that cement their class trajectory...While evidence can be mustered to defend this position, it is equally important to consider that street gangs in late modernity can change and may constitute counter-hegemonic forms and moments of both individual and collective resistance organized deep within the poorest, subaltern communities. (Brotherton 2008, p. 56)

While there was little evidence of politicization of this kind in Langview, Brotherton's approach points the way to an open-ended cultural analysis of gangs that envisages the possibility of change, be it deliberate or not, over time.

Lo (2012), writing from a Hong Kong perspective, has addressed the process through which gang identities continue through a perspective based on age and socialization. Basing his findings on several tranches of data collection with young people who identify with local triad associations, Lo argues that in marginalized housing estates they undergo a process of 'triadization' as they grow up:

Triadization is a process in which individuals gradually inherit and adapt triad norms and values through interaction with their friends in youth gangs under the umbrella of triad societies. Engaging with a group of bold and alienated youths makes the youth gang members much more vulnerable to triadization as they are exposed to an aggressive and rebellious atmosphere. Eventually, as the triad subculture provides normative support for delinquent behaviours, individual gang members' attitudes towards triad attachment will begin to change. (Lo 2012, p. 560)

In Lo's formulation, patterns of age and social development interact with the illicit opportunity structure available through triad societies. While street-based youth groups may form in a pattern similar to Thrasher's 'gangs in embryo' (1963), their subsequent development is contingent on the broader ecology of organized crime in the community. The open-ended nature of this model, crucially, suggests that not only are gang formations specific to particular cities, but that continuity and change can coexist.

Unlike Chicago or Hong Kong, illicit opportunity structures for young people are not well developed in Glasgow; youth gangs have seldom evolved into more organized groups through drug sales, racketeering, or organized crime. Rather, through a relatively closed loop of social reproduction which reflects the persistence of inequality in Glasgow's communities, groups of young people are socialized into a street habitus that limits available routes to high status. Growing up in street-based environments with age-based hierarchies, identification with a gang becomes a temporary route to status and distinction consistent with the logic of local models of masculinity. As a result, like the 'fighting gangs' identified by Cloward and Ohlin (1960), groups have retreated to violence.

In the UK, several recent studies have pointed to the divergent historical development of gangs in different cities. Based on their study in an anonymous English city, Medina and colleagues (2013) note that 'very few empirical studies that assess gang stability, document the process of transformation that gangs experience, or provide explanations for those changes' (Medina et al. 2013, p. 197). The authors point to long histories of particular gangs, comparable to Glasgow, yet with significant changes occurring since the 1980s, with groups becoming 'more institutionalised, more oriented toward profit activities built around participation in drug markets, and to have increased their level of participation in serious violence' (Medina et al. 2013, pp. 200–1). While there may be superficial similarities between gangs in different UK cities, this suggests that the particular nature and form of gangs is contingent on local levers of difference. In London, Pitts (2008) and Densley similarly argue that identification with a gang has a long history but that it has fundamentally altered in recent years. Densley (2013) argues that street-based youth groups in London have evolved into more organized gang structures, in the context of the available economic opportunities offered by the drug trade. While these claims have been disputed vehemently by other London-based researchers (Hallsworth 2013), at the very least these debates suggest the need to analyse the divergent trajectories of gangs within the context of the particular historical, cultural, and spatial contexts of different cities, avoiding generalizations about 'gangs in the UK' to examine the specific histories of different urban environments.[2]

Unlike accounts of gang evolution in England, gangs in Glasgow have not developed into organized criminal organizations. Rather, they are best conceived as an adaptive response to ongoing structural and cultural conditions, reproduced through age-graded hierarchies that perpetuate through generations in a pattern that involves both continuity and change.

Continuity and change

For certain groups of boys and young men growing up in Glasgow—bored, with limited leisure opportunities, in search of identity and transgressive activity—gang identity is learned as an available persona and experimented with in various ways. Like a hand-me-down, it is a loose and baggy fit at first but by degrees,

---

[2] For a history of street gang identification in a range of British cities, see Humphries (1981).

groups of young people make it their own, establishing in-group solidarity through communicative codes and symbols. As discussed in Chapter 5, for some 'the gang' played a purely symbolic function, connecting young people both with one another, and with the area. For young males in their early teens, 'the gang' becomes more closely tied to area identity, masculinity, and the acting out of group dynamics, status politics, and developing gender identities. This process represents a gradual development, consolidation, and refinement of gang identification becoming more or less fixed and central to self-definition during this process of development. Gangs play a different role at different stages of social development, reflecting not only a type of violent masculinity and territorial attachment, but play, group identity, community attachment, and solidarity. Critically, however, many young people detach from gang identity as they grow older, shedding this form of violent territorialism as they mature and reflect on the consequences of this behaviour.

Nonetheless, just as one group begins to mature and change their patterns of behaviour, so another may come of age and start to act out the same territorialism. The cyclical nature of this pattern suggests a 'closed loop' in the social reproduction of gang identity, a tightly interlocking sequence that persists in social environments where there are few opportunities in either the licit or illicit marketplace almost independent of broader social changes. This pattern suggests that gang identification cannot be viewed in isolation. A broader set of socio-spatial relationships and cultural contexts needs to be analysed in order to understand a gang's particular historical and cultural lineages. Bannister and colleagues, for example, point to the embeddedness of violent territorialism as a cultural response to structural exclusion, drawing specific attention to the inter-generational of gang identification across a number of sites, including Glasgow (Bannister et al. 2013). This pattern of reproduction, however, should not be read as being fixed, determined, or static, but subject to change at both an individual and city level.[3] As demonstrated in Chapter 3, gangs have

---

[3] Bourdieu's model of social reproduction has been criticized, particularly from a British perspective, as being overly deterministic (Jenkins 2002), lending weight to the much-criticized 'cultures of poverty' argument (Lewis 1959; Leacock 1971). Bourdieu has roundly disputed these claims (Bourdieu 2005); habitus can, in certain circumstances, adapt, or—as with the *habitus clivé*—become riven with internal contradiction and tension.

reconfigured over time in Glasgow according to a broad-based set of vectors—changing economic circumstances, and shifting economies of crime and justice—just as an individual's gang identification alters during the life-course (Farrington 2003).

In this context, it may be productive to envisage a *generational* model of gang persistence. Where young people may grow in and out of gang identities in a more or less cyclical loop, broad-based changes to the nature and form of gangs may be distinguished at a more general level.[4] Broadly, *industrial-era gangs* were characterized by sectarian rivalries, the ability to mobilize large numbers, and non-territorial identity (Davies 2013). *Depression-era gangs* were more closely related to territory, smaller in size, older in age, and sufficiently flexible to exhibit entrepreneurialism in the illicit economy (Sillitoe 1956; Davies 2013). *Post-war gangs* were younger, more violently territorial, and less criminally oriented. While certain aspects of gang identity have persisted through these generations—violent masculinities, territorial identity, and location in Glasgow's more disadvantaged communities—these differences suggest alterations to gangs that have been responsive to the broader social, economic, and cultural conditions of the day.

In a collaborative project with an oral historian (Bartie and Fraser 2014a, 2014b) I have recently been investigating gang identification in the 1960s in an effort to interrogate these processes of continuity and change.[5] One participant, Danny, had grown up in a post-war housing estate where territorial gang violence was particularly intense. For Danny, involvement in gangs and fighting was just something you were expected to do. In response to a question asking what the gangs got up to, he replied:

it was just reputations I think probably...Bravado and things like that just to get a bit of respect and a name for yourself so that you could be left alone.... [Pause] I don't know how the guys that didnae get involved in a gang coped, you know. They must have just sat doonstairs on the bus an' the hood up type of thing and kept...Fair play but I couldnae have done it, I couldnae have done that, you know.

---

[4] One of the few longitudinal studies of gang identification in Scotland found marked alterations over young people's teenage years (Smith and Bradshaw 2005; McVie 2010): 20 per cent said they were in a gang by the age of 13, declining to 12 per cent by age 16, and 5 per cent by age 18 (McVie 2010).

[5] Funded by the British Academy.

Like the Langview Boys, for Danny older role models helped to shape his perception and understanding of what it is to be a man. This included older teenagers in the area, but also his father, who still kept a weapon behind his door in his 80s.

[I]n those days…if you come up and get a doing as a kid your dad gave you a choice. You either get back down and get in again or he would have beat you down, so that, that was pretty much the, the culture then. You either get down then and you go back down there and you hit him back then or 'I'll be giving you a skud', you know. And that, that's, that's how you knew not to go up to your dad again because if you've got a real chance of getting a little lamp off your dad, you know. So you had to go back down.

Danny's experiences demonstrate the repeating pattern of gang identification in Glasgow, and the critical role of 'hardman' masculinities in replicating this form of territorialism. Like the Langview Boys, however, Danny 'grew out' of gangs while others in his peer groups graduated into more organized forms of criminality. Violent masculinities, territorial identity, and neighbourhood nationalism all run deep in the gangs of Glasgow's cultural and economic history, and gang identity is perhaps best understood as a youthful articulation of these trajectories. Recent research similarly suggests strong intergenerational aspects to gang identification. Frondigoun and colleagues (2008), for example, quote respondents saying that 'grandparents, parents, brothers have all been in the gang'. Similarly, a recent research report concluded that:

[i]n the West of Scotland in particular, most interviewees pointed to the longstanding presence of gangs in their local area. Indeed, the existence of gangs was taken as a given whilst growing up. Many, though not all, pointed to the participation of their fathers and older siblings in gangs and gang-related fighting. Indeed, several gang members reported that they had been introduced to the gang by their older siblings. The witnessing of gang fighting, directly or indirectly through story-telling, appeared to emphasize the normality of gangs. (Bannister et al. 2010, p. 33)

The directors of Scotland's Violence Reduction Unit, John Carnochan and Karen McCluskey (2010), come to similar conclusions. Discussing the minimal impact of policing strategies of the 1930s, they argue that 'in contemporary times there are still the same gangs, with the same names, in largely the same locations' (Carnochan and McCluskey 2010, p. 409).

While there are clear continuities between past and present, however, there are also marked differences. Deliberate interventions from the police and community organizations have had an impact at various points in history, while broader shifts in work, leisure, education, and housing have also resulted in change, particularly the move to multi-neighbourhood schools and decline in street-based leisure (Sweeting and West 2003).

Gangs in post-industrial Glasgow

> Bored, drunk and drugged, packs of thugs run wild on our streets in an echo of darker times. Children aged six brandish bricks and iron bars. Sons follow fathers into violence and girls are just as brutal as boys. This is Scotland's gang culture in 2001.
>
> (Daily Record, 2001)

This item in the *Daily Record* newspaper—at the time having the largest readership in Scotland—announced a building of renewed popular concern over youth gangs in post-industrial Glasgow. This was to mark the beginning of a gradual build-up of media, public, political, and academic attention to the issue. The Glasgow-based newspaper, the *Evening Times*, ran a full week of coverage in 2006 on the 'new face' of Glasgow gangs; the front page was splashed with images of graffiti, accompanied with the following tag lines: 'Not just part of Glasgow's history. Today there are 110 active gangs with more than 2000 members. Fighting over borders is a daily occurrence. It is nothing more than recreational violence'. This was followed by a week-long 'special investigation', including a map of gang territories—including the LYT—with 110 different groups across the city, alongside countless images of young men in tracksuits, standing menacingly, eyes blocked out. Since then, a series of television documentaries, practitioner conferences, and academic articles have emerged in relation to the gang phenomenon.[6] In 2009, the Scottish Government commissioned the first ever Scotland-wide study of 'Troublesome Youth Groups, Gangs and Knife-Carrying in Scotland' (Bannister et al.

---

[6] Herald (2008) '300 'booze and blade' gangs blighting Scotland: numbers revealed for first time'. Available at: <http://www.heraldscotland.com/300-booze-and-blade-gangs-blighting-scotland-1.875815> [Accessed 9 August 2014].

2010), and released dedicated funding for youth projects dealing with gangs.[7]

Amidst the increase in interest and attention, rates of violence in general, and youth violence in particular, appear to have been gradually declining in Glasgow and Scotland more generally (Fraser et al. 2010). Part of the explanation for this disjuncture lies in the rapid increase in interest in the UK gang phenomenon and its role, as Davies notes, as a 'focal point for a host of economic, social and cultural anxieties' (Davies 2007a, p. 409). In the context of popular fears over youth disorder and knife crime, the gang has emerged as an all-purpose folk devil for the twenty-first century (Hallsworth 2013). As gangs have become a central focus for law and order rhetoric in the wider national context, so Glasgow has attracted attention, and a looping effect between media representation, political discourse, and policing response has developed.

Nonetheless, it is clear that there are some unique configurations of gang identity in post-industrial Glasgow that bear further investigation. First, the role of the media—and in particular social media—has altered the communicative meanings associated with gangs. While in previous generations gang fights might be reported 'inna papirs' (Patrick 1973), today gang identity can be projected through any number of online platforms; and area reputations staked and claimed in similar fashion. In this context, media representations can have a clear impact on young people's area identity. For example, the pride with which the Langview Boys speak about Langview comes in the knowledge of its media reputation for gang activity. In the following discussion, Kev talks with pride of a poll that rated the main street in Langview as the 'dirtiest street in Scotland'. In this way, the reputation of Langview—feeding into a version of masculinity that prizes violence—is appropriated as a badge of reputation for the group:

DYLAN: Lang St Number One (thumps table twice)
KEV: There's only one. It's the worst street in Glesga.
AF: Where did you get that?
KEV: In the newspaper.
AF: Worst for what?

---

[7] Violence Reduction Unit (2010) 'New helpline service for parents worries about gangs'. Available at <http://www.actiononviolence.co.uk/node/160> [Accessed 29 August 2010].

KEV: Ah don't know. Just every'hin. The blackest. Aw the litter, an abandoned shoaps an every'hin. An plus aw the graffiti.

JAMES: What do you want it tae be dirty for?

KEV: No the dirty bit. It just says 'worst street in Glesga', so it makes us look worse, 'hnnnggg' (noise made like when straining to tense muscles). Kiddin' oan.

I heard of a young woman mistakenly labelled as a 'gang member' in a media investigation, who suffered from extreme bullying as a result. The reflection and refraction of gang identity in the media-made 'hall of mirrors' (Ferrell 1999, p. 397) has thrown up new forms of rivalry, social organization, and labelling that are particular to the post-industrial context.

Second, the broad-based shifts in work and leisure described in earlier chapters have doubtless had a significant impact on gang identity in the post-industrial city. The neoliberal changes to the streets of Glasgow described in Chapter 5 (exclusion, securitization, gentrification) coupled with broad-based alterations to leisure in the post-industrial economy—particularly the increase in privatized leisure, and decrease in street-based leisure—have had an impact on the extent to which young people spend time on the streets. Since the street is the primary environment through which street habitus is developed and gang identity enacted, it follows that these changes to street life may diminish the extent to which young people become habituated to street-based violence.

Third, however, these changes to the economic field in Glasgow have created marked challenges to models of street masculinity that is rooted in former industrial working cultures. The dialectical confrontation between young people's street habitus and the needs of the service sector—symbolizing the broader rupture seen in the city's shift from industrial to post-industrial economy—has resulted in both continuities and changes in gang identity. While the generative grammar of habitus has persisted, the field of economic and gender relations has altered, resulting in these forms of masculine disposition being at times counter to the needs of the local marketplace. As Hall argues of young men similarly disenfranchised in the north-east of England: 'the hard, unskilled graft is all but gone, as are the fundamental conditions of its initial establishment, leaving the hard lad howling in a desperate wilderness where one of the few places of acceptance and comfort to be found is within the criminal economy' (Hall 1995, p. 59). These shifts have may have created space for alternative models of masculinity that no longer rely on the residual culture of industrial 'hardness', but they may also have exacerbated reliance on these forms of machismo as a defensive response to change.

Finally, changes in the nature of policing in the post-industrial city have had an important impact on gangs. The shift from policing 'hunch' and 'prejudice' to policing by 'intelligence' (Waddington 2007, p. 130) has created new opportunities for social interventions in violence.[8] Glasgow's flagship gang policing strategies—the Gangs Taskforce, and the Community Initiative to Reduce Violence[9]—have achieved reductions in violence for participants, and as a result the Prime Minister has stated that learning from these policies would form part of the 'national priority' of action in relation to youth gang violence.[10] Multi-agency cooperation between community organizations that previously operated in isolation and the evolution of hard-working local charities into more developed community organizations have also played an important part.[11]

[8] Although these are not without their own problems. See Fraser and Atkinson (2014) for a critical discussion.

[9] During the period of fieldwork, Strathclyde Police was piloting the Community Initiative to Reduce Violence (CIRV) initiative, in which gang members—as identified by police intelligence—were invited to participate in a series of 'call-ins' at the High Court in Glasgow. These sessions consist of a series of motivational talks and emotional entreaties from ex-gang members, facial trauma surgeons, family members of victims, and police. At these sessions individuals are offered a 'no violence' contract in return for access to the CIRV team, composed of a range of police, health, social work, and education workers offering professional advice and support. The criterion for access to this range of services was, during this pilot period, that the individual has an intelligence marker in the police database for gang membership. For more information see Donnelly and Tombs (2008) and Deuchar (2013).

[10] Herald (2013). Available at: <http://www.heraldscotland.com/news/home-news/cameron-vows-to-learn-from-scotland-over-riots.14706619> [Accessed 4 November 2013].

[11] The Violence Reduction Unit have, however, themselves been responsible for changes in the policing of gangs in Glasgow; work that would appear to be having an impact on the lives of those involved in the CIRV programme (Deuchar 2013). Along with the work of one-to-one mentoring agencies such as Includem (Seaman 2012), it is clear that gang identification is not a fixed or static aspect of young people's lives, but under the right circumstances is amenable to change.

Conclusion

Previous chapters have aimed, in various ways, to demonstrate both continuity and change in young people's gang identities in Glasgow, emphasizing the role of structure, agency, and social change. Focusing on the everyday lives of the Langview Boys, I have sought to dislodge the assumption that gangs in Glasgow are self-evident, homogenous, or static entities; on the contrary, gang identity is a situational enactment of street habitus which cannot be understood apart from the broader experience of growing up in the area. Boredom and leisure, group dynamics and status rivalry, sport and character contests, computer gaming and hanging around: these constitute the mainstay of life for the boys and young men involved in the study. Gang identities, where they exist, are densely woven into these activities and are only explicable through them. These forms of territorial loyalty, place attachment, and street masculinities that structure instances of gang violence, moreover, run deep in Glasgow's history. Territorial youth gangs have been reported for over a century in Glasgow, most often in areas marked by significant social and economic disadvantage, and demonstrate marked continuities over this period. Despite significant changes to the landscape of work and leisure in the 'new Glasgow', these forms of youthful collectives have survived.

Against this backdrop, this chapter has sought to develop a framework through which to understand continuity and change in the Glasgow gang phenomenon. Gang identification has persisted through a repeating pattern of age-based, hierarchically structured street culture that replicates some of the most deeply embedded aspects of Glaswegian history, particularly that of persistent inequality, territorial identity, and violent masculinities, in a social environment where there are few alternative routes to status or distinction. This repeating pattern should not be viewed in isolation, however, but as a particular symptom of a broader network of inequalities. Nonetheless, the nature and form of gangs in Glasgow have altered over time, according to broader social, cultural, and economic conditions. It is therefore possible not only to talk of individual but also generational change in gang activity, drawing attention to the open-ended nature of gang identification over time.

9

Come On, Die Young?

Glasgow 2014. This year, the city relived its former status as 'Second City' of Empire by hosting the Commonwealth Games. Rather than sending off ships to the four corners of the British Empire, though, in a strange reversal the city played host to plane-loads of athletes from those same territories. This reversal powerfully symbolizes the changed place of Glasgow in the world and the changing nature of the global economy itself. The concentration of power in a small number of nations—controlling trade routes through a tightly controlled network of strategic foreign territories—has been replaced by a much more complex and fragmented landscape of global power and geopolitics. In this context, where Glasgow once benefited from the economic heft of the British Empire, the city must now compete on a more even playing field with other world cities.

In the wake of these shifts in the global economy, the jobs available to young people have undergone a series of changes. From an economy premised on physical labour to a job market premised on service, Glasgow has adapted to the vicissitudes of the global economy through a process of rebranding. For many young people growing up in the city, however, the sand-blasted image of a prosperous and modern city does not tally with the everyday realities of social and spatial immobility. For the Langview Boys, their Glasgow was not a cosmopolitan tourist destination but a small patch of residential housing. While the city shifted into the realm of post-industrialism, the Boys inherited a long tradition of street-based masculinities that would prepare them not for work in the 'new Glasgow', but for an uncertain future in a precarious economic climate.

The street-based culture that the Langview Boys reproduced represents one strand in a web of replicating behaviours and activities. Through a shared childhood spent on the streets of Langview, the Boys developed a deep-seated connection to the bounded physical and symbolic space of Langview, a connection which can be read as an instance of 'space-fixing' (Bauman 2000b) amid a changing social landscape. This street habitus, while emphasizing an inclusive group and area identity, is bounded by symbolic borders between Langview and neighbouring communities, resulting in processes of territoriality and exclusion towards young people from these areas. These boundaries operate as spaces in which developing masculinities and gang identities are acted out in the context of risk-seeking behaviours. The Langview Boys' ubiquity in public space, however, created fears and anxieties amongst other groups of young people in Langview, resulting in further restrictions on the mobility of already disadvantaged youth.

At the same time, traditional leisure pursuits in Langview have reconfigured—becoming increasingly commercial, privatized, and removed from the local area—squeezing the Langview Boys into an increasingly limited range of leisure activities. In this context, the Boys switch between different leisure activities, pin-balling from one to another in a cycle of boredom relief, re-enacting some leisure habits from the past and reimagining others in the context of new neoliberal spaces. New risks and challenges are continually created and contested through the invention of edgework activities (Lyng 1990, 2005). In this context, 'weird ideas' (Corrigan 1979) such as setting off fire hydrants, or throwing eggs at strangers, emerge spontaneously. Unlike the 'lads' in Willis study, however, the Boys are not 'learning to labour' in the post-industrial economy, but 'learning to leisure' amid a fragmented archipelago of work and leisure opportunities.

These shifts have posed clear challenges to the street-based masculinities that the Langview Boys embody. These 'ways of being'—being a 'gemmie', taking a slagging, being 'best at stuff', being 'in the know', and being 'wan ae the boays'—represent a contemporary configuration of masculinity that connects with previous incarnations in Glasgow, stretching back to the industrial era. They represent localized forms of street-based masculinities that are marked by Glasgow's unique trajectory of social, cultural, and economic development. Nonetheless, as call centre and other service work has come to replace manual labour, some young men have experienced a dialectical confrontation between these 'ways of being' and the ways of earning available in the post-industrial city. While this has resulted in adaptation for some, for others the disjuncture has heightened experiences of exclusion and marginalization.

Against this backdrop, gang identities have 'survived' as a root of identity—and route to masculinity—in communities with limited employment opportunities, where street-based leisure remains the least worst option for young people. In a post-industrial city where socio-spatial inequality is a defining feature, young people are growing up in a society that has little place for them, in communities that, despite their best efforts, cannot provide enduring economic opportunities. In this context, the cultivation of street masculinities and physical capital is a defensive response to this future—preparing for the worst, making a virtue of necessity. While some young people are adapting to the times, others are left behind. For these latter groups, violence and gang reputations are a symbolic form of compensation for this broader network of inequalities.

In this context, it must be remembered that gang violence is not the only adaptive response to these conditions. The age-old battle-cry for Glasgow gangs—'Come On, Die Young'—is also reflected in the health statistics. Glasgow has exceptionally high rates of morbidity and mortality, even when compared to similar post-industrial cities such as Liverpool and Manchester. Rates of alcoholism, smoking-related disease, and drug-related deaths are staggeringly high, leading researchers to talk of a 'Glasgow Effect', referring to persistently high rates of ill health and mortality, to an extent that is neither predicted nor explained by the most sophisticated statistical analysis (Walsh et al. 2010). This effect has been attributed to deeply entrenched habits through which health behaviours are transmitted between generations.

These arguments present a complex and complicating picture to visions of the 'global gang' and pathologizing accounts of the 'gang menace'. Gang-related violence causes real and lasting harm to communities, limiting mobility and causing fear and injury to other young people, however it cannot be understood outside the structural violence that has been visited on communities across the country. In the following sections, I summarize the key contributions and implications of these arguments which aim to incorporate history and social change, diversity and difference, and structure and agency into accounts of gangs, reconnecting gang research with a sociological imagination.

Homologies of habitus

Across the globe, the youth gang phenomenon has become an important and sensitive public issue. In communities from Los Angeles to Rio, Cape Town to London, the local realities of violent groups present complex dangers and instability for children and young people and generate high levels of public fear and anger. Nonetheless, like a great deal of criminological research which is deemed to be applicable worldwide, many of these accounts are produced in the global North, specifically in the US, UK, Australia, Canada, and mainland Europe (Aas 2011). Like the classic Mercator world map, criminological research is over-whelmingly skewed away from countries in Asia and the global South (Cain, 2000; Agozino 2003; Connell 2007). In this context, doubts have been raised as to the relevance and applicability of Western concepts to the global South, and the corresponding potential for harm[1] (Bowling 2011). At worst, this form of 'travelling reason' (Aas 2011) suggests a form of intellectual colonialism, in which research sites in the global South are viewed as sites of 'parochial wisdom, or antiquarian traditions, of exotic ways and means' (Comaroff and Comaroff 2012, p. 1).

Where most accounts of gangs in a 'global' context proceed from an *assumed similarity*, I have argued for the need to start from an *understanding of difference*. While globalization has led to convergences in neoliberal economic policy making and corresponding convergences in socio-spatial inequality, gangs are fundamentally rooted in the unique cultural and political histories of their home cities. In re-invigorating the sociological imagination (Mills 1959) within a global context, the conceptual tools of habitus, field, and capital are posited as a means of making sense of this similarity and difference. This account of habitus offers a framework for understanding the emergence of comparable social formations in a wide range of contexts, countries, and cultures. If it is true that national boundaries are no longer the governing force in individual identities and that global forces are creating marked similarities in distant communities, it follows that there may exist

---

[1] Bowling develops the concept of 'criminological iatrogenesis' to indicate the negative impacts involved in the transplantation of criminal justice policy, drawing particularly on examples of drugs policy exported from the US (Bowling 2011).

homologies of habitus between these diverse locations. In this sense, it may be productive to envisage the importance of *scale* and the nesting of forms of habitus at micro, meso, and macro levels.

Crucially, this approach to understanding gangs in a global context is rooted in situated meaning and embedded understanding of the divergent meanings of gangs in different contexts. *Habitus* represents a set of deeply embedded, historically rooted, and culturally specific traits and dispositions. As such, while comparative research is necessary, it must proceed from a deep knowledge of the history and context of gangs in different cities. As Sheptycki notes:

> the task of the comparative criminologist is not merely to compare and contrast the findings (hard data) produced by positivistic social scientists. Rather, it becomes an attempt to compare the social, cultural and institutional context in which certain acts become defined as criminal and measured as crimes. (Sheptycki 2005, p. 76)

In this way, knowledge production can proceed from a basis in which dialogue and debate is possible between North and South. In linking the global and local in this way, approaching gangs from the perspective of urban history and city-based characteristics is instructive.

City as lens

In connecting the dots between the macro level of global economic change and the micro level of everyday experience, I have argued for the importance of the meso level of the city in mediating between the two. The city, in this context, becomes a lens through which global and national forces become refracted and gang identities are situated within history. Unlike accounts of youth gangs that stress universal characteristics, criminal orientations, and static meanings, this book has emphasized the shifting and historically contingent nature of gangs, distinguishing the clear-cut divergences between gangs in different global contexts and the difficulties inherent in efforts to delineate 'the gang' as a universal form. On the contrary, I have argued that gang identification can and must be understood as an articulation of local cultural processes, temporally and spatially specific, that represent an adaptation to broader structural forces. Gang identification therefore has divergent historical lineages and unique configurations in different urban contexts, depending on the particular social, political, and economic opportunity structures available. As such, rather than relying on consensual definitions of gangs, we must delve deeply into the urban history of gangs in specific cities, locating these collectives within the broader context of space, class, and political economy in the urban milieu.

In making this argument, I have sought to lay the foundations for a critical approach to gangs in the UK that is sensitive to history, biography, and culture—a global sociological imagination—in making sense of the gang phenomenon. In stemming the tide of 'gang panic' that has emerged recently in the UK, it is necessary to balance the critical traditions of youth research with new theoretical and methodological approaches. In this way, the shifts I identified in gang research—street to database, ethnography to dataset, subcultures to crime, and local to global—are not *reversed* as much as *negotiated*. This book should not be read as a call for a return to the past in making sense of the new, but the revisiting and reinterpreting of ideas in the context of new circumstance, blending past and present in a way that contributes to the long arc of historical ideas that compose the contemporary field of sociology. In this way, it is to be hoped, a critical counterweight to the new US-style gang policies can be built.

A theory of gang persistence

As public and political debate has become increasingly carried away with the obsession with an apparent 'new gang menace', we have forgotten that similar groups have existed in the UK for over a century. The history of gangs in Glasgow tells a story of striking persistence in gangs over time, despite major changes to the fabric of the city. While gangs have changed according to broader economic and political forces—from the industrial era to the Depression, from the post-war era to the post-industrial—they continue to represent a cultural response to structural disadvantage, embodying values of community, solidarity, and friendship as well as enmity, violence, and danger. I have argued for a model of the persistence of gangs that is rooted in the particular characteristics of the city of Glasgow, reproduced in a way that is both open-ended and subject to change; an 'open system of cultural codification' (Delanty 2003) that re-embodies a masculine habitus contiguous with Glasgow's industrial past. In short, this is a theory of gang identification as an adaptive response to economic disadvantage, learned and re-enacted through growing up amid an age-graded social hierarchy on the streets. Gang identification represents one method through which to gain status in the context of an embedded street habitus. However, gang identification waxes and wanes during the life-course, and for some it is a rite of passage that is discarded as one grows up.

The processes through which dispositions are learned and reproduced are located within the context of street-based age hierarchies in which groups of young people are continually tested and re-tested within their own peer group as well as by older and younger groups in the local area. This has the effect of embedding a deep-seated attachment to the local area, inscribing a locally specific model of street masculinities. While these processes encourage collectivism, insofar as they forge powerful bonds between peers, they are also individualizing, as each member of the group must continually defend their status and seek individual distinction. In this context, gang activity serves to solidify group bonds while creating space for individual reputation. This experience should not be thought of as entirely negative; in many ways, young people might grow as individuals through the processes of group loyalty, community identification, and local pride which form the core of gang identity. In a social and cultural environment characterized by change, gang identities form a source of fixity through which to act out important aspects of social development. These individual and group processes, moreover, do not occur in a structural vacuum.

As has been argued, gang identification in Glasgow is rooted in the city's long history of migration, politics, and sectarian tensions—as well as the social clubs which came to represent these competing interests—but also in social and economic inequality which continues to this day. In Glasgow's most marginalized communities, gangs have formed a continuing source of status and reputation in a city that was reconfiguring away from the industries that once fed those areas. The travesty is that the violence caused by this form of territorialism is directed at other, similarly marginalized, young people and not at the social system that perpetuates this form of inequality. The history of gangs in Glasgow tells a story of persistent marginalization, poverty, and violence but, with a few exceptions, seldom a story of political organization or resistance.

Implications

These conclusions have important implications for the field of gang research. Reconceptualizing approaches to gangs in this way opens the door to a reframing of gang research beyond the traditional criminological gaze, moving 'beyond the gang' to incorporate to incorporate broader sociological theories of globalization, youth, space, class, and identity. Disaggregating the 'global gang phenomenon' in this way draws attention to the contingency of gang development on broader cultural, social, and economic changes in the city, opening the way to more sophisticated comparative analyses. In what follows, I draw attention to several key implications of this conclusion for research and practice communities.

First, the synthesis of classical studies of British youth cultures with the social theory of Bourdieu is intended to build a new critical vocabulary for understanding gangs in the UK. To date, researchers have struggled to locate the apparent upsurge in youth violence within Birmingham School traditions with fierce epistemological debates bedevilling the development of new knowledge. The building blocks that Bourdieu's schema enables—history and social change, diversity and difference, and structure and agency—offer a way of approaching gangs that recognizes both continuity and change, rebellion and reproduction, in making sense of the contemporary gang phenomenon.

Second, the deep-seated attachments that young people formed with the Langview community, despite large-scale alterations to the socio-spatial fabric of the community, suggests the need for more detailed focus on the relationship between *space, place, and territory* in gang research. The concept of a stable territory, or 'turf'—understood as a static, geographically delimited and defended space, in which control is exerted over activity and access—has formed a central component in criminological definitions of 'gangs' since the very earliest forays in the field and remains integral to both popular and academic accounts of youth 'gangs' (Spergel 1990; Klein et al. 2001). However, global processes of globalization, gentrification, and displacement have resulted in shifting boundaries and more fluid conceptions of 'turf' (Aldridge et al. 2011), while de-industrialization and ghettoization have intensified the spatial immobility of many. There is a need to reorient our perspectives on gangs to account for these reconfigured relations between space, place, and gang identity.

Third, paradoxically, given the long qualitative tradition in gang research, this increase in attention coincides with a marked decline in first-hand accounts of youth gangs in a global context. Grounded accounts have become sidelined as quantitative methodologies have become the new orthodoxy in both US-based and comparative gang research. At a time when theoretically innovative and methodologically rigorous accounts of gangs and social change are most needed, ethnographic studies have become increasingly marginalized. As Alexander notes:

There is very little sustained qualitative work into 'gangs' in Britain, while sociological accounts of youth cultures and identities have been excluded from the discussions. There is an urgent need for more intensive and long term empirical investigation into youth identities and violence that takes as its focus the mundane encounters of everyday life and conflict. (Alexander 2008, p. 17)

There is therefore a pressing need for more grounded accounts of the complex meanings and motivations attached to gang activity, that are sensitive to global, national, and local dimensions in the response to youth gangs.

Fourth, the role of age, learning, and social development in young people's gang identification represents an important future research trajectory. Research on the processes through which children learn, play with, and enact gang identities would offer considerable insights into the historical continuities, suggesting appropriate ways of harnessing the positive aspects of gang identities while intervening in the more problematic, violent elements. Similarly, the process through which young people 'desist' from gang identities bears further exploration. There is little research on the reasons and processes by which former gang members move away from former involvement, and a great deal can be gained from integrating the rich criminological 'desistance' literature with that of gang research. In this context, the role of *resilience* among young people who actively rejected gang fighting is a particularly productive avenue.

Fifth, there are clear gaps in knowledge in relation to several aspects of youth gangs and crime in Glasgow. Most obvious in this context is the dearth of knowledge of the ecology of organized crime in the city and the connections (or lack thereof) with youthful collectives. Without a grasp of the broader landscape of structures of criminality in the city, it is difficult to assess the nature of gang institutionalization and changes over time. More broadly, there is a need to investigate the deep-seated nature of violent masculinities in the city and their relation to a range of problematic behaviours—health issues being foremost among them. Gangs form part of a broader city culture that goes well beyond those who participate. We would do well to heed Conquergood's advice, to see gang identities as 'magnifying mirrors in which we can see starkly the violence, territoriality and militarism within all of us' (Conquergood 1994b, p. 219).

Sixth, while this study has focused primarily on young men of ethnically white Scottish origin, the research has also highlighted the impact that gangs have on the lives, experiences, and mobilities of young women in Langview, and young men of non-white origin. There is therefore a clear need for the development of knowledge of young women's involvement and participation in gangs, and the role of ethnicity in structuring gang rivalries and conflicts, particularly in light of the changing demographics in the city of Glasgow, and the potential for increases in racialized conflict. Further, there is a need for more detailed knowledge of the broader impact of gangs on the mobility of young people—both spatial and social—who do not participate in gang activity.

Finally, the analysis has important implications for policing and policy responses. This framework opens the way for understanding the divergent trajectories of gangs in varying global contexts, and for locating critical points of social intervention at individual, city, and global scales. Lessons from the study suggest an approach to youth violence that moves 'beyond the gang', in policy as well as research, focusing not on arbitrary, universal definitions and responses but rather on approaches that recognize the individual nature of gang identities and the positive role that these may play in the social development of children and young people. Potential avenues for intervention might focus, for example, on early intervention, alternative models of masculinity, and rejection of violence while retaining the communit spirit, solidarity, and attachment to place that underpin gang identification in Glasgow.

References

Aas, K.F. (2007). Analysing a World in Motion: Global Flows Meet 'Criminology of the Other'. *Theoretical Criminology* 11(2):283–303.

Aas, K.F. (2010). Global Criminology. In: E. McLaughlin and T. Newburn (eds). *The Sage Handbook of Criminological Theory*. London: Sage, pp. 427–46.

Aas, K.F. (2011). Visions of Global Control: Cosmopolitan Aspirations in a World of Friction. In: M. Bosworth and C. Hoyle (eds). *What is Criminology?* Oxford: Oxford University Press, pp. 406–22.

Aas, K.F. (2012). 'The Earth is One but the World is Not': Criminological Theory and Its Geopolitical Divisions. *Theoretical Criminology* 16(1):5–20.

Adamson, C. (2000). Defensive Localism in White and Black: A Comparative History of European-American and African-American Youth Gangs. *Ethnic and Racial Studies* 23(2):272–98.

Adler, P.A., and Adler, P. (1998a). Foreword: Moving Backward. In: J. Ferrell and M.S. Hamm (eds). *Ethnography at the Edge*. Boston, MA: Northeastern University Press, pp. xii–xvi.

Adler, P.A., and Adler, P. (1998b). *Peer Power: Preadolescent Culture and Identity*. New Brunswick, NJ; Rutgers University Press.

Agar, M. (1980). *The Professional Stranger: An Informal Introduction to Ethnography*. London: Academic Press.

Agozino, B. (2003). *Counter-Colonial Criminology: A Critique of Imperialist Reason*. London: Pluto.

Akram, S. (2014). Recognizing the 2011 United Kingdom Riots as Political Protest: A Theoretical Framework Based on Agency Habitus, and the Preconscious. *British Journal of Criminology* 54(3):375–92.

Aldridge, J., Medina, J., and Ralphs, R. (2007). Youth Gangs in an English City: Social Exclusion, Drugs and Violence. Full Research Report ESRC End of Award Report, RES-000-23-0615. Swindon: ESRC.

Aldridge, J., Medina, J., and Ralphs, R. (2008). Dangers and Problems of Doing 'Gang' Research in the UK. In: F. van Gemert, D. Peterson, and I-L. Lien (eds). *Street Gangs, Migration and Ethnicity*. Cullompton: Willan.

Aldridge, J., Ralphs, R., and Medina, J. (2011). Collateral Damage: Territory and Policing in an English Gang City. In: B. Goldson (ed.). *Youth in Crisis? 'Gangs', Territoriality and Violence*. Abingdon: Routledge, pp. 72–88.

Alexander, C. (2000). *The Asian Gang: Ethnicity, Identity, Masculinity*. Oxford: Berg.

Alexander, C. (2008). *(Re)thinking Gangs*. London: Runnymede Trust.

Anderson, B. (2006). *Imagined Communities: Reflections on the Origin and Spread of Nationalism*. London: Verso.

Anderson, E. (1999). *Code of the Street: Decency, Violence, and the Moral Life of the Inner City*. New York, NY: Norton.

Anderson, E. (2006). Jelly's Place. In: R. Hobbs and D. Wright (eds). *The Sage Handbook of Fieldwork*. London: Sage, pp. 39–59.

Anderson, N. (1923). *The Hobo: The Sociology of the Homeless Man*. Chicago, IL: University of Chicago Press.

Appadurai, A. (1996). *Modernity At Large: Cultural Dimensions of Globalization*. London, MN: University of Minnesota Press.

Archibald, M. (2013). *Glasgow: The Real Mean City*. Edinburgh: Black & White Publishing.

Aries, P. (1967). *Centuries of Childhood: A Social History of Family Life*. New York, NY: Vintage.

Armstrong, G., and Wilson, M. (1971). Social Control, Deviance and Dissent: Social Problems, Social Control and the Case of Easterhouse. Presentation to the British Sociological Association, London, 14–16 April, 1971.

Armstrong, G., and Wilson, M. (1973a). City Politics and Deviance Amplification. In: I. Taylor and L. Taylor (eds). *Politics and Deviance: Papers from the National Deviance Conference*. Middlesex: Pelican, pp. 61–89.

Armstrong, G., and Wilson, M. (1973b). Delinquency and Some Aspects of Housing. In: C. Ward (ed.). *Vandalism*. London: Architectural Press, pp. 64–84.

Asbury, H. (1927). *The Gangs of New York: An Informal History of the Underworld*. Garden City, NY: Garden City Publishing Company.

Back, L. (1996). *New Ethnicities and Urban Culture: Racisms and Multiculture in Young Lives*. London: UCL Press.

Baird, A. (2012). Negotiating Pathways to Manhood: Rejecting Gangs and Violence in Medellin's Periphery. *Journal of Conflictology* 3(1):30–41.

Balkind, N. (ed.) (2013). *World Film Locations: Glasgow*. Bristol: Intellect Books.

Ball, R., and Curry, G. (1995). The Logic of Definition in Criminology: Purposes and Methods for Defining 'Gangs'. *Criminology* 33(2): 225–45.

Bannister, J., and Fraser, A. (2008). Youth Gang Identification: Learning and Social Development in Restricted Geographies. *Scottish Journal of Criminal Justice Studies* 14, July:96–114.

Bannister, J., Pickering, J., and Kintrea, K. (2013). Young People and Violent Territorial Conflict: Exclusion Culture and the Search for Identity. *Journal of Youth Studies* 16(4):474–90.

Bannister, J., Pickering, J., Batchelor, S., et al. (2010). *Troublesome Youth Groups, Gangs and Knife-Carrying in Scotland*. Edinburgh: Scottish Government.

Barbalet, J.M. (1999). Boredom and Social Meaning. *British Journal of Sociology* 50(4):631–46.

Bartie, A. (2010). Moral Panics and Glasgow Gangs: Exploring 'the New Wave of Glasgow Hooliganism', 1965–1970. *Contemporary British History* 24(3):385–408.

Bartie, A., and Fraser, A. (2014a). Speaking to the 'Hard Men': Masculinities, Violence and Youth Gangs in Glasgow, c.1965–75. *Exploring Masculinities in Scottish History Conference*. University of St Andrews, 14 March 2014.

Bartie, A., and Fraser, A (2014b). The Easterhouse Project: Youth Gangs, Social Justice and the Arts in Glasgow, 1968–1970. *Scottish Justice Matters*. Available at: <http://scottishjusticematters.com/the-journal/march-2014-arts-and-justice-issue/>.

Batchelor, S. (2001). The Myth of Girl Gangs. In: *Criminal Justice Matters* 43:26–7; Reprinted in Y. Jewkes and G. Letherby (eds). (2002). *Criminology: A Reader*. London: Sage.

Batchelor, S. (2007). Prove Me the Bam!: Victimisation and Agency in the Lives of Young Women Who Commit Violent Offences. PhD thesis: University of Glasgow.

Batchelor, S. (2009). Girls, Gangs and Violence: Assessing the Evidence. *Probation Journal* 56(4):399–414.

Batchelor, S. (2011). Beyond Dichotomy: Towards an Explanation of Young Women's Involvement in Violent Street Gangs. In: B. Goldson (ed.). *Youth in Crisis? 'Gangs', Territoriality and Violence*. London: Routledge, pp. 110–28.

Bauman, Z. (1998). *Work, Consumerism and the New Poor*. Oxford: Oxford University Press.

Bauman, Z. (2000a). *Liquid Modernity*. Cambridge: Polity Press.

Bauman, Z. (2000b). *Globalization: The Human Consequences*. New York, NY: Columbia University Press.

Bauman, Z. (2002). In the Lowly Nowherevilles of Liquid Modernity: Comments on and around Agier. *Ethnography* 3(3):343–9.

BBC News (2011). 'Riots: David Cameron's statement in full'. Available at: <http://www.bbc.co.uk/news/uk-politics-14492789> [Accessed 23 July 2013].

BBC News (2011a). 'Scottish Youths Arrested over Facebook 'Riot' messages', 9 August. Available at: <http://www.bbc.co.uk/news/uk-scotland-glasgow-west-14461393>.

BBC News (2011b). 'Glasgow Boy, 16, Charged with Incitement', 10 August. Available at: <http://www.bbc.co.uk/news/uk-scotland-glasgow-west-14481665> [Accessed 26 February 2014].

Beck, U. (1999). *World Risk Society*. Cambridge: Polity Press.

Becker, H.S. (1963). *Outsiders: Studies in the Sociology of Deviance.* New York, NY: Free Press of Glencoe.

Becker, H.S. (1967). Whose Side Are We On? *Social Problems* 14(3):239–47.

Becker, H.S. (1982). *Art Worlds.* Berkeley, CA: University of California Press.

Behar, R (2003). Ethnography and the Book That was Lost. *Ethnography* 4(1):15–39.

Behnke, C., and Meuser, M. (2001). Gender and Habitus: Fundamental Securities and Crisis Tendencies among Men. In: H. Kotthof and B. Baron (eds). *Gender in Interaction: Perspectives on Masculinity and Femininity in Ethnography and Discourse.* Amsterdam: John Benjamins Publishing, pp. 153–74.

Bennett, T. (2007). Habitus Clivé: Aesthetics and Politics in the Work of Pierre Bourdieu. *New Literary History* 38(1):201–28.

Bennett, T., and Holloway, K. (2004). Gang Membership, Drugs and Crime in the UK. *British Journal of Criminology* 44(3):305–23.

Best, J. (2005). Lies, Calculations and Constructions: Beyond 'How to Lie with Statistics'. *Statistical Science* 20(3):210–14.

Bloch, H., and Niederhoffer, A. (1958). *The Gang.* New York, NY: Philosophical Library.

Bourdieu, P. (1977). *Outline of a Theory of Practice.* Cambridge: Cambridge University Press

Bourdieu, P. (1984). *Distinction.* London: Routledge Kegan Paul.

Bourdieu, P. (1990). *The Logic of Practice.* Translated by Richard Nice. Cambridge: Polity Press.

Bourdieu, P. (1991). *Language and Symbolic Power.* Cambridge, MA: Harvard University Press.

Bourdieu, P. (1997). Masculine Domination Revisited. *Berkeley Journal of Sociology* 41:189–203.

Bourdieu, P. (1998). *Practical Reason: On the Theory of Action.* Stanford, CA: Stanford University Press.

Bourdieu, P. (2000). *Pascalian Meditations.* Cambridge: Polity.

Bourdieu, P. (2001). *Masculine Domination.* Cambridge: Polity.

Bourdieu, P. (2005). Habitus. In: J. Hillier and E. Rooksby (eds). *Habitus: A Sense of Place* (2nd edn). Aldershot: Ashgate, pp. 43–52.

Bourdieu, P., and Wacquant, L. (1992). *An Invitation to Reflexive Sociology.* Cambridge: Polity.

Bourgois, P. (1995). *In Search of Respect: Selling Crack in El Barrio.* Cambridge University Press: Cambridge.

Bourgois, P. (1996). In Search of Masculinity: Violence, Respect and Sexuality among Puerto Rican Crack Dealers in East Harlem. *British Journal of Criminology* 36(3):412–27.

Bowling, B. (2011). Transnational Criminology and the Globalization of Harm Production. In: M. Bosworth and C. Hoyle (eds). *What is Criminology?* Oxford: Oxford University Press, pp. 361–79.

Boyle, J. (1977). *A Sense of Freedom.* London: Canongate.

Boyle, M., McWilliams, C., and Rice, G. (2008). The Spatialities of Actually Existing Neoliberalism in Glasgow, 1977 to Present. *Human Geography* 90(4):313–25.

Bradshaw, P. (2005). Terrors and Young Teams: Youth Gangs and Delinquency in Edinburgh. In: S.H. Decker and F.M. Weerman (eds). *European Street Gangs and Troublesome Youth Groups.* Walnut Creek, CA: AltaMira Press, pp. 241–74.

Brenneman, R. (2012). *Homies and Hermanos: God and Gangs in Central America.* Oxford: Oxford University Press.

Brotherton, D. (1996). 'Smartness', 'Toughness', and 'Autonomy': Drug Use in the Context of Gang Female. *Journal of Drug Issues* 26(1):261–77.

Brotherton, D. (2007). Proceedings from the Transnational Street Gang/ Organization Seminar. *Crime Media Culture* 3(3):372–81.

Brotherton, D. (2008). Beyond Social Reproduction: Bringing Resistance Back in Gang Theory. *Theoretical Criminology* 12(1):55–77.

Brotherton, D., and Barrios, L. (2004). *The Almighty Latin King and Queen Nation: Street Politics and the Transformation of a New York City Gang.* New York, NY: Columbia University Press.

Brubaker, R., and Cooper, F. (2000). Beyond Identity. *Theory and Society* 29(1):1–47.

Bryce-Wunder, S. (2003). Of Hard Men and Hairies: No Mean City and Modern Scottish Urban Fiction. *Scottish Studies Review* 4(1):112–25.

Burawoy, M. (2009). *The Extended Case Method: Four Countries, Four Decades, Four Great Transformations, and One Theoretical Tradition.* Berkeley, CA: University of California Press.

Burawoy, M. (ed.) (2000). *Global Ethnography: Forces, Connections and Imaginations in a Postmodern World.* Berkeley, CA: University of California Press.

Burman, M., and Batchelor, S. (2009).). Between Two Stools: Responding to Young Women Who Offend. *Youth Justice* 9(3):270–85.

Burrowes, J. (1998). *Great Glasgow Stories.* Edinburgh: Mainstream Publishing.

Cain, M (2000). Orientalism, Occidentalism and the Study of Crime. *British Journal of Criminology* 40(2):239–60.

Campbell, A. (1984). *The Girls in the Gang.* Oxford: Basil Blackwell.

Campbell, T.C., and McKay, R. (2001). *Indictment: Trial by Fire.* London: Canongate.

Carnochan, J., and McCluskey, K. (2010). Violence, Culture and Policing in Scotland. In: D. Donnelly and K. Scott (eds). *Policing Scotland.* Abingdon: Willan Publishing, pp. 399–424.

Castells, M. (2000). *The Information Age: Economy, Society and Culture.Volue III: End of Millennium*, vol. 3. Malden, MA: Blackwell.

Castles, S., and Miller, M.J. (2009). *The Age of Migration*. London: Palgrave-MacMillan.

Centre for Social Justice (2008). *Breakthrough Glasgow: Ending the Cost of Social Breakdown*. London: Centre for Social Justice.

Centre for Social Justice (2009). *Dying to Belong: An In-Depth Review of Street Gangs in Britain*. London: Centre for Social Justice.

Charlesworth, S. (2000). *A Phenomenology of Working Class Experience*. Cambridge: Cambridge University Press.

Checkland, S.G. (1981). *The Upas Tree: Glasgow 1875–1975...And After*. Glasgow: University of Glasgow Press.

Chesney-Lind, M., and Hagedorn, J. (1999). *Female Gangs in America: Essays on Girls, Gangs and Gender*. Chicago, IL: Lake View Press.

Childress, H. (2004). Teenagers, Territory and the Appropriate of Space. *Childhood* 11(2):195–205.

Clarke, J. (1975). The Skinheads and the Magical Recovery of Community. In: S. Hall and T. Jefferson (ed.). *Resistance through Rituals*. Birmingham: Centre for Contemporary Cultural Studies, pp. 99–118.

Clifford, J. (1988). *Predicament of Culture: Twentieth-Century Ethnography, Literature, and Art*. Cambridge, MA: Harvard University Press.

Clifford, J., and Marcus, G. (eds). (1986). *Writing Culture: The Poetics and Politics of Ethnography*. Berkeley, CA: University of California Press.

Cloward, R., and Ohlin, L. (1960). *Delinquency and Opportunity*. New York, NY: The Free Press.

Coffey, A. (1999). The Ethnographic Self: Fieldwork and the Representation of Identity. London: Sage.

Cohen, A. (1955). *Delinquent Boys: The Culture of the Gang*. Glencoe: Free Press.

Cohen, P. (1972). Subcultural Conflict and Working-Class Community. *Working Papers in Cultural Studies* 2 (Spring):5–52.

Cohen, S. (1972). *Folk Devils and Moral Panics: The Construction of the Mods and Rockers*. London: MacGibbon and Kee.

Cohen, S. (1973). Property Destruction: Meanings and Motives. In: C. Ward (ed.). *Vandalism*. London: Architectural Press, pp. 23–53.

Collinson, D.L. (1988). Engineering Humour: Masculinity, Joking and Conflict in Shop-floor. *Organization Studies* 9:181.

Collison, M. (1996). In Search of the High Life: Drugs, Crime, Masculinities and Consumption. *British Journal of Criminology* 36(3):428–44.

Comaroff, J., and Comaroff, J. (2012). *Theory from the South: Or, How or, How Euro-America is Evolving toward Africa*. Boulder, CO: Paradigm Publishers.

Connell, R.W. (2007). *Southern Theory: The Global Dynamics of Knowledge in Social Science.* Malden, MA: Polity.

Connell, R.W. (1995). *Masculinities.* Cambridge: Polity.

Connell, R.W. (2002). On Hegemonic Masculinity and Violence: Response to Jefferson and Hall. *Theoretical Criminology* 6(1):89–99.

Connell, R.W., and Messerschmidt, J. (2005). Hegemonic Masculinity: Rethinking the Concept. *Gender and Society* 19(6):829–59.

Conquergood, D. (1991). Rethinking Ethnography: Towards a Critical Cultural Politics. *Communication Monographs* 58:179–94.

Conquergood, D. (1994a). Homeboys and Hoods: Gang Communication and Cultural Space. In L. Frey (ed.). *Group Communication in Context: Studies of Natural Group.* Hillsdale, NJ: Lawrence Erlbaum Associates, pp. 23–56.

Conquergood, D. (1994b). For the Nation! How Street Gangs Problematize Patriotism,I In D. Simon and M. Billig (eds). *After Postmodernism: Reconstructing Ideology Critique.* London: Sage, pp. 200–21.

Conquergood, D. (1996). The Power of Symbols. *One City.* Chicago Council on Urban Affairs: Chicago. Available at: <http://www.gangresearch.net/GangResearch/Media/Power.hm> [Accessed 26 September 2010].

Conrad, P. (1997). It's Boring: Notes on the Meaning of Boredom in Everyday Life. *Qualitative Sociology* 20(4):465–75.

Corrigan, P. (1979). *Schooling the Smash Street Kids.* London: Macmillan.

Corrigan, P. (1995). What Do Kids Get out of Pop Music and Football? In: C. Critcher, P. Branham, and A. Tomlinson (eds). *Sociology of Leisure: A Reader.* London: E. & F.N. Spon, pp. 71–7.

Cottrell-Boyce, J. (2013). 'Ending Gang and Youth Violence: A Critique', *Youth Justice* 13(3):193–206.

Coughlin, B.C., and Venkatesh, S. (2003). 'The Urban Street Gang after 1970', *Annual Review of Sociology* 29:41–64.

Cressey, P.B. (1932). *The Taxi-Dance Hall: A Sociological Study in Commercialized Recreation and City Life.* Chicago, IL: University of Chicago Press.

Croall, H., and Frondigoun, L. (2010). Race, Ethnicity, Crime and Justice in Scotland. In: H. Croall, G. Mooney, and M. Munro (eds). *Criminal Justice in Contemporary Scotland. Cullompton.* Abingdon: Willan, pp. 111–31.

Crossley, N. (2001). The Phenomenological Habitus and its Construction. *Theory and Society* 30:81–120.

Crow, G., and Maclean, C. (2000). Community. In: G. Payne (ed.). *Social Divisions* (2nd edn). Basingstoke: Palgrave, pp. 305–24.

Cumbers, A., Helms, G., and Keenan, M. (2009). *Beyond Aspiration: Young People and Decent Work in the De-Industrialised City,* Discussion Paper. Glasgow: University of Glasgow GES/Urban Studies.

Currie, E. (1997). Market, Crime and Community: Toward a Mid-Range Theory of Post-Industrial Violence. *Theoretical Criminology* 1 (2):147–72.

Daily Record (2001). 'Gangs on the warpath'. Available at: <http://www.thefreelibrary.com/GANGS+ON+WARPATH%3B+Bored,+drunk+ and + drugged, + packs + of + thugs + run + wild . . . -a076193828> [Accessed 6 August 2014].

Daily Record (2011). 'Glasgow gangland: How 1970s saw street battles turn to organised crime'. Available at: <http://www.dailyrecord.co.uk/news/uk-world-news/glasgow-gangland-how-1970s-saw-1092584> [Accessed 6 August 2014].

Damer, S. (1989). *From Moorepark to 'Wine Alley': The Rise and Fall of a Glasgow Housing Scheme*. Edinburgh: Edinburgh University Press.

Damer, S. (1990a). *Glasgow: Going for a Song*. London: Lawrence & Wishart.

Damer, S. (1990b). No Mean Writer? The Curious Case of Alexander McArthur. In: K. McCarra and H. Whyte, *A Glasgow Collection: Essays in Honour of Joe Fisher*. Glasgow: Glasgow City Libraries, pp. 24–42.

Damer, S. (1992). *'Last Exit to Blackhill': The Stigmatization of a Glasgow Housing Scheme*. Glasgow: University of Glasgow, Centre for Housing Research.

Danson, M., and Mooney, G. (1998). Glasgow: A Tale of Two Cities? Disadvantage and Exclusion on the European Periphery. In: S. Hardy, P. Lawless, and R. Martin (eds). *Unemployment and Social Exclusion: Landscapes of Labour Inequality and Social Exclusion*. London: Routledge, pp. 217–34.

Davies, A. (1998). Street Gangs, Crime and Policing in Glasgow during the 1930s: The Case of the Beehive Boys. *Journal of Social History* 23 (3):251–67.

Davies, A. (2007a). Glasgow's 'Reign of Terror': Street Gangs, Racketeering and Intimidation in the 1920s and 1930s. *Contemporary British History* 21(4):405–27.

Davies, A. (2007b). The *Scottish Chicago*? From 'Hooligans' to 'angsters' in Inter-War Glasgow. *Cultural and Social History* 4(4):511–27.

Davies, A. (2008). *The Gangs of Manchester: The Story of the Scuttlers, Britain's First Youth Cult*. Preston, Milo Books.

Davies, A. (2013). *City of Gangs: Glasgow and the Rise of the British Gangster*. London: Hodder & Stoughton.

Davis, M. (1998). *City of Quartz: Excavating the Future in Los Angeles*. London: Pimlico.

Davis, M. (2006). *Planet of Slums*. London: Verso.

de Lima, P. (2005). An Inclusive Scotland? The Scottish Executive and racial inequality. In: G. Mooney and G. Scott (eds). *Exploring Social Policy in the 'New' Scotland*. Bristol: Policy Press, pp. 135–56.

Decker, S., and Pyrooz, D. (2013). Contemporary Gang Ethnographies. In: F.T. Cullen and P. Wilcox (eds). *The Oxford Handbook of Criminological Theory*. Oxford: Oxford University Press, pp. 274–93.

Decker, S., van Gemert, F., and Pyrooz, D. (2009). Gangs, Migration and Crime: The Changing Landscape in Europe and the USA. *International Migration and Integration*. 10:393–408.

Delanty, G. (2003). *Community*. London: Routledge.

Deleuze, G., and Guatarri, F. (1984). *Anti-Oedipus: Capitalism and Schizophrenia*. London: Athlone Press.

Densley, J. (2013). *How Gangs Work: An Ethnography of Youth Violence*. London: Palgrave-MacMillan.

Deuchar, R. (2009). *Gangs, Marginalised Youth and Social Capital*. Sterling, VA: Trentham Books.

Deuchar, R. (2011). 'People Look at Us, the Way We Dress, and They Think We're Gangsters': Bonds, Bridges, Gangs and Refugees—A Qualitative Study of Inter-Cultural Social Capital in Glasgow. *Journal of Refugee Studies* 24(4):672–89.

Deuchar, R. (2013). *Policing Youth Violence: Transatlantic Connections*. London: Institute of Education Press.

Deuchar, R., and Holligan, C. (2010). Gangs, Sectarianism and Social Capital. *Sociology* 44(1):13–30.

Dinsmor, A., and Goldsmith, A. (2010). Scottish Policing: A Historical Perspective. In: D. Donnelly and K. Scott (eds). *Policing Scotland*. Abingdon: Willan Publishing.

Donnelly, P. (2010). Evaluating Gang Rehabilitation and Violence Reduction in Glasgow's East End. Presentation to 18th UKPHA Annual Public Health Forum, *Bournemouth International Conference Centre*, 24–25 March 2010. Available at: <http://www.ukpha.org.uk/media/2973/B2.3%20P.Donnelly.%20Evaluating%20gang%20reha-bilitation%20and%20violence.pdf> [Accessed 26 September 2010].

Donnelly, P.D., and Tombs, J. (2008). An Unusual Day in Court. *British Medical Journal*. 337:a2959.

Dorling, D., and Pritchard, J. (2010). The Geography of Poverty, Inequality and Wealth in the UK and Abroad: Because Enough is Never Enough. *Applied Spatial Analysis* 3:81–106.

Douglas, M. (1966). *Purity and Danger: An Analysis of the Concepts of Pollution and Taboo*. London: Routledge.

Dowdney, L. (2007). *Neither War Nor Peace: International Comparisons of Children and Armed Youth in Organised Armed Violence*. UN: COAV. Available at: <http://www.coav.org.br/publique/media/NewAll.pdf> [Accessed 26 September 2010].

Downes, D. (1966). *The Delinquent Solution: A Study in Subcultural Theory*. London: Routledge & Kegan Paul.

Downes, D., and Rock, P. (2003). *Understanding Deviance* (4th edn). Oxford: Oxford University Press.

Elias, N., and Scotston, J. (1994). *The Established and the Outsiders* (2nd edn). London: Sage.

Epstein, D., Kehily, M., Mac an Ghaill, M., et al. (2001). Boys and Girls Come Out to Play: Making Masculinities and Femininities in School Playgrounds. *Men and Masculinities* 4(2):158–72.

Ericson, R., and Haggerty, K. (1997). *Policing the Risk Society*. Toronto: University of Toronto Press.

Eveslage, S., and Delaney, K. (1998). Talkin' Trash at Hardwick High: A Case Study of Insult Talk on a Boys' Basketball Team. *International Review for the Sociology of Sport* 33:239–53.

Faris, R.E.L. (1967). *Chicago Sociology, 1920–1932*, San Francisco, CA: Chandler Pub. Co.

Farrington, D. (2003). Key Results from the First Forty Years of the Cambridge Study in Delinquent Development. In: T.P. Thornberry and M.D. Krohn (eds). *Taking Stock of Delinquency: An Overview of Findings from Contemporary Longitudinal Studies*. New York: Kluwer Academic/Plenum Publishers, pp. 137–83.

Feeley, M., and Simon, J. (1992). The New Penology. *Criminology* 30(4):449–74.

Feinstein, J., and Kuumba, N.I. (2006). *Working with Gangs and Young People: A Toolkit for Resolving Group Conflict*. London: Jessica Kingsley Publishers.

Ferrell, J (1999). Cultural Criminology. *Annual Review of Sociology* 25:395–418.

Ferrell, J. (2009). Kill Method: A Provocation. *Journal of Theoretical and Philosophical Criminology* 1(1):1–22.

Ferrell, J. (2012a). Outline of a Criminology of Drift. In: S. Winlow and S. Hall (eds). *New Directions in Criminological Theory*. Abingdon: Routledge, pp. 241–56.

Ferrell, J. (2012b). Autoethnography. In D. Gadd, S. Karstedt, and S.F. Messner (eds). *The SAGE Handbook of Criminological Research Methods*. London: Sage.

Ferrell, J., and Hamm, M. (1998). *Ethnography at the Edge: Crime, Deviance and Field Research*. Boston: Northeastern University Press.

Ferrell, J., Hayward, K., and Young, J. (2008). *Cultural Criminology: An Invitation*. London: Sage.

Ferris, P., and McKay, R. (2001). *The Ferris Conspiracy*. Edinburgh: Mainstream Publishing.

Fine, G.A. (ed.). (1995). *A Second Chicago School? The Development of a Postwar American Sociology*. Chicago, IL: University of Chicago Press.

Fitzpatrick, S.A.T. (1972). *Myths and Rituals Surrounding Delinquent Gangs in Edinburgh and Dundee*. PhD thesis, University of Edinburgh.

Foucault, M. (1977). *Discipline and Punish: The Birth of the Prison*. London: Allen Lane.

Fox, K.J. (1991). The Politics of Prevention: Ethnographers Combat AIDS among Drug Users. In: M. Burawoy, B. Burton, and A.A. Ferguson, et al. (eds). *Ethnography Unbound*. Berkeley, CA: University of California Press.

Fraser, A. (2009). Skills Development Scotland Debrief Report. London: Uffindell West Ltd.

Fraser, A. (2010). Deviation from the Mean? Cultural Representations of Glasgow since No Mean City. In: A. McNair and J. Ryder (eds). *Further from the Frontiers: Cross-Currents in Irish and Scottish Studies*. Aberdeen: AHRC Centre for Irish and Scottish Studies.

Fraser, A. (2012). Review of 'Youth in Crisis? Gangs, Territoriality and Violence' (ed. Barry Goldson; London: Routledge, 2011). *British Journal of Criminology* 52(1): 227–30.

Fraser, A. (2013a). Street Habitus: Gangs, Territorialism and Social Change in Glasgow. *Journal of Youth Studies* 16(8):970–85.

Fraser, A. (2013b). Ethnography at the Periphery: Redrawing the Borders of Criminology's World-Map. *Theoretical Criminology* 17(2):251–60.

Fraser, A., and Atkinson, C. (2014). Making Up Gangs: Looping, Labelling and the New Politics of Intelligence-Led Policing. *Youth Justice* 14(2):154–70.

Fraser, A., and Piacentini, T. (2013). We Belong to Glasgow: The Thirdspaces of Youth 'Gangs' and Asylum Seeker, Refugee and Migrant Groups. In: C. Phillips and C. Webster (eds). *New Directions in Race, Ethnicity and Crime*. London: Routledge, pp. 55–79.

Fraser, A., Burman, M., and Batchelor, S., with McVie, S. (2010). *Youth Violence in Scotland: A Literature Review*. Edinburgh: Scottish Government.

Frondigoun, L., Nicholson, J., Robertson, A., et al. (2008). *Building Safer Communities: An Evaluation of the Enhanced Policing Plan in Shettleston, Baillieston and the Greater Easterhouse Area*. Glasgow Caledonian University/Strathclyde Police.

Furlong, A., and Cartmel, F. (2004). *Vulnerable Young Men in Fragile Labour Markets: Employment, Unemployment and the Search for Long-Term Security*. York: Joseph Rowntree Foundation.

Furlong, A., and Cartmel, F. (2007). *Young People and Social Change: New Perspectives* (2nd edn). Maidenhead: McGraw-Hill/Open University Press.

Gabriel, Y. (1998). An Introduction to the Social Psychology of Insults in Organisations. *Human Relations* 51(11):1329–54.

Garcia, B. (2005). Deconstructing the City of Culture: The Long-Term Cultural Legacies of Glasgow 1990. *Urban Studies* 42 (5/6):841–68.

Garland, D. (2001). *The Culture of Control: Crime and Social Order in Contemporary Society.* Oxford University Press: Oxford.

Garot, R. (2007). Where You From: Gang Identity as Performance. *Journal of Contemporary Ethnography* 36(1):50–84.

Garot, R. (2010). *Who You Claim: Performing Gang Identity in School and on the Streets.* New York, NY: New York University Press.

Geertz, C. (1967). Under the Mosquito Net. *The New York Review of Books* Vol. 9, No. 4, September 14, 1967.

Geertz, C. (1990). *Works and Lives: The Anthropologist as Author.* Stanford, CA: Stanford University Press,

Giddens, A. (2000). *Runaway World: How Globalisation is Reshaping Our Lives.* London: Profile.

Glasgow Anti-Racist Alliance (GARA). (2009). *The State of The Nation: Race and Racism in Scotland 2008.* Glasgow: GARA. Available online: <http://www.crer.org.uk/index.php?option = com_content&view = article&id = 73:state-of-the-nation&catid = 47&Itemid = 81> [Accessed 16 July 2012].

Glasgow Centre for Population Health (2008). *Community Health Profiles of Greater Glasgow and Clyde.* Glasgow: GCPH. Available at: <http://www.gcph.co.uk/assets/0000/0390/GCPH_briefing_paper_FS_14_Web.pdf>.

Goffman, E. (1959). *The Presentation of Self in Everyday Life.* New York: Double Day.

Goldson, B. (ed.). (2011). *Youth in Crisis? 'Gangs', Territoriality and Violence.* London: Routledge.

Gouldner, A. (1968). The Sociologist as Partisan: Sociology and the Welfare State. *The American Sociologist* 3:103–16.

Grant, B.K. (2003). *Fritz Lang: Interviews.* Jackson, MS: University of Mississippi Press.

Gray, A. (1981). *Lanark: A Life in Four Books.* Edinburgh: Canongate.

Gray, N., and Mooney, G. (2011). Glasgow's New Urban Frontier: 'Civilising' the Population of 'Glasgow East'. *City* 15(1):4–14.

Guardian (2008). 'Lonely planet rates Glasgow as one of the world's top ten cities', *Guardian*, 15 October 2008. Available at: <http://www.guardian.co.uk/travel/2008/oct/15/glasgow-scotland> [Accessed 28 September 2008].

Guardian (2009). 'Gangbos become the latest measure for fighting antisocial behaviour'. *Guardian*, 21 November 2009. Available at: <http://www.guardian.co.uk/uk/2009/nov/21/gangbos-antisocial-behaviour-policing-pledge> [Accessed 17 September 2010].

Guardian (2010). 'The scheme: Gritty TV or poverty porn?' for further discussion. Available at: http://www.theguardian.com/tv-and-radio/tvandradioblog/2010/may/28/the-scheme-bbc> [Accessed 9 August 2014].

Guardian (2011). 'Glasgow gangs chose route to peace in face of tough Crackdown'. Available at: <http://www.theguardian.com/uk/2011/aug/11/glasgow-gangs-peace-crackdown> [Accessed 8 August 2014].

Guardian (2014). 'The death of the American shopping mall'. Available at: <http://www.theguardian.com/cities/2014/jun/19/-sp-death-of-the-american-shopping-mall> [Accessed 25 June 2014].

Gunter, A. (2008). Growing Up Bad: 'Road' Culture and Badness in an East London Neighbourhood. *Crime Media Culture* 4(3):349–66.

Gunter, A., and Watt, P. (2009). Grafting, Going to College and Working on Road: Youth Transitions and Cultures in an East London Neighbourhood. *Journal of Youth Studies* 12(5):515–29.

Hacking, I. (2004). Between Michel Foucault and Erving Goffman: Between Discourse in the Abstract and Face-to-Face Interaction. *Economy and Society* 33(3):277–302.

Hagedorn, J. (1998a). Frat Boys, Bossmen, Studs and Gentlemen. In: L. Bowker (ed). *Masculinities and Violence: Research on Men and Masculinities*. London: Sage.

Hagedorn, J. (1998b). *People and Folks: Gangs, Crime and the Underclass in a Rustbelt City* (2nd edn). Chicago: Lake View Press.

Hagedorn, J. (ed). (2007). *Gangs in the Global City: Alternatives to Traditional Criminology*. Chicago, IL: University of Illinois Press.

Hagedorn, J. (2008). *A World of Gangs: Armed Young Men and Gangsta Culture*. Minneapolis, MN: University of Minnesota Press.

Hagedorn, J. (2009). A Genealogy of Gangs in Chicago: Bringing the State Back into Gang Research. Presentation to *Global Gangs Conference*, Geneva, Switzerland. Available at: <http://gangresearch.net/Archives/hagedorn/articles/genealogy.pdf>. [Accessed 9 August 2014].

Hagedorn, J., and Rauch, B. (2007). Housing, Gangs, and Homicide: What We Can Learn from Chicago. *Urban Affairs Review* 42(4):435–56.

Hall, S. (1995). Grasping at Straws: The Idealisation of the Material in Liberal Conceptions of Youth Crime. *Youth and Policy* 48:49–63.

Hall, S. (2002). Daubing the Drudges of Fury: Men, Violence and the Piety of the 'Hegemonic Masculinity' Thesis. *Theoretical Criminology* 6(1):35–61.

Hall, S., Winlow, S., and Ancrum, C. (2008). *Criminal Identities and Consumer Culture: Crime, Exclusion and the New Culture of Narcissism*. Cullompton: Willan Publishing.

Hall, S.M. (1996). Introduction: Who Needs Identity? In: S. Hall and P. du Gay (eds). *Questions of Cultural Identity*. London: Sage.

Hall, S.M., and Jefferson, T. (1976). *Resistance through Rituals: Youth Subcultures in Post-War Britain*. London: Hutchinson.

Hall, S.M., Critcher, C., Jefferson, T., et al. (1978). *Policing the Crisis: Mugging, the State and Law and Order*. London: Macmillan.

Hallsworth, S. (2011). Gangland Britain? Realities, Fantasies and Industry. In: B. Goldson (ed). *Youth in Crisis? 'Gangs', Territoriality and Violence.* London: Routledge, pp. 183–97.

Hallsworth, S. (2013). *The Gang and Beyond: Interpreting Violent Street Worlds.* Basingstoke: Palgrave Macmillan.

Hallsworth, S., and Brotherton, D. (2011). *Urban Disorder and Gangs: A Critique and a Warning.* London: Runnymede Trust.

Hallsworth, S., and Young, T. (2008). Gang Talk and Gang Talkers: A Critique. *Crime Media Culture* 4(2):175–95.

Hanley, L. (2007). *Estates: An Intimate History.* London: Granta.

Haria, J. (2014). Near the Start of Our Journey. *Scottish Left Review (Special Issue: Black Scotland)* Issue 80:4–6.

Harvey, D. (2000). Globalization in Question. In: J.D. Schmidt and J. Hersh (eds). *Globalization and Social Change.* London: Routledge.

Hayward, K., and Yar, M. (2006). The 'Chav' Phenomenon: Consumption, Media and the Construction of a New Underclass. *Crime Media Culture* 2(1):9–28.

Hayward, K.J. (2004). *City Limits: Crime, Consumer Culture and the Urban Experience.* London: Glasshouse Press.

Hayward, K.J. (2012). Five Spaces of Cultural Criminology. *British Journal of Criminology.* 52(3):441–62.

Hayward, K.J., and Young, J. (2004). Cultural Criminology: Some Notes on the Script. *Theoretical Criminology* 8(3):259–85.

Held, D. (2000). Regulating Globalization? The Reinvention of Politics. *International Sociology* 15(2):394–408.

Hebdige, D. (1979). *Subculture: the meaning of style,* London: Methuen.

Herald (2008). '300 'booze and blade'gangs blighting Scotland: numbers revealed for first time'. Available at: <http://www.heraldscotland.com/300-booze-and-blade-gangs-blighting-scotland-1.875815> [Accessed 9 August 2014].

Herald (2012). 'Scotland's FBI warns 25 foreign mafia gangs are now at large'. Available at: <http://www.heraldscotland.com/news/home-news/scotlands-fbi-warns-25-foreign-mafia-gangs-are-now-at-large.16460653> [Accessed 6 August 2014].

Herald (2013). 'Cameron vows to learn from Scotland'. Available at: <http://www.heraldscotland.com/news/home-news/cameron-vows-to-learn-from-scotland-over-riots.14706619> [Accessed 4 November 2013].

Hillier, J., and Rooksby, E. (2005). *Habitus: A Sense of Place* (2nd edn). Aldershot: Ashgate.

Hind, A. (2001 [1966]). *The Dear Green Place.* Birlinn: Edinburgh.

HM Government (2010). *Safeguarding Children and Young People Who May Be Affected by Gang Activity.* London: Home Office.

HM Government (2011). 'PM's speech on the fightback after the riots'. Available at: <https://www.gov.uk/government/speeches/pms-speech-on-the-fightback-after-the-riots> [Accessed 23 July 2013].

HM Government (2011). *Ending Gang and Youth Violence*. London: Home Office.

Hobbs, D. (1997). Going Down the Glocal: The Local Context of Organised Crime. *The Howard Journal* 37(4):407–22.

Hobbs, D. (2000). Researching Serious Crime. In: R. King and E. Wincup (eds). *Doing Research on Crime and Justice*. Oxford: Oxford University Press, pp. 153–82.

Hobbs, D. (2001). Ethnography and the Study of Deviance. In: P. Atkinson, A. Coffey, S. Delamont, et al. (eds). *Handbook of Ethnography*. London: Sage.

Hobbs, D. (2013). *Lush Life: Constructing Organized Crime in the UK*. Oxford: Oxford University Press.

Hobbs, D., Hadfield, P., and Lister, S. (2003). *Bouncers: Violence and Governance in the Night-Time Economy*. Oxford: Oxford University Press.

Hodgkinson, J., Marshall, S., Berry, G., et al. (2009). Reducing Gang Related Crime: A Systematic Review of 'Comprehensive' Interventions. London: Social Science Research Unit.

Holloway, S., and Valentine, G. (eds). (2000). *Children's Geographies: Playing, Living, Learning*. London: Routledge.

Houchin, R. (2005). Social Exclusion and Imprisonment: A Report. Glasgow: Glasgow Caledonian University. Available at: <http://www.scotpho.org.uk/downloads/SocialExclusionandImprisonmentinScotland.pdf>.

Hudson, N., Liddell, G., and Nicol, S. (2012). *Youth Unemployment: Key Facts*. Scottish Parliament Briefing Paper. Available at: <http://www.scottish.parliament.uk/ResearchBriefingsAndFactsheets/S4/SB_12_19rev.pdf> [Accessed 23 March 2015].

Humphries, S. (1981). *Hooligans or Rebels? An Oral History of Working-Class Childhood and Youth 1889–1939*. Oxford: Blackwell.

Ilan, J. (2010), If You Don't Let Us In, We'll Get Arrested: Class-Cultural Dynamics in the Delivery of, and Resistance to, Youth Justice Work. *Youth Justice* 10(1):25–39.

Ilan, J. (2013). Street Social Capital in the Liquid City. *Ethnography* 14(1):3–24.

Jacobs, J. (2009). Gang Databases: Contexts and Questions. *Criminology and Public Policy* 8(4):705–9.

James, A., Jenks, C., and Prout, A. (1998). *Theorising Childhood*. London: Polity Press.

Jefferson, T. (1975). Cultural Responses of the Teds: The Defence of Space and Status. In: S. Hall and T. Jefferson (eds). *Resistance through Rituals*; Birmingham: Centre for Contemporary Cultural Studies, pp. 81–6.

Jefferson, T. (1997). Masculinities and Crime In: M. Maguire, R. Morgan, and R. Reiner (eds). *The Oxford Handbook of Criminology* (2nd edn). Oxford: Oxford University Press.

Jenkins, R. (2002). *Pierre Bourdieu*. London: Routledge.

Jenkins, R. (2008). *Social Identity* (3rd edn). London: Routledge.

Jenks, C. (1996). *Childhood*. London: Routledge.

Jephcott, P. (1967), *Time of One's Own*. Edinburgh: Oliver & Boyd.

Joe-Laidler, K., and Hunt, G. (2012). Moving beyond the Gang-Drug-Violence Connection. *Drugs: Education, Prevention and Polic*, 19(6):442–52.

Johnston, R., and McIvor, A. (2004). Men at Work: Oral History and the Glasgow Hard Man. Presented at *European City in Comparative Perspective: Seventh International Conference on Urban History*, Panteion University, Athens, Greece, 27–30 October. Available at: <pan-demos.panteion.gr/index.php?op=record&pid=iid:474&lang=en>.

Jones, G. (2002). *The Youth Divide: Diverging Pathways to Adulthood*. York: Joseph Rowntree.

Jones, T., and Newburn, T. (2007). *Policy Transfer and Criminal Justice: Exploring US Influence over British Crime Control Policy*. Open University Press: Berkshire.

Katz, C.M., and Webb, V.J. (2006). *Policing Gangs in America*. Cambridge: Cambridge University Press.

Katz, J. (1988). *Seductions of Crime: Moral and Sensual Attractions in Doing Evil*. New York, NY: Basic Books.

Katz, J., and Jackson-Jacobs, C. (2004). The Criminologists' Gang. In: C. Summer (ed.). *The Blackwell Companion to Criminology*. Oxford: Blackwell, pp. 91–124.

Kehily, M.J., and Nayak, A. (1997). 'Lads and Laughter': Humour and the Production of Heterosexual Hierarchies. *Gender and Education* 9(1):69–88.

Kelman, J. (1984). *The Bus-Conductor Hines*. Edinburgh: Polygon.

Kelman, J. (1994). *How Late It Was, How Late*. London: Secker and Warburg.

Kelman, J. (2009). *Kieron Smith, Boy*. London: Hamish Hamilton/Penguin.

Kemp, D. (1990). *Glasgow 1990: The True Story behind the Hype*. Gartocharn: Famedram.

Kennedy, D.M. (2009). Gangs and Public Policy: Constructing and Deconstructing Gang Databases. *Criminology and Public Policy* 8(4):711–16.

King, E. (1987). Popular Culture in Glasgow. In: R.A. Cage (ed.). *The Working Class in Glasgow, 1750–1914*. Beckenham: Croom Helm, pp. 142–87.

Kintrea, K., Bannister, J., Pickering, J., et al. (2008). *Young People and Territoriality in British Cities*. York: Joseph Rowntree Foundation.

Kintrea, K., Bannister, J., and Pickering, J. (2011). 'It's Just an Area—Everybody Represents It': Exploring Young People's Territorial Behaviour in British Cities.I In: B. Goldson (ed.). *Youth in Crisis? 'Gangs', Territoriality and Violence*. London: Routledge, pp. 55–71.

Klein, M. (ed.). (1967). *Juvenile Gangs in Context: Theory, Research, and Action*. Englewood Cliffs, NJ: Prentice-Hall.

Klein, M. (1971). *Street Gangs and Street Workers*. Englewood Cliffs, NJ: Prentice-Hall.

Klein, M. (1995). *The American Street Gang: Its Nature, Prevalence, and Control*. New York, NY: Oxford University Press.

Klein, M. with Kerner, H-J., Maxson, C.L., and Weitekamp, E.G.M. (eds). (2001). *The Eurogang Paradox*. London: Kluwer Academic Press.

Law, A., and Mooney, G. (2012). The De-Civilizing Process and the Urban Working Class in Scotland. *Social Justice* 38(4):106–26.

Law, A., Mooney, G., and Helms, G. (2010). Urban 'Disorders', 'Problem Places' and Criminal Justice in Scotland. In: H. Croall, G. Mooney, and M. Munro (eds). *Criminal Justice in Scotland*. Abingdon: Willan, pp. 43–64.

Leach, N. (2005). Belonging: Towards a Theory of Identification with Space. In: J. Hillier and E. Rooksby (eds). *Habitus: A Sense of Place* (2nd edn). Aldershot: Ashgate, pp. 297–314.

Leacock, E.B. (ed.). (1971). *The Culture of Poverty: A Critique*. New York, NY: Simon & Schuster.

Lee-Treweek, G., and Linkogle, S. (eds). (2000). *Danger in the Field: Risk and Ethics in Social Research*. London: Routledge.

Lefebvre, H. (1974). *The Production of Space*. Oxford: Blackwell Publishing.

Leonard, M. (2006). Teens and Territory in Contested Spaces: Negotiating Sectarian Interfaces in Northern Ireland. *Children's Geographies* 4(2):225–38.

Letherby, G. (2000). Dangerous Liaisons: Auto/Biography in Research and Research Writing. In: G. Lee-Treweek and S. Linkogle (eds). *Danger in the Field: Risk and Ethics in Social Research*. London: Routledge, pp. 91–113.

Lewis, O. (1959). *Five Families: Mexican Case Studies in the Culture of Poverty*. New York, NY: Basic Books.

Ley, D., and Cybriwsky, R. (1974). Urban Graffiti as Territorial Markers. *Annals of the Association of American Geographers* 64(4):491–505.

Lo, T.W. (2012). Triadization of Youth Gangs in Hong Kong. *British Journal of Criminology* 52(3):556–76.

Loader, I. (1996). *Youth, Policing and Democracy*. Basingstoke: Macmillan.

Lofland, J. (1971). *Analysing Social Settings: A Guide to Qualitative Observation and Analysis*. Belmont, CA: Wadsworth.

Loseke, D.R. (2003). *Thinking about Social Problems*. New York, NY: Aldine de Gruyter.

Lynch, K. (1960). *The Image of the City*. Cambridge, MA: MIT Press.

Lyng, S. (1990). Edgework: A Social Psychological Analysis of Voluntary Risk Taking. *American Journal of Sociology* 95(4):851–86.

Lyng, S. (2005). *Edgework: The Sociology of Risk Taking.* London: Routledge.

Mac an Ghaill, M. (1994). The Making of Black English Masculinities. In H. Brod and M. Kaufman (eds). *Theorizing Masculinities.* Thousand Oaks, CA: Sage, pp. 183–99.

MacCallum, R.G. (1994). *Tongs Ya Bas: The Explosive History of Glasgow's Street Gangs.* Glasgow: New Glasgow Library.

MacDonald, R., and Marsh, J. (2005). *Disconnected Youth? Growing Up in Britain's Poor Neighbourhoods.* London: Palgrave Macmillan.

MacDonald, R., and Shildrick, T. (2007). Street Corner Society: Leisure Careers, Youth (Sub)Culture and Social Exclusion. *Leisure Studies* 26(3):339–55.

MacDonald, R., Mason, P., Shildrick, T., et al. (2001). Snakes and Ladders: In Defence of Studies of Youth Transition. *Sociological Research On-line 5.*

MacDonald, R, Shildrick, T., Webster, C., et al. (2005). Growing Up in Poor Neighbourhoods: The Significance of Class and Place in the Extended Transitions of 'Socially Excluded' Young Adults. *Sociology* 39(5):873–91.

Mack, J.A. (1958). Crime. In: J. Cunnison and J.B.S. Gilfillan (eds). *The Third Statistical Account of Scotland. Glasgow,* Vol. 5. Glasgow: Collins.

MacLeod, G. (2002). From Urban Entrepreneurialism to a 'Revanchist City'? On the Spatial Injustices of Glasgow's Renaissance. *Antipode* 34(3):02–24.

Malinowski, B. (1967). *A Diary in the Strict Sense of the Term.* London: Routledge & Kegan Paul.

Malkki, L. (1992). National Geographic: The Rooting of Peoples & the Territorialization of National Identity among Scholars & Refugees. *Cultural Anthropology* 7(1):24–45.

Maruna, S. (2001). *Making Good: How Ex-Convicts Reform and Rebuild Their Lives.* Washington DC: American Psychological Association.

Matthews, H., Limb, M., and Percy-Smith, B. (1998). Changing Worlds: The Microgeographies of Young Teenagers. In: *Tijdschrift voor Economische en Sociale Geografie* 89(2):193–202.

Matthews, H., Limb, M., and Taylor, M. (2000). The 'Street as Thirdspace'. In: S. Holloway and G. Valentine (eds). *Children's Geographies: Playing, Living, Learning.* London: Routledge, pp. 63–79

Matza, D. (1964), *Delinquency and Drift.* New York, NY: Wiley.

Maver, I. (2000), *Glasgow.* Edinburgh: Edinburgh University Press.

McArthur, A., and Kingsley Long, H. (1956). *No Mean City.* London: Transworld Publications.

McCrone, D. (2001). *Understanding Scotland: The Sociology of a Nation.* London: Routledge.

McDonald, K. (2003). Marginal Youth, Personal Identity, and the Contemporary Gang: Reconstructing the Social World? In: L. Kontos, D. Brotherton, and L. Barrios (eds). *Gangs and Society: Alternative Perspectives.* New York, NY: Columbia University Press, pp. 62–74

McDowell, L. (2003). *Redundant Masculinities? Employment Change and White Working Class Youth.* Malden, MA: Blackwell.

McIlvanney, W. (1983). *The Papers of Tony Veitch.* London: Hodder and Stoughton.

McIlvanney, W. (1985). *The Big Man.* Kent: Hodder and Stoughton.

McIlvanney, W. (1987). Where Greta Garbo Wouldn't Have Been Alone. In: O. Marzaroli and W. McIlvanney (eds). *Shades of Grey: Glasgow 1956–1987.* Edinburgh: Mainstream Publishing, pp. 13–36.

McIvor, A. (2010). Forging the male body: masculinities in the Scottish heavy industries, c1930–1980s. Presentation to Royal Society of Edinburgh, Seminar on Scottish Masculinity in a Historical Perspective, University of Glasgow, 20 September 2010.

McKay, J. (undated). 'Modern times: 1950s to the present day', *The Glasgow Story.* Available at: <http://www.theglasgowstory.com/storyf.php> [Accessed 28 September 2010].

McKay, R. (2006). *Murder Capital: Life and Death on the Streets of Glasgow.* Edinburgh: Black and White Publishing.

McKinlay, W., Forsyth, A.J.M., and Khan, F. (2009). *Alcohol and Violence among Young Male Offenders in Scotland.* SPS Occasional Paper No. 1/09. Edinburgh: Scottish Prison Service.

McLay, F. (ed.). (1988). *Worker's City: The Real Glasgow Stands Up.* Glasgow: Clydeside Press.

McLay, F. (ed.). (1990). *The Reckoning: Beyond the Culture City Rip-Off.* Glasgow: Clydeside Press.

McNay, L. (2001). Meditations on Pascalian Meditations. *Economy and Society* 30, 1:39–54.

McRobbie, A. (1980). Settling Accounts with Subcultures: A Feminist Critique. *Screen Education* 34:37–49.

McRobbie, A., and Garber, J. (1976). Girls and Subcultures: An Exploration. In: S. Hall and T. Jefferson (eds) *Resistance through Rituals.* London: Hutchison, pp. 209–22.

McVie, S. (2010). *Gang Membership and Knife Carrying: Findings from the Edinburgh Study of Youth Transitions and Crime.* Edinburgh: Scottish Government.

Mead, G.H. (1934). *Mind, Self and Society: From the Standpoint of a Social Behaviourist.* Chicago, IL: University of Chicago Press.

Medina, J., Aldridge, J., and Ralphs, R. (2013). Gang Transformation, Changes or Demise: Evidence from an English City. In: C.L. Maxson, A. Egley Jr, J. Miller, et al. (eds). *The Modern Gang Reader*. Los Angeles, CA: Oxford University Press, pp. 197–209.

Mendoza-Denton, N. (2008). *Homegirls: Language and Cultural Practice among Latina Youth Gangs*. Malden, MA: Blackwell.

Merton, R.K. (1957). *Social Theory and Social Structure*. New York: Free Press.

Messerschmidt, J. (2002). On Gang Girls, Gender and Structured Action Theory: A Reply to Miller. *Theoretical Criminology* 6(4):461–75.

Miles, R. (1993). *Racism after 'Race Relations'*. London: Routledge.

Miller, J. (2001). *One of the Guys: Girls, Gangs and Gender*. Oxford University Press: Oxford.

Miller, J. (2002). The Strengths and Limits of 'Doing Gender' for Understanding Street Crime. *Theoretical Criminology* 6(4):433–60.

Miller, W. (1958). Lower Class Culture as a Generating Milieu of Gang Delinquency. *Journal of Social Issues* 4:5–19.

Miller, W. (1975). *Violence by Youth Gangs and Youth Gangs as a Crime Problem in Major American Cities*. Washington DC: Department of Justice.

Miller, W.J. (2005). Adolescents on the Edge: The Sensual Side of Delinquency. In: S. Lyng (ed.). *Edgework: The Sociology of Risk-Taking*. London: Routledge, pp. 153–71.

Mills, C.W. (1959). *The Sociological Imagination*. New York, NY: Oxford University Press.

Mitchell, I. (2005). *This City Now: Glasgow and Its Working Class Past*. Edinburgh: Luath Press.

Mooney, G. (2012). 'The 'Broken Society' Election: Class Hatred and the Politics of Poverty and Place in Glasgow East. *Social Policy and Society* 8(4):437–50.

Mooney, G., Croall, H., and Munro, M. (2010). Social Inequalities, Criminal Justice and Discourses of Social Control in Scotland. In: H. Croall, G. Mooney, and M. Munro, M. (eds). *Criminal Justice in Contemporary Scotland. Cullompton*. Abingdon: Willan, pp. 21–42.

Moore, J. (1998). Understanding Youth Street Gangs: Economic Restructuring and the Urban Underclass. In: M.W. Watts (ed.). *Cross-Cultural Perspectives on Youth and Violence*. Stanford, CT: JAI Press Inc, pp. 65–78.

Morgan, R. (2007). Gangs and Criminal Justice: Challenges and Risks: Keynote address to *University of Manchester Conference*, 6 July 2007, 'Dealing with Youth Gangs'.

MORI Scotland (2003). Glasgow Youth Survey 2003: Final Report. Glasgow: Glasgow City Council.

MORI Scotland (2005). *Being Young in Scotland 2005: Young People's Participation in Youth Work, Arts, Culture and Sport.* Edinburgh: Scottish Executive.

Mullins, C. (2006). *Holding Your Square: Masculinities, Streetlife, and Violence*; Cullompton: Willan.

Mungham, G., and Pearson, G. (1976). *Working Class Youth Culture.* London: Routledge & Kegan Paul.

Murray, W.J. (1996). *The Old Firm: Sectarianism, Sport, and Society in Scotland.* Edinburgh: J. Donald Publishers.

Nash, R. (1999). Bourdieu, 'Habitus', and Educational Research: Is It All Worth the Candle? *British Journal of the Sociology of Education* 20(2):175–87.

Nayak, A. (2003). 'Boyz to Men': Masculinities, Schooling and Labour Transitions in De-Industrial Times. *Educational Review* 55(2):147–59.

Nayak, A. (2006), Displaced Masculinities: Chavs, Youth and Class in the Post-Industrial City. *Sociology* 40:813–31.

Nayak, A. (2007). Critical Whiteness Studies. *Sociology Compass* 1/2:737–55.

Nellis, M. (2010). Prose and Cons: Autobiographical Writing by British Prisoners. In: L. Cheliotis (ed.). *The Arts of Imprisonment: Essays on Control, Resistance and Empowerment.* Abingdon: Ashgate, pp. 189–210.

Newman, D. (2005). World Society, Globalization and a Borderless World: The Contemporary Significance of Borders and Territory. *World Society Focus Paper Series.* Zurich: World Society Foundation.

NHS Scotland (2004). *Langview: A Community Health and Wellbeing Profile.* Health Scotland: Edinburgh.

Nilan, P., and Feixa, C. (2006). *Global Youth? Hybrid Identities, Plural Worlds.* Abingdon: Routledge.

Nurge, D. (2003). Liberating yet Limiting: The Paradox of Female Gang Membership. In: L. Kontos, D. Brotherton, and L. Barrios (eds). *Gangs and Society: Alternative Perspectives.* Columbia, NY: Columbia University Press, pp. 161–82.

O'Malley, P. (2001). Policing Crime Risks in the Neo-Liberal Era. In: K. Stenson and R. Sullivan (eds). *Crime, Risk and Justice: The Politics of Crime Control in Liberal Democracies.* Cullompton: Willan, pp. 89–103.

O'Malley, P., and Mugford, S. (1994). Crime, Excitement and Modernity. In: G. Barak (ed.). *Varieties of Criminology: Readings from a Dynamic Discipline.* Westport: Praeger, pp. 189–211.

Oakley, C.A. (1946). *The Second City.* London: Blackie & Son Ltd.

Opie, I., and Opie, P. (1969). *Children's Games in Street and Playground.* Oxford: Clarendon Press.

Parker, H. (1974). *View From the Boys: A Sociology of Down-Town Adolescents.* Newton Abbot: David and Charles Holding.

Paton, K. (2009). *The hidden injuries and hidden rewards of urban restructuring on working-class communities: a case study of gentrification in Partick, Glasgow*; PhD Thesis: University of Glasgow.

Paton, K., Mooney, G., and McKee, K. (2012). Class, Citizenship and Regeneration: Glasgow and the Commonwealth Games 2014. *Antipode* 44(4):1470–89.

Patrick, J. (1973). *A Glasgow Gang Observed.* London: Eyre-Methuen.

Pearson, G. (1983). *Hooligan: a History of Respectable Fears.* London: Macmillan.

Pearson, G. (1993). Talking a Good Fight: Authenticity and Distance in the Ethnographer's Craft. In: D. Hobbs and T. May (eds). *Interpreting the Field: Accounts of Ethnography* Oxford: Clarendon Press, pp. vii–xx.

Pearson, G. (2006). Disturbing Continuities: 'Peaky Blinders' to 'Hoodies'. *Criminal Justice Matters* Issue 65, Autumn:6–7.

Pearson, G. (2011). Perpetual Novelty: Youth, Modernity and Historical Amnesia. In: B. Goldson (ed.). *Youth in Crisis? 'Gangs', Territoriality and Violence.* London: Routledge, pp. 128–44.

Percy-Smith, B., and Matthews, H. (2001). Tyrannical Spaces: Young People, Bullying and Urban Neighbourhoods. *Local Environment* 6(1):49–63.

Petrie, D. (2004). *Contemporary Scottish Fictions: Film, Television and the Novel.* Edinburgh: Edinburgh University Press.

Phillips, C. (2003). Who's Who in the Pecking Order: Aggression and 'Normal Violence' in the Lives of Girls and Boys. *British Journal of Criminology* 43(4):710–28.

Piaget, J. (1955). *The Child's Construction of Reality.* London: Routledge & Kegan Paul.

Pickering, J., Kintrea, K., and Bannister, J. (2012). Invisible Walls and Visible Youth: Territoriality among Young People in British Cities. *Urban Studies* 49(5):945–60.

Pitts, J. (2008). *Reluctant Gangsters: The Changing Face of Youth Crime.* Cullompton: Willan Publishing.

Pitts, J. (2011). Mercenary Territory: Are Youth Gangs Really a Problem? In: B. Goldson (ed). *Youth in Crisis? 'Gangs', Territoriality and Violence.* London: Routledge, pp. 161–82.

Polsky, N. (1967). *Hustlers, Beats, and Others.* Harmondsworth: Penguin.

Poole, L., and Adamson, K. (2008). Report on the Situation of the Roma Community in Govanhill, Glasgow. Glasgow: Oxfam <http://www.oxfam.org.uk/resources/ukpoverty/downloads/roma_report.pdf> [Accessed 4 July 2012].

Presdee, M. (1994). Young People, Culture and the Construction of Crime: Doing Wrong versus Doing Right. In: G. Barak (ed.). *Varieties of Criminology: Readings from a Dynamic Discipline.* Westport: Praeger, pp. 179–88.

Presdee, M. (2000). *Cultural Criminology and the Carnival of Crime.* London: Routledge.

Quintini, G., Martin, J.P., and Martin, S. (2007). *The Changing Nature of the School-to-Work Transition Process in OECD Countries.* Discussion Paper No. 2582; Bonn: Institute from the Study of Labour (IZA).

Raban, J. (1974). *Soft City.* London: William Collins and Sons.

Ralphs, R., Medina, J., and Aldridge, J. (2009). Who Needs Enemies with Friends Like These? The Importance of Place for Young People Living in Known Gang Areas. *Journal of Youth Studies* 12(5):483–500.

Roberts, B. (1976). Naturalistic Research into Subcultures and Deviance. In: S. Hall and T. Jefferson (eds). *Resistance through Rituals.* London: Hutchinson, pp. 243–52.

Roberts, K. (2012). The Leisure of Young People in Contemporary Society. *Arbor Cencia: Pensamiento y Cultura* 188(754):327–37.

Robertson, R. (1995). Glocalization: Time–Space and Homogeneity–Heterogeneity. In: M. Featherstone, S. Lash, and R. Robertson (eds). *Global Modernities.* London: Sage, pp. 25–44

Robins, D., and Cohen, P. (1978). *Knuckle Sandwich.* Harmondsworth: Penguin.

Robson, G. (1997). *Class, Criminality and Embodied Consciousness: Charlie Richardson and a South East London Habitus.* London: Goldsmiths College.

Rogaly, B., and Taylor, B. (2011). *Moving Histories of Class and Community: Identity, Place and Belonging in Contemporary England.* London: Palgrave MacMillan.

Rojek, C. (1995). *Decentring Leisure: Rethinking Leisure Theory.* London: Sage.

Rojek, C. (2005). Leisure and Tourism. In: C. Calhoun, C. Rojek, and B. Turner (eds). *The SAGE Handbook of Sociology.* London: Sage, pp. 302–14.

Ross, N.J., Hill, M., and Shilton, A. (2008). 'One Scotland, Many Cultures': The Views of Young People from White Ethnic Backgrounds on Multiculturalism in Scotland. *Scottish Affairs* 64:97–116.

Runnymede (2009). *Who Cares about the White Working Class?* London: Runnymede Trust.

Rutherford, J. (1988). Introduction: Avoiding the Bends. In: R. Chapman and J. Rutherford (eds). *Male Order: Unwrapping Masculinity.* London: Lawrence & Wishart, pp. 3–20.

Sack, R.D. (1983). Human Territoriality: A Theory. *Annals of the Association of American Geographers* 73(1):55–74.

Sanchez-Jankowski, M. (2003). Gangs and Social Change. *Theoretical Criminology* 7(2):191–216.

Sanchez-Jankowski, M. (1991). *Islands in the Street: Gangs and American Urban Society*. Berkeley, CA: University of Berkeley Press.

Sandberg, S. (2008). Street Capital: Ethnicity and Violence on the Streets of Oslo. *Theoretical Criminology* 12(2):153–71.

Sandberg, S., and Pederson, W. (2011). *Street Capital: Black Cannabis Dealers in a White Welfare State*. Bristol: Policy Press.

Sanders, T. (2004). Controllable Laughter: Managing Sex Work through Humour. *Sociology* 38(2):273–91.

Sassen, S. (1991). *The Global City*. Princeton, NJ: Princeton University Press.

Sassen, S. (2007). The Global City: One Setting for New Types of Gang Work and Political Culture? In: J. Hagedorn (ed). *Gangs in the Global City: Alternatives to Traditional Criminology*. MN: University of Minnesota Press, pp. 97–119.

Scotsman (2008). 'The changing face of gangland crime'. Available at: <http://www.scotsman.com/news/the-changing-face-of-gangland-crime-1-1158587> [Accessed 6 August 2014].

Scott, P. (1956). Gangs and Delinquent Groups in London. *British Journal of Delinquency* 7:4–26.

Scottish Census Online Warehouse (Undated). Available at: <http://www.scrol.gov.uk/scrol/warehouse/warehouse?actionName=choose-area> [Accessed 1 May 2008].

Scottish Executive (2006). Scottish Index of Multiple Deprivation: General Report. Available at: <http://www.rics.org/Practiceareas/Property/Regeneration/scottishindex_multipledeprivation2006_enewsnov06.htm> [Accessed 2 May 2008].

Scottish Government (2007). *Recorded Crime in Scotland 2006–2007*. Available at: <http://www.scotland.gov.uk/Publications/2008/03/06120248/14> [Accessed 29 August 2008].

Scottish Government (2009). *Recorded Crime in Scotland*. Available at: <http://www.scotland.gov.uk/Publications/2009/09/28155153/0> [Accessed 28 July 2010].

Scottish Government (2013). *Homicide in Scotland, 2011–12*. Available at: <http://www.scotland.gov.uk/Publications/2012/11/6428/downloads#res-1> [Accessed 20 March 2013].

Scottish Index of Multiple Deprivation (2012). *SIMD 2012 Results*. Available at: <http://simd.scotland.gov.uk/publication-2012/simd-2012-results/overall-simd-results/key-findings/> [Accessed 9 August 2014].

Scottish Neighbourhood Statistics (2014). Available at: <http://www.sns.gov.uk/Simd/Simd.aspx> [Accessed 7 July 2014].

Scottish Police Authority (2014). *SPA Board Meeting Minutes* [not protectively marked]. Available at: <http://www.spa.police.uk/assets/126884/225921/item241>.

Seaman, P. (2012). *Exploring the Use of Assets in Practice: The Includem Gangs Intervention*, Glasgow: Glasgow Centre for Population Health. Available at: <http://www.gcph.co.uk/assets/0000/3462/GCPHBP34forweb.pdf>.

Seaman, P., Turner, K., Hill, M., et al. (2005). *Parenting and Children's Resilience in Disadvantaged Communities*. London: National Children's Bureau.

Sharp, C., Aldridge, J., and Medina, J. (2006). *Delinquent Youth Groups and Offending Behaviour: Findings from the 2004 Offending, Crime and Justice Survey*. London: Home Office.

Shaw, C. (1966). *The Jackroller: A Delinquent Boy's Own Story*. Chicago, IL: University of Chicago Press.

Shaw, C., and McKay, H.D. (1942). *Juvenile Delinquency and Urban Areas*. Chicago, IL: University of Chicago Press.

Sheptypcki, J. (2005). Relativism, Transnationalisation and Comparative Criminology. In: J. Sheptycki and A. Wardak (eds). *Transnational and Comparative Criminology*. London: Glasshouse Press, pp. 69–88.

Shildrick, T.A., and MacDonald, R. (2007). Street Corner Society: Leisure Careers, Youth (Sub)Culture and Social Exclusion. *Leisure Studies* 26(3):399–55.

Short, J.F. (ed.). (1968). *Gang Delinquency and Delinquent Subcultures*. Chicago, IL: Harper and Row.

Short, J.F., and Strodtbeck, J.R. (1965). *Group Process and Gang Delinquency*. Chicago, IL: University of Chicago Press.

Sibley, D. (1995). *Geographies of Exclusion*. London: Routledge.

Sillitoe, P. (1956). *Cloak without Dagger*. London: Cassell.

Simmel, G. (2002). The Metropolis and Mental Life. In: G. Bridge and S. Watson (eds). *The Blackwell City Reader*. Oxford: Blackwell Publishing, pp. 11–19.

Simpson, B. (2006). 'You Don't Do Fieldwork, Fieldwork Does You': Between Subjectivation and Objectivation in Anthropological Fieldwork. In: D. Hobbs and R. Wright (eds), *The Sage Handbook of Fieldwork*. London: Sage, pp. 125–38.

Smethurst, P. (2000). *The Postmodern Chronotope: Reading Space and Time in Contemporary Fiction*. Amsterdam: Rodopi.

Smith, D.J., and Bradshaw, P. (2005). 'Gang Membership and Teenage Offending', Edinburgh Study of Youth Transitions and Crime; Publication Number 8. Available at: <http://www.law.ed.ac.uk/cls/esytc/findings/digest8.pdf> [Accessed 30 July 2007].

Smith, N. (1996). *The New Urban Frontier: Gentrification and the Revanchist City*. London: Routledge.

Smith, O. (2013). Holding Back the Beers: Maintaining 'Youth' Identity within the British Night-Time Economy. *Journal of Youth Studies* 16(8):1069–83.

Smithson, H., Ralphs, R., and Williams, P. (2013). Used and Abused: The Problematic Usage of Gang Terminology in the United Kingdom and Its Implications for Ethnic Minority Youth. *British Journal of Criminology* 53(1):113–28.

Snodgrass, J. (1976). Clifford R. Shaw and Henry D. McKay: Chicago Criminologists. *British Journal of Criminology* 16(1):1–19.

Soja, E.W. (1998). *Thirdspace: Journeys to Los Angeles and Other Real and Imagined Places*. Cambridge, MA: Blackwell.

Spergel, I. (1990). Youth Gangs: Continuity and Change. *Crime and Justice* 12:171–275.

Spergel, I. (2009). Gang Databases: To Be or Not to Be. *Criminology and Public Policy* 8(4):667–74.

Spring, I. (1990). *Phantom Village: The Myth of the New Glasgow*. Edinburgh: Polygon.

Squires, P., Silverstri, A., with Grimshaw, R., and Solomon, E. (2008). *Street Weapons Commission: Knives and Street Violence*. London: Centre for Crime and Justice Studies.

Standing, G. (2011). *The Precariat: The New Dangerous Class*. London: Bloomsbury.

Steele, J. (2002). *The Bird That Never Flew*. Mainstream: London.

Streicher, R. (2011). *The Construction of Masculinities and Violence: 'Youth Gangs' in Dili, East Timor*. Working Paper No.2, Center for Middle Eastern & North African Politics, Berlin: Freie Universität Berlin.

Stumpf, J. (2006). The Crimmigration Crisis: Immigrants, Crime, and Sovereign Power. *American University Law Review* 56:367–419.

Suttles, G. (1990). *The Man-Made City: The Land-Use Confidence Game in Chicago*. Chicago, IL: University of Chicago Press.

Suzuki, N. (2007). *Sport and Neighbourhood Regeneration: Exploring the Mechanisms of Social Inclusion through Sport*. Unpublished PhD thesis: University of Glasgow.

Sweeting, H., and West, P. (2003). Young People's Leisure and Risk-Taking Behaviours: Changes in Gender Patterning in the West of Scotland during the 1990s. *Journal of Youth Studies* 6(4):391–412.

Taylor (2013). Street Gangs in the Interwar Gorbals: The Jewish Experience. *Contemporary British History* 27(2):214–31.

Taylor, I., Evans, K., and Fraser, P. (1996). *A Tale of Two Cities: Global Change, Local Feeling and Everyday Life in the North of England: A Study in Manchester and Sheffield*. New York: Routledge.

Taylor, P., and Bain, P. (2003). 'Subterranean Worksick Blues': Humour as Subversion in Two Call Centres. *Organization Studies* 24:1487–509.

Thompson, T. (1995). *Gangland Britain*. London: Hodder & Staughton.

Thornberry, T., Krohn, M., Lizotte, A., et al. (2003). *Gangs and Delinquency in a Developmental Perspective*. Cambridge: Cambridge University Press.

Thornton, S. (1995). *Club Cultures: Music, Media and Subcultural Capital*. Cambridge: Polity Press.

Thorpe, H. (2010). Bourdieu, Gender Reflexivity, and Physical Culture: A Case of Masculinities in the Snowboarding Field. *Journal of Sport and Social Issues* 34(2):176–214.

Thrasher, F. (1963). *The Gang: A Study of 1,313 Gangs in Chicago* (2nd edn). Chicago, IL: University of Chicago Press.

Travlou, P. (2003). *Teenagers and Public Space: Literature Review*. Edinburgh: OPENSpace.

Treadwell, J. (2008). Call the (Fashion) Police: How Fashion Becomes Criminalised. *Papers from The British Criminology Conference*. British Society of Criminology, Vol 8. pp. 117–33.

Treadwell, J., Briggs, D., Winlow, S., et al. (2013). Shopocalypse Now: Consumer Culture and the English Riots of 2011. *British Journal of Criminology* 53(1):1–17.

Tsing, A. (2005). *Friction: An Ethnography of Global Connection*. Princeton, NJ: Princeton University Press.

Turner, K.M., Hill, M., Stafford, A., et al. (2006). How Children from Disadvantaged Areas Keep Safe. *Health Education* 106(6):450–64.

UK Government (2011). *PM's Speech on the Fightback after the Riots*. Available at: https://www.gov.uk/government/speeches/pms-speech-on-the-fightback-after-the-riots [Accessed 23 July 2013].

van Gemert, F. (2005). Youth Groups and Gangs in Amsterdam: A Pretest of the Eurogang Expert Survey. In: S. Decker and F. Weerman (eds). *European Street Gangs and Troublesome Youth Groups*. Oxford: AltaMira Press, pp. 147–68.

Venkatesh, S. (2003). A Note on Social Theory and the American Street Gang. In: L. Kontos, D. Brotherton, and L. Barrios (eds). *Gangs and Society: Alternative Perspectives*. New York, NY: Columbia University Press, pp. 3–11.

Venkatesh, S. (2008). *Gang Leader for a Day: A Rogue Sociologist Crosses the Line*. London: Allen Lane.

Venkatesh, S., and Kashimir, R. (2007). *Youth, Globalisation and the Law*. Palo Alto, CA: Stanford University Press.

Vigil, D. (1988). *Barrio Gangs: Street Life and Identity in Southern California*. Austin, TX: University of Texas Press.

Vigil, D. (2002). *A Rainbow of Gangs*. Austin, TX: University of Texas Press.

Wacquant, L.J.D. (2007). Territorial Stigmatization in the Age of Advanced Marginality. *Thesis Eleven* 91:66–77.

Wacquant, L.J.D. (2008a). *Urban Outcasts: A Comparative Sociology of Advanced Marginality*. London: Polity Press.

Wacquant, L.J.D. (2008b). Pierre Bourdieu. In: R. Stones (ed.). *Key Sociological Thinkers*. London: Macmillan, pp. 261–77.

Waddington, P.A.J. (2007). Public Order: Then and Now. In A.H. Smith and D.J. Smith (eds). *Transformations of Policing*. Aldershot: Ashgate, pp. 113–42.

Walsh, D., Bendel, N., Jones, R., et al. (2010). *Investigating a 'Glasgow Effect': Why Do Equally Deprived UK Cities Experience Different Health Outcomes?* Glasgow: Glasgow Centre for Population Health.

Watt, P., and Stenson, K. (1998). The Street: 'It's a Bit Dodgy around There': Safety, Danger, Ethnicity and Young People's Use of Public Space. In: T. Skelton and G. Valentine (eds). *Cool Places*. London: Routledge, pp. 249–66.

Weaver, A. (2008). *So You Think You Know Me?* Waterside Press: Hampshire.

Webb, J., Schirato, T., and Danaher, G. (2002). *Understanding Bourdieu*. London: Sage.

Webster, C. (2008). Marginalised White Ethnicity, Race and Crime. *Theoretical Criminology* 12(3):293–312.

Weerman, F., Maxson, C., Esbensen, F-A., et al. (2009). *Eurogang Program Manual: Background, Development and Use of the Eurogang Instruments in Multi-Site, Multi-Method Comparative Research*. Available at: <http://www.umsl.edu/ccj/eurogang/EurogangManual.pdf> [Accessed 5 March 2013].

White, R. (2008). Disputed Definitions and Fluid Identities: The Limitations of Social Profiling in Relation to Ethnic Youth Gangs. *Youth Justice* 8(2), 149–61.

Whittaker, L., and Batchelor, S. (2014). Commonwealth City: Challenging or Reinforcing Stereotypes of Glasgow's East End? Available at: <http://reimaginingyouth.wordpress.com> [Accessed 9 August 2014].

Whyte, W.F. (1993). (1943). *Street Corner Society: The Social Structure of an Italian Slum* (4th edn). Chicago, IL: University of Chicago Press.

Williams, R. (1976). *Keywords: A Vocabulary of Culture and Society*. New York, NY: Oxford University Press.

Willis, P., and Trondman, M. (2000). Manifesto for Ethnography. *Ethnography* 1:5–16.

Willis, P. (1977). *Learning to Labour: How Working Class Kids Get Working Class Jobs*. Hampshire: Gower.

Willis, P. (2000). *The Ethnographic Imagination*. Cambridge: Polity.

Wilmott, P. (1966). *Adolescent Boys of East London*. Harmondsworth: Penguin.

Winlow, S. (2001). *Badfellas: Crime, Tradition and New Masculinities*. Oxford: Berg.

Winlow, S., and Hall, S (2009a). Retaliate First: Memory, Humiliation and Male Violence. *Crime, Media Culture* 5(3):285–304.

Winlow, S., and Hall, S. (2006). *Violent Night: Urban Leisure and Contemporary Culture*. Oxford: Berg.

Winlow, S., and Hall, S. (2009b). Living for the Weekend: Youth Identities in Northeast England. *Ethnography* 10:91–113.

Winton, A. (2005). Youth, Gangs and Violence: Analysing the Social and Spatial Mobility of Young People in Guatemala City. *Children's Geographies* 3(2):167–84.

Wirth, L. (1928). *The Ghetto*. Chicago, IL: University of Chicago Press.

Witschi, B. (1991). *Glasgow Urban Writing and Postmodernism: A Study of Alasdair Gray's Fiction*. Frankfurt am Main: Peter Lang.

Yablonsky, L. (1962). *The Violent Gang*. London: Collier-MacMillan.

Young, J. (1999). *The Exclusive Society: Social Exclusion, Crime and Difference in Late Modernity*. London: Sage Publications.

Young, J. (2003). Merton with Energy, Katz with Structure. *Theoretical Criminology* 7(3):388–414.

Young, J. (2004). Voodoo Criminology and the Numbers Game. In: J. Ferrell, W. Morrison, and M. Presdee (eds). *Cultural Criminology Unleashed*. London: Glasshouse Publishing.

Young, J. (2012). *The Criminological Imagination*. Cambridge: Polity.

Young, M., and Wilmott, P. (1957). *Family and Kinship in East London*. London: Kegan Paul.

Young, T. (2009). Girls and Gangs: 'Shemale' Gangsters in the UK? *Youth Justice* 9(3):224–38.

Young, T. (2011). In Search of the 'Shemale' Gangster. In: B. Goldson (ed.). *Youth in Crisis? 'Gangs', Territoriality and Violence*. London: Routledge, pp. 128–44.

Young, T., FitzGerald, M., Hallsworth, S., et al (2007). *Groups, Gangs and Weapons*. London: Youth Justice Board. Available at:<http://www.yjb.gov.uk/publications/Resources/Downloads/gangs%20Guns%20and%20Weapons%20Summary.pdf> [Accessed 1 August 2013].

Zedner, L. (2009). *Security*. London: Routledge.

Zijderveld, A.C. (1983). The Sociology of Humor and Laughter. *Current Sociology* 31(3).

Zorbaugh, H.W. (1929). *The Gold Coast and the Slum: A Sociological Study of Chicago's Near North Side*. Chicago, IL: University of Chicago Press.

Feature films

Comfort and Joy (1984). (Director: John Mackenzie, Writer: Jimmy Boyle and Peter McDougall, Producer: Jeremy Isaacs, Raymond Day).

Deathwatch (1980). (Director: Betrand Tavernier, Writer: David Compton, David Rayfiel and Bertrand Tavernier, Producer: Elie Kfouri).

Just Another Saturday (1975). (Director: John Mackenzie, Writer: Peter MacDougall, Producer: Graeme McDonald).

Metropolis (1927). (Director: Fritz Lang, Writer: Thea von Harbou, Producer: Erich Pommer).

Neds: Non-Educated Delinquents (2010). (Director: Peter Mullan, Writer: Peter Mullan, Producers: Olivier Delbosc, Alain de la Mata, Marc Missonier).

Ratcatcher (1999). (Director and Writer: Lynne Ramsay, Producer: Gavin Emerson).

Red Road (2006). (Director: Andrea Arnold, Writers: Andrea Arnold, Anders Thomas Jensen, Lone Scherfig, Producer: Carrie Comerford).

Small Faces (1996). (Director: Gillies MacKinnon, Writers: Billy M.acKinnon, Gillies MacKinnon, Producers: Billy MacKinnon, Steve Clark Hall).

Under the Skin (2013). (Director: Jonathan Glazer, Writers: Jonathan Glazer and Walter Campbell, Producer: Reno Antoniades).

World War Z (2013). (Director: Mark Forster; Writer: Matthew Carnahan; Producer: Brad Simpson).

Television series

Ross Kemp on Gangs (2006–2008). Sky One.

Taggart (1983–2011). (Director: Lawrence Moody, Richard Holthouse, Writer: Glenn Chandler, Barry Appleton, Producer: Robert Love, John G. Temple).

Documentary sources

BBC Scotland (2010–2011). *The Scheme*. Broadcast 18 May 2010–30 May 2011.

BBC Scotland (2014). *Commonwealth City*. Broadcast 8–21 July 2014.

BBC Two (2010). *Revealed: Glasgow's Gang War*. Broadcast 12 June 2010.

Channel Five (2005). *MacIntyre Uncovered*. Broadcast 19 April 2005.

Channel Four (2009). *Dispatches: The War against Street Weapons*. Broadcast 3 August 2009.

Radio source

BBC Radio 4 (2008). *Thinking Allowed: Gang Culture*. Broadcast 31 December 2008. Available at: <http://www.bbc.co.uk/programmes/b00g4zk7>.

Websites

<http://www.actiononviolence.co.uk/>
<http://www.ckdgalbraith.co.uk/glasgow-calling>

\<http://www.scottishcinemas.org.uk/\>
\<http://www.scottishcinemas.org.uk/\>
\<http://www.scrol.gov.uk/scrol/warehouse/warehouse?actionName=
   choose-area\>
 \<http://www.gangresearch.net\>
\<http://www.theglasgowstory.com/image.php?inum=TGSA00847\>

Index